Thorneythwaite Farm

Borrowdale

The 1,000 year story of a Lakeland Farm and its valley

Ian Hall

Orchard House Books

Published by Orchard House Books 2017

Orchard House Books
Raven Lane
Applethwaite
Keswick
CA12 4PN

The right of Ian Hall to be identified as the author of this work
has been asserted by him in accordance with the
Copyright, Design and Patents Act 1988

A CIP catalogue record is available from the British Library

In memory of my parents, Jim & Betty Hall
who farmed Thorneythwaite 1960 - 1975

Author's note

Skeletons are preserved for much longer than the bodies which are built upon them. So it is with history. The dateable events of a nation's life, a valley's life, a farm's life, and the lives of those involved are recordable and so recorded, and of huge interest to generations as yet unborn. Yet compared to the motives, appetites, religious drive, loves, hatreds, and the myriad other emotional and psychological factors that make up a person the skeleton is but a pale indicator.

In this story there is a skeleton – history as recorded in pollen analysis, archaeology, abbey records, church records, legal documents and so on, and to the best of my ability I have been faithful to the skeleton. Every name (from 1562 onwards), every date of birth, marriage and death is as meticulously researched as I could manage. Every major event in Borrowdale's history finds a place: from the early clearances, the gradual forest erosion, the twin influences of Fountains and Furness Abbeys' 350 years of dominance; to the German miners who opened up the valley in the latter half of the 16th Century, the phenomenal prosperity of graphite mining in the Seathwaite Wad Mines – and its attendant temptations to pilfer and steal. National events likewise impinged upon the valley even back in the 16th century. The dissolution of the Monasteries under Henry VIII brought fresh landlords as Fountains and Furness were stripped of their assets, and the subsequent Great Deed of Borrowdale (after a further 75 years) changed the basis of tenancy and freehold yet again.

Even before the Civil War the accession of King James I brought its own peculiar influence on the valley, in the form of Sir Wilfrid Lawson who schemed and plotted his way into Lordship of the Manor and ownership of a great many tenements and farms, building on his patronage by the king, who made him leader of the Crown Colony set up to dismantle the last of the Border Reivers.

Onto this skeleton I have sought to build a body – the various lives of the perhaps forty generations of farmers, miners, quarrymen and their womenfolk who have inhabited Thorneythwaite Farm. I have tried to be faithful to the entire skeleton as preserved in the records, but beyond that the story is, of course, fictional. Intertwined with the ongoing one-thousand-year saga is the story of my own parents' tenancy of Thorneythwaite, from Lady Day (25th March) 1960 to Lady Day 1975 – which is also my own coming-of-age, from eleven to twenty-six.

In an attempt to preserve and demonstrate the skeleton of the story, I have provided at the back of the book 'Historical Notes', which give details of whichever records form the basis of each chapter, for those who look for a bit more rigour. They begin on page 186.

Prologue

The auction room was laid out with at least a hundred and fifty chairs – they were expecting a full house I guessed, after all, the publicity had been very professional, with a glossy colour brochure featuring a photo from a drone that accentuated the charm of the long farmhouse with its attendant barns, and the magnificent backdrop of the head of Borrowdale, with the flat valley-bottom fields leading the eye to the brooding mountains behind. Jen and I slid in almost apologetically: we weren't here to buy, simply to see my old childhood home move on to its next incarnation.

There was none of the usual buzz of a sale-room – in fact, the auctioneer and his team looked distinctly uncomfortable as a tiny trickle of potential customers spread themselves around the room. There were no farmers lining the back wall, possible bidders or just valuing their own properties, no chattering gatherings of auction groupies, there for the tingle of excitement that comes with a bidding war in the hundreds of thousands of pounds, and very few of the well-heeled, well-groomed professional classes the brochure had surely been aimed at. For this wasn't just a local auction, with PF&K officiating – they were sharing the honours with Savills, a major national firm. And this wasn't just another Lake District property, this was Thorneythwaite, a fell-farm whose history stretched back over centuries, at least a thousand years, to the Cistercian Monks of Furness Abbey and beyond.

I counted us up, as the clock moved on to 2.00 pm, the allotted time for the farm's fate to be decided. There were eighteen of us who could be regarded by the auctioneer as potential buyers. Jen and I had a row near the back to ourselves, with only a group of four behind us. A couple of rows in front was another group of four, including Peter Edmondson, the tenant of Seathwaite Farm – Thorneythwaite's neighbour at the head of the valley, owned by the National Trust. On the other side of the central aisle were the Blands on the back row – three generations. Stuart, who followed my parents as tenant and stayed thirty-five years before handing on to his son Jonny, there with him and with his own son Campbell. In front of them a single professional-looking man talking to a counterpart woman who moved defiantly to the front row just before proceedings started; and a couple of rows in front of him the only potential 'off-comer' buyers, a couple in their late forties.

I began to think the old farm might not be sold, and the auctioneer must have wondered the same as he launched into his preamble, for he passed over the usual tension-mounting descriptions of the merits of the farm and all the various intricacies of the sale particulars, assuring us and himself that we had had ample time to peruse them beforehand. He did remind us that there was a reserve price, and of the nature of the sale. That was, as is so often the case with a small farm, that he would first offer the house, buildings and the thirteen acres immediately surrounding it. He would then offer Lot two, the 303.41 acres of land, common rights and hefted flock of 470 Herdwick sheep. He would then offer the farm as a whole, starting from the total price offered for lots one and two together. He was careful to make sure we knew that he would only then return to lots one and two separately if Thorneythwaite didn't sell as a whole. If it did then that would be its fate, this time.

Optimistically, he invited an opening bid of 800,000 pounds – well all right then, 750? No, where then? He took a bid of £650,000 either from the group of four behind us or 'from the back wall' – I couldn't tell. The next bid was clear, though, 700,000 from the offcomers across the aisle, quickly followed by 720 from the group behind us. Back and forth it went, between them, to 760 before the back row gave up. With a resigned sigh the auctioneer pencilled the bid in and announced that we would move on to the land. PF&K and Savills had jointly been a little over-optimistic with their guide price for the house and buildings: I couldn't imagine the land would now make anything near the £700,000 guide they had put on it. That had been before June 23rd, 2016, when a majority of the voters in the referendum on Britain's continued membership of the European Union said no! As far as I could see, virtually the only financial value of these 303 acres lay in the fulsome amount of cash they attracted annually from the Common Agricultural Policy – that's Common to all members of the EU, not to a post-Brexit Britain. I suspected the auctioneer had come to the same conclusion, as he rather hesitantly started at 650,000 pounds, clearly expecting to come down some way before he'd get a bid.

Clearly, in a voice which rang around the room, the professional-looking lady who'd taken up her position on the front row enunciated 'Nine hundred and fifty thousand pounds'. There have not been many moments in my life when it has felt as if the world has suddenly stopped: this was one. There was a profound silence of three and a half hours – I suppose only that many seconds in truth, and then the sound of eighteen people jointly letting out their breath. To his credit the auctioneer recovered first, and manfully called for further bids. Am I offered a million anywhere? No, he wasn't. The group of four behind were whispering feverishly – National Trust, she's National Trust. The whisper went round the room in less time than the silence had lasted. The National Trust – what the hell were they playing at?

Meanwhile, as if nothing unusual had happened, the auctioneer went through a performance of adding the two figures together and announcing to us all that the total for the two lots came to 1.71 million pounds. As if we didn't know. 'So, what am I now bid for the farm as a whole – shall we start with 1750 thousand pounds... am I offered 1750 thousand? Well, 1720 thousand then... No, then Thorneythwaite will be sold in two lots. That might have been that, with the couple opposite getting house, buildings and thirteen acres for £760,000, but that Peter Edmondson put in 780. Now the tension that should have been there from the beginning built spontaneously, the sale was on, and the price was getting high. The couple responded, after a moment or two's deliberation, with 800,000, and after significant deliberation Peter put in 825,000, but it was clear he was far from happy at this price. With a slightly hesitant nod, the lady of the pair signalled their willingness at 850,000 pounds, and with a surely feigned air of resignation the auctioneer pronounced the time-honoured "Going at eight hundred and fifty thousand pounds, ladies and gentlemen, going, going – gone!" There should have been a gavel, but it wasn't that sort of auction.

He went through the motions of once again offering the land, knowing full well that £950,000 was not going to be beaten. "Thank you very much, ladies and gentlemen. Could the purchasers please come to the desk where we will exchange contracts and take the ten per cent deposits for your purchases. Thank you once again, ladies and gentlemen."

Dazed, the rest of us made our way to the back of the room – the Lodore Hotel's function suite – and set to dissecting what had happened. Peter stormed out, face thunderous, clearly very disappointed. Stuart Bland and I looked at each other in disbelief. Nine hundred and fifty thousand pounds for that useless, bare pile of rock, bracken and boggy ground that would scarcely support the 470 sheep that went with it? Stuart had a theory that sounded plausible. "I reckon the Trust really wanted the land, but really didn't want the house and buildings. Otherwise they'd have had to keep it as a farm, and we both know it's far too small to make a decent living."

"Well, fine, but why start so high? They could probably have had the land for half a million."

"Ah, but could they? Half a million would just make the total, what, 1.26 million. Somebody might well have bid more to keep it all together, then they'd have missed their chance." Stuart had a point, I could see, but still..."Hell of a high price, though, for fifty poor acres and two hundred and fifty completely useless acres." We both knew, from hard experience, just what a hard place Thorneythwaite was, and had always been.

Chapter one

Betty Hall 1960

Betty Hall fired up the old Grey Fergie and thought herself back in heaven. She loved the little tractor, it was her sort of size, and yet superbly versatile. Today she was going to plough Horse Close, the five acre field by the lane up to Thorneythwaite. The Fergie was just the same as the one she remembered from Myreground, petrol to start it then after five minutes or so, when it was warmed up, switch over to TVO – tractor vaporising oil – so much cheaper than petrol. It was September, 1960, and she had just turned forty. She could still hardly believe she and Jim had been taken on as tenants. Most of the farms in the valley, well, in the whole of Cumberland really, were farmed by the sons of farmers, who were themselves sons of farmers… and so back and back. She giggled to herself, remembering the old school rhyme 'Bigger fleas have smaller fleas upon their backs to bite 'em, and smaller fleas have smaller fleas – and so ad infinitum'. Jim was at least the son of a farm labourer, and no doubt came from a long line of farm labourers, but she – she was the daughter of a grocer, and not even a Cumbrian grocer. She came from Bristol, and was a tax inspector in real life, before the war. And before the war he had been a clerk in a Carlisle fabric factory.

The war: the war had changed everything. Six years of not knowing whether you might be killed, your loved ones killed, whether the Nazis would win and life become unbearable. Six years of protracted stress that left everybody changed, every value questioned. For Jim it meant throwing over a smart clerk's life, a life indoors, a paper life. He wanted to be back to the earth that had nourished his ancestors, probably for ever. But he wasn't farm labourer material. Eight years of office life and six years as an army sergeant had given him ambition – or maybe he'd always had it.

Jim set up the plough for her as she did a few experimental yards, the little two-furrow plough (the same grey as the tractor) bucking and gybing as it hit stone after stone. Jim turned it up a bit – they'd be better turning over as little as possible in these conditions. Finally he was satisfied: it wasn't going to be pretty, with lovely long straight furrows but most of the sod was turning, and any deeper just made it jump too often. He left her to it, just as she liked it! For long hours the sod slowly turned over, and her thoughts likewise. Many a time she hit a bigger stone and had to reverse and dig in again, disturbing her train of thought. Many a time her thoughts hit a painful memory, and her mental plough bucked. The war years that had so distressed her; her long on-off long courtship with Jim;

4

the unbelievable pain of her first childbirth, when it had taken four days, ending in a Caesarean, to produce Ian – and then the agony of her still-born second son, his birth confirming what her heart had known for a fortnight but her brain had refused to contemplate.

That had been at Myreground, their first tenancy, just after the war, starting Lady Day 1947. On his demob Jim had enrolled in a Labour government scheme to train farmers, working for peanuts as a farm labourer in Distington but with teaching thrown in. What a year that had been! Betty was still working in the tax office – removed to Colwyn Bay for safety reasons, and never returned to Bristol. It was a long way from Colwyn Bay to Cumberland, but the trains were good, and she visited as often as she could.

She looked back over the slowly expanding area of exposed soil. Gawd, but there were a hell of a lot of stones. It hadn't been like that at Myreground, down on the West Cumbrian coastal strip. There the plough drove straight and deep, with hardly a stone to trouble it. The acre she had ploughed here looked for all the world like a plate of meat, potatoes and peas, with stones and unturned grass all over it. A dog's dinner. Still, there was no turning back now. Just as she had felt after the war. They had met just before it, July 1939, both on walking holidays in Ireland, and somehow she had held onto him 'for the duration'. She didn't kid herself that he'd been hers alone – just as, if she was honest, nor had she been his alone.

Harry Grice had given them their chance, letting them have the tenancy of Myreground for all Jim's meagre qualifications and her complete lack. Perhaps it was for that very reason? Harry was 'county', and as a couple they were, let's face it, a cut above your average dyed in the wool farming stock. And it was a brave new world, and even agriculture was getting paper qualifications and a need to understand the War Ag forms and the complexities of new-fangled feeding formulae. Perhaps a couple who had perforce to 'do it by the book' was just what he was looking for?

It was late, and she was tired with all that looking back over her shoulder and her life, and the continual backing up and re-starting. She couldn't believe only about half the five-acre field was brown side up. At Myreground she'd have finished easily, but Thorneythwaite was no Myreground, able to support a milking herd and a flock of cheviot sheep. Here the stock was 470 Herdwick ewes, and about twenty beef cows and Charlie, the Hereford bull. The book said fields should be ploughed and seeded with rye grass to increase the yield, and Horse Close was the first one they'd tackled. It took her four days to produce what might pass for a tilth, going over it, once she'd finished ploughing, with first the disc

5

harrows to cut the sods up – several times! – and then the chain harrows. By the time she'd finished it looked more like Brighton Beach than a seed-bed, but the year was getting old so they sewed the rye grass, rolled it in as best they could, and hoped the stones might sink away.

Next Spring, after lambing, in the school Whit Week half term holiday, they spent the week picking off as many of the stones as possible, before rolling it with the roller piled as heavy as the Fergie could pull, and hoping they didn't break too many mower teeth at hay-time. The man who wrote the book didn't come from Borrowdale. The farmers who did come from Borrowdale never ploughed a field. Well, not in that century, anyway. But the walls around Horse Close are often six feet thick, essentially two walls filled with the accumulated stone of a dozen pickings. Clearing the land must have been a back-breaking job, and it must have gone on over long years.

The choice of Whit week for the clearance wasn't accidental. Ian was twelve now, nearly thirteen, and keen as mustard to join in the farming. With his army training behind him, Jim was a hard taskmaster with a young squaddie, while in her heart of hearts Betty half hoped Ian would cavil at the back-breaking work. He loved the tractor as much as she did, and she could see herself being displaced very soon, if he kept up his enthusiasm. Anyway, she had higher ambitions for him than farming – even if it was what she and Jim had chosen for themselves. Part of the reason they had moved to Thorneythwaite was that Keswick School was so good, and he had passed the eleven-plus to gain entry. He revelled in the work, shirt off and young muscles hardening almost visibly, and she was relegated to driving the twenty yard stretches between stops to fill the trailer.

That Winter – 1961/2 – they joined the History Society which met each Monday evening in 'The Institute', the village hall in Rosthwaite, where a well-known local archaeologist was giving a series of lectures on the valley's history. For one thing, there was electric light and power in Rosthwaite, but none further up the valley. Betty mused, a little disconsolately, that since marrying and moving to these wild Northlands she'd lived in three farms none of which had electricity. Even her beloved grandfather's house in Bristol had had electricity long before she was born, in 1920. The problem was the Friends of the Lake District, she sniffed, all living in their centrally heated glowing little houses demanding that any power lines in Borrowdale must be underground. Well, it was underground to Rosthwaite, but the CEGB said the cable was too thin to take any more power further up the valley – and to put a new one in underground was far too expensive for the few farms and houses of Stonethwaite, Seatoller,

Seathwaite – and Thorneythwaite. It would come, some day, but meanwhile it was calor gas and candles in the farmhouse.

Tonight's lecture was on the hillfort on top of Castle Crag. Jim gave her one of his 'old-fashioned' glances that were a sort of question mark. No, she had never realised why it was called Castle Crag either. Ian sat between them lapping up the lecturer's words, he was a precocious kid, always thirsty for new knowledge. Again she had a sharp pang of regret that his brother had been still-born – it would have been good for him to have someone to play with, he was getting far too serious. Still, at least he had a girl-friend now! At thirteen she didn't suppose it would last, but Jennifer seemed a nice girl, and was already a regular visitor.

Around 500 BC, the archaeologist was saying, the valley supported several communities of Celtic people, sometimes called Briganti, who built hillforts to retreat to when danger loomed – danger that was generally a neighbouring tribe looking for a fresh supply of women and cattle! Two forts had been discovered in the valley: Castle Crag, the subject of his lecture; and Reecastle, a less-easily defended fort high up above the present road into Watendlath. It was outside his remit for tonight, he said, but there was also an earlier fort, or cairn at least, from the Bronze Age, on a hillside above the West bank of Watendlath Tarn. But tonight was about these Iron Age people.

Ian's hand was up almost involuntarily – a by-product of Keswick School teaching methods. 'Yes?' the professor condescended. "Please Sir, what about the Stone Age people? Surely with Castlerigg Stone Circle on the doorstep they must have been in the valley?" Betty squirmed in her seat, but the lecturer was perhaps pleased to have some feedback.

"You're right, of course, but they were a long time before the hillfort on Castle Crag. We don't know much about them, whether they actually lived in the valley bottom, because you must remember it was covered in trees, marsh and scrubland. But what we do know is that they made stone axes – thousands of them – up on the slopes of Glaramara, in the boulder fields on the side of Thorneythwaite Fell." She could feel her young son glowing with the pride of possession – a Stone Axe factory, on their land!

Ian lost most of the rest of the lecture, his imagination running rife with the vision of men 5,000 years ago up on the steep intakes above the farm, chipping that particular volcanic rock, tuff, that would split so sharply, roughing out a boxful of axe heads for transporting down to the coast to be smoothed with the sandstone there into gleaming stone axes, used to chop down big trees to make all sorts of useful things. Oh yes, Borrowdale was a great place and always had been; and now he lived here, was a part of something amazing. He caught the last few words, before the polite applause from the mix of locals and visitors who had gathered.

"And yet, as far as we can tell, these Iron Age settlers either died out or moved on to gentler pastures. The Romans left no records of anyone living in the valley, though it does seem as if they climbed Castle Crag itself, for some shards of Roman pottery have been discovered there."

That night, after blowing out his candle and settling down in his bed, Ian had the strangest, but very lucid, dream…

Betty Hall on her beloved 'Grey Fergie' with Jim and Ian on an ancient hay-rake. 1961.

8

Chapter two

Ragnar, Freya and Ingmar. 960 AD

Thank God it was a clear night, with a full Harvest moon. Ragnar and Freya and their son Ingmar crept round the hamlet of Cese-wic aiming for the lake. It was unlikely anyone else would be about – it had been dark for hours – but there were always dogs ready to raise the alarm. So they kept well outside the limits, suffering the bogs and brambles as far preferable to being caught, for that would be death for Ragnar. No matter that Hagen had deserved to die; Norse justice demanded blood for blood, and Ragnar would rather live an outlaw than leave Freya and Ingmar to face the world without their man. At least a world without Hagen in it would be just that little safer for women. They should be safe as far up Borgar Dalr – the valley of the fort – as they could get, for the very reason that getting far up it was nearly impossible. The valley was a vast tangle of scrub, bogs, and fallen trees under a canopy of tall oak, elm and silver birch all competing for the light, leaving the valley floor dark and impenetrable. It was also home to wolves, wild boar and fierce wildcats that they would need to keep a sharp watch for.

By the time they reached the lake they were soaked several times over and badly scratched, but at least they made it without being discovered. Now the going was much easier, for Ragnar's plan was to use the stony shore where little grew as their highway. Sometimes they had to wade in the cold water, when crags or scrub grew right to the edge, but the lake was as warm at this end of Summer as it would ever be. Soon he had to carry little Ingmar, for the boy was only five summers old, and the cold and briars took their toll on him. He stopped so suddenly that Freya, following close behind, bumped into him and gave a low curse.

"Whisht, woman," he hissed, and pointed ahead to where a family of wild boar had come to the water's edge to drink, no more than thirty yards away. Fortunately they were downwind of the pigs, who seemed unaware of their presence, but the sight, even by moonlight, of those savage tusks was enough to keep them stock-still for what seemed an age, till the pigs had drunk their fill and melted back into the tangle of trees and the night. Ragnar felt at his belt for his axe – their only weapon – and hoped they met nothing else that night. The boy grew heavier as his legs grew colder, and he was aware of Freya's weariness as she carried the pack he had had to abandon. They would have to stop soon, yet he needed to be well away from Cese-wic before day-break.

At the head of the lake progress became impossible. Ragnar's plan was to follow the river up the valley – there was bound to be a river – but, quite suddenly, the stony edge of the lake gave way to deep water. There was no way between the scrubby, dense growth on the bank and the water too deep for them to wade. Exhausted, Freya laid down the burden, all their worldly goods strapped up in a leathern belt with a further belt to shoulder the load, and sat sobbing quietly on it. Ragnar too laid down his load, their sleepy son, and spread his woollen cloak over the three of them, as they huddled together, cold, wet, homeless, and very miserable. The moon sank below the Western fell and the darkness closed around them.

Only the boy slept. Freya and Ragnar would have had a hard enough time sleeping so roughly, but it was their thoughts that robbed them of sleep. Freya's terror as Hagen broke into their hut knowing Ragnar was out hunting with their neighbouring menfolk. He had been eyeing her for weeks, but she never thought he would act on his obvious lust. The rape had been brutal but mercifully short, but the pain of his penetration made the desperate journey up the lakeside doubly difficult. Had Ragnar returned a few minutes earlier she would have been spared the humiliation and perhaps Hager would still live. As it was he had burst in, warned by some instinct of her desecration, and with a single blow from that mighty axe had split Hagen's head in two.

Now, with the enforced rest, the full shock of that brief, momentous event made Freya tremble uncontrollably, reinforcing the natural shivers of the cold night. Ragnar held her close, as if to smother the shaking, but he too had his demons that night. He had never killed a man before, and the image of Hagen's brains spilling out on the earth floor of their hut almost made him vomit again, as he had so violently immediately after the blow. They had gathered up the boy, and as many possessions as they could easily carry, and crept away into the evening light. Who knew how long it would be before the hue and cry would begin, but with luck they would be well away by then.

Small wonder, then, that as soon as it was light enough they were ready to push on. Leaving the impassable lake-shore they turned into the taller trees and found the going tolerably easy. The canopy of leaves overhead, turning red, orange and yellow as Autumn drained the green from them, stopped any undergrowth, and the only real obstacles were the rotting trunks of long fallen trees, home to insects and fungi – and a source therefore of food for those who knew how to tell tasty from toxic – and the thousands of strewn boulders fallen from the crags above. They hurried on Southwards, with the steep fells always on their left, glimpsed now and then through a tear in the multi-coloured roof above them, past a tinkling

10

waterfall that was clearly just a shadow of what it would be in spate, and worked their way up the valley floor.

By and by they came upon a truly huge boulder, bigger by far than the ship Ragnar's grandfather had crossed the sea from the homeland in, and which he never tired of describing to his young kinsman. This 'gurt bowder' as Freya called it was the height of seven men surely, and far longer than the longship Grandfather had described – yet it was curiously ship-shaped, resting precariously on a keel. Ingmar was entranced, and cried when they insisted on moving on, after a short rest. They could hear the river chuckling to itself somewhere down to their right, and, again glimpsed from time to time through the eternal leaf-roof overhead was the strange hill they had seen so many times from Cese-wic – the Borgar crag, where the stories said was an ancient fort from the old days. If there was indeed such a thing, Ragnar couldn't see who might have built it or needed it, for there was no trace of human life in this dense forest.

The terrain pushed them down to the riverside, and to a confluence. It would have been simpler to follow the left tributary, but it very soon led to a swamp and scrubland, whereas they could see that across the main river the forest continued, looking a lot more inviting. Once across the river, that is. Bare feet found the stony river-bed hard going indeed, especially as Freya once again shouldered the baggage so that Ingmar could be carried, but once across they felt somehow lighter, as if they had put a barrier between themselves and any who might pursue them. Perhaps it was just that they could now see some distance. From their river-bank, under the trees, they could see a vast valley of marshy land stretching South-East from them, ringed by tree-covered fells and mighty crags. Never, in all their time in Cese-wic, had they suspected such a place existed. From there the Borgar crag hid all behind it, and yet here was a land where they could surely make a home. They sat, drying off and drinking in the unexpected vista.

As if to order there was a thicket of briars nearby, and they filled their empty bellies with the juicy brambles, young Ingmar dribbling purple all down his chin and jerkin. For once Freya hadn't the heart to chide. Here on the river-side was perhaps the only patch of ground around open to the sun, and, bellies full, they lay for a while soaking up its heat, letting it smooth away the horrors of yesterday and the night. It wasn't long however till the sun moved over the trees, and the chill wind urged them on. Not that Ragnar needed any urging: he wouldn't rest easy till he was as far from Cese-wic as the valley would allow. So once again they worked their way through the forest, the sun just visible enough from time to time to know they still headed South. They kept the river on their left, almost as

11

a trusted companion, as they worked their way around the unknown valley bottom.

It was almost evening when they came to the next marshland, nearly at the head of the valley. Much smaller than the valley floor where they had eaten, this swamp was held tightly by the high fells that crowded in on either side, and by the range they could see from the hut in Cese-wic, so much bigger now at close quarters. There was no point in going further; beyond the marsh was nothing but fell, nowhere to build a hut and a new life. The river here was much narrower, and took little effort to ford, and they made their way along the edge of the marsh, a steep little hillock running alongside it on their left, covered in trees and, once again, thorn briars, laden with brambles. Picking again, they found themselves atop the small hillock, and suddenly in the lea on its Northern rim, for this strange ridge ran like a spine from the river towards the fell. It seemed a good place to shelter for the night at least, and in the gathering darkness they fashioned a shelter from the fallen branches. Once again they lay together on the mossy forest floor, Ragnar's cloak pulled over them, and stiffened together as the wolves started their ghostly howling, greeting the night. Ragnar's hand tensed around his axe-shaft, yet strangely they slept, and slept on till dawn sought them out again.

The next morning they awoke to a hoar frost, the ground sparkling underfoot. Hidden as they were under the seamless canopy, with the hillock to their backs, the world might have disappeared whilst they slept, and it was tempting for the adults to lie still, warm under the cloak, and put off the business of food and shelter as long as possible. Ingmar would have none of this lassitude, and bounded up the small ridge crying out as he reached the top "Come and look! I can see right to the fells."

He was right: the forest gave way to the marsh they had seen the evening before, but now there was time to take an informed look. Freya was fascinated. "Look, you can see how this little ridge has curved all the way across the valley. It must have enclosed a lake once, before the river broke through where we came in last night."

"That's why it's still so marshy, I suppose" agreed Ragnar, " It'll be good for us – there must be all sort of fruit among the scrub, and isn't it good to be able to see a distance." It was true: looking South there were views, but to the North nothing but the eternal forest, easy to get lost in – but surely good for hunting and for building materials. He had his trusty axe so it must be possible to make a decent shelter for his family. And a bow. They needed meat, there was only so long you can keep going on brambles. One of the trees nearby was a yew – and an old yew at that, with its heart long gone, but strong still with its vast hollow trunk supporting new growth. Ragnar selected a stout, straight shoot and trimmed it down to an arm's span bow. Ferreting about in the baggage they had brought with them he found a length of good hemp rope to string the bow, and cut several arrows from a hazel growing nearby. He was ready.

"What will you shoot, father?" asked Ingmar, wide-eyed. He was much too young to have been on a hunt yet. "Let's see what we can find." murmured Ragnar, thoughtfully. The marsh might well be the best place – at least he could see some distance there.

"Freya, take the lad down and out into the swamp, if you can, and when you're as far out as you can get, turn and start back, shouting. Let's see if anything moves down there." He settled himself at the edge, watchful, as Freya and Ingmar made a wide sweep, often up to their knees in mud. They got about fifty yards out before turning and breaking out into a fine hullabaloo. Startled, a young roe deer – this year's calf – erupted from a clump of reeds and ran from them, straight at Ragnar. He was a skilled bowman, and at that range could hardly miss. The doe was dead before it hit the ground, pierced in the breast. They would eat well that night.

They did, but that night for the first time since they set out from Cese-wic the rain came. And what rain! It soon broke through the pitiful shelter they had made against the huge fallen oak, and before long their teeth chattered in unison beneath the soaking cloak. It was as well they had good meat in their bellies, and the fire they had cooked venison on or they might well have been dead of cold by morning. The rain stopped, eventually, as light began to seep through the russet trees, and Freya was up and fretting at the fire to warm her young son, who shivered still. There would be no dry tinder for the flint now; thank Odin they had lit it yesterday. She made Ingmar jump and run and skip till he warmed, though they were all still in soaked clothing. A waterproof shelter was vital, and they set out as a family to decide just where it should be.

Obviously the marsh was of no use, but Freya was fearful of the dense forest and the wolves they had heard in the night. Looking East from where they stood the forest seemed lighter – almost as if it had been cleared in some dim and distant past. Hoisting the pack Ragnar set out through the trees, Freya holding young Ingmar's hand, as much for her comfort as his. Sure enough they soon came upon what was, if not a clearing, at least a much less densely wooded area, containing a lot of scrub and bramble and patches of nettle. They had gone no more than a hundred paces, but this felt like a place for a home. They cast about the area, which seemed another hundred paces across, coming on the remains of old stone walls. A tear glistened on Freya's eye as she took in the implication: their long outlawed trek had somehow brought them to a place of sanctuary. She could feel it in her whole being. This was a place that had been loved – long ago, to be sure, but here she felt safe. To the East the fell rose rapidly, promising shelter, and the clearing itself nestled among huge boulders in the lea of the same ridge they had come up last night.

National Trust map of the Iron Age settlement. The four thick lines are modern walls. The outer bank goes into all four quadrants and is easiest seen in the Western quarter, and can then be traced into three quarters of a circle. (Used with permission.)

It was Ingmar who found what was to be their home, hidden away in a huge patch of nettles a stone walled circle standing four feet high, with an obvious doorway. The South side snuggled into a mighty boulder, a man's height. Ragnar gave a cry of delight and vigorously

14

tousled his son's red curls. Cutting hazel sticks they laid low the nettlebed, dragged away the bedraggled fallen stems, and stamped the stumps to flatten them. Freya and Ingmar searched around for ferns to lay on the floor while Ragnar used the fallen stones around the wall to rebuild and heighten it. By midday it was ready for a roof. Steady work with his axe produced a number of sturdy ash poles and many more hazel rods which Freya and Ingmar wove into the cross poles. Soon they had a lattice that would bear sods – enough hopefully to keep out any rain. In this regrown clearing the tree cover was light enough to allow a grassy undergrowth, and before darkness fell they had a roof worthy of the name, and a shelter to call a home. In the last of the light they ate their fill of brambles Freya had sent Ingmar off to pick, and managed to light a fire of reeds that had dried enough in the day to catch from the flint. It felt almost like home, and from then on it would indeed be home.

It had no name, but a little later, when other Norsemen made their way up the valley and such places needed to be called something they called it 'the clearing in the thorns' after the briars that had nourished them in those first desperate days – or, in their own language, Thorney-thwaite

Chapter three

Jim 1960 – 63

After the Horse Close debacle Jim sought advice on ploughing – or rather, on which fields to plough. Not from his neighbours, but from the professional agricultural advisors to be found at the Ministry of Agriculture's establishment at Pen-y-Cuik, near Edinburgh. His historic link with farming was broken: true enough his father, old Tom Hall, had been an agricultural labourer all his life, but Jim had been a city boy till the war and he was a strong believer in good advice, and plenty of it. Giving, as well as taking, as Ian often found. Mr Ollerenshaw duly arrived and Jim and Betty set off round the bottom land with him. Mr Ollerenshaw got more and more excited as they made the tour.

"Do you realise what you're sitting on here? It's a complete geography and geology lesson within a few small acres! Look, where the farmyard sits, in the lee of that ridge – that's a terminal moraine left by the Ice Age." Betty looked quizzical; the school certificate in Bristol hadn't covered the Ice Age.

"When the glaciers that scoured out this U-shaped valley started to melt they were carrying immeasurable tons of rock and debris they'd cut away from the hillsides, and where they stopped and melted all that debris piled up, and that's what you've got here. The ridge behind the house is made from millions of tons of rocks that got dumped there." It was Jim's turn to look quizzical.

"And does that have an effect on where we should plough, then?"

"Most certainly! Because the moraine has gone right across the valley floor there would be a lake behind it – all the way up to Seathwaite. So all this land to the South, in the obvious dip, was a lake bottom, and will be full of silt – maybe many feet deep. That's where to plough. Let's go along to those fields – what is it you call them?"

"The big six-acre is Noon Bank, and the four-acre beyond is Nookem, or Neukum – take your choice." Once in Noon Bank Mr Ollerenshaw theatrically poised his walking stick, and thrust it into the ground. Putting his full weight on the top he pushed and rotated, as it sank its full length into the soil. Betty felt moved to clap at such a performance, while Jim helped pull it out again against the considerable suck of the rather sticky clay.

"Of course, the problem is drainage" puffed Mr O. "They're always going to be difficult, and obviously that next field, nearer to the

16

moraine, is completely saturated." He was right, Overclose Bottom as it was nudgingly known was a mass of sieves and bog, with a choked gutter running through it. Even the field on the opposite side of Black Syke, the stream that ran through all these fields, bore a lot of rushes and wet patches.

"I'll bet that lot has been drained, once upon a time, but unless you spend a fortune to re-do them I doubt you'll ever be able to use that one. How big did you say it was?"

"Oh, I guess there must be six acres there, but it would have to be a landlord's job to drain it, and I can't see them going to that expense." Just two years into their tenancy Jim and Betty had discovered that if you want something done on a tenanted farm, you'd best do it yourself.

"Well, you could certainly plough Noon Bank and… Nookem, did you say it was called? That would give you ten acres of improved grazing. And in a dry year you could probably do that field between the river and Black Syke. What a magnificent name for a beck!" One thing you could say for Mr O, he was enthusiastic.

"One thing more" he added "before you plough Noon Bank, I would mole drain it, it'll help the drainage no end." Betty looked blank, so he explained. "It's a deep burrow like as if a mole had made a run two feet down. You pull the machine behind the tractor, and it has a solid metal cylinder about three inches in diameter below a strong sharp plate that cuts a channel so water can trickle down to the 'mole run'." Jim nodded sagely, he knew the machine, and it shouldn't be expensive – it was just a lump of metal really, no moving parts except for the disc that cut the sod.

That autumn, Jim attached their brand-new mole drainer to the back of the Fergie, and Betty carefully drew it from the beck right across to the far fence, cutting a drain every yard, as Mr O had instructed. The field looked a bit like lined paper, as the mole plough raised a weal every yard along the length of the field. Never mind, once she had ploughed it and made a proper seed-bed it would look beautiful. All that draining and she hadn't hit a single stone – after Horse Close it was a great relief.

Next day a GPO van drew into the yard and asked if there was any reason they could think of why the telephone line to Seathwaite Farm, up the valley wasn't working. With a dawning realisation they looked at each other.

"You'd better come along to Noon Bank" said Jim, leading the way in the old Land Rover. The man in the van took one look at all those neat cuts, every yard along the field, and said "Yep, I guess that would do it!"

"Bloody silly place to put a telephone line," muttered Jim.

Jim had good reasons for wanting to improve the grass, bringing in a rye-grass mixture. Already they had discovered just how hard it is to make hay in a climate with an average 140 inches of rain a year – the wettest in England – and they were keen to move on to silage, which could be cut one day and moved into a silo the next. They'd also discovered how difficult it is to persuade a landlord to invest in such a silo, and had to agree to fund it themselves with an understanding that they would receive disbursements for it if they left the tenancy. That meant doing all the building work themselves, and as cheaply as possible. The obvious place to put the silo was in the stackyard behind the smaller barn, but as Mr Ollerenshaw had pointed out that was on the terminal moraine, with hard rock pressed down and overflowing.

The silo needed a roof, and the roof needed ten stanchions: one-foot diameter larch trunks, to be set at least three feet into the ground. Jim started the first hole with a pick and spade. "Here Ian, you're always saying you want to build up your muscles. See what you can do with this." Ian was thirteen, his Dad forty-five. Perfect opportunity to show what he was made of. Together they got down nearly a foot, after a whole afternoon, and now it was impossible to pick and hammering a crowbar in did nothing either. Jim looked at his sweating son. "Well, what do you reckon?"

"Dynamite!" Ian was kidding, but that's what they would do in the adventure books he loved.

"D'you know, that's not a bad idea." One call to his pal Mr Ollerenshaw to explain the problem, and soon a certificate came through permitting them to buy dynamite 'for the purposes of agricultural excavation'. Imagine a young boy's delight at being allowed to use explosives – so much better than a cap-gun. They quickly established a decent method. Jim would drive the crowbar as far down as he could achieve – sometimes only a few inches, such was the compaction of the boulder clay they were working in, and allow Ian to cut an 18 inch length of fuse, clamp on a detonator, insert it into a stick of dynamite and feed the stick into the hole Jim had made. They stuffed a bale of straw on top, to direct as much blast downwards as possible, then cut an inch long slit in the end of the fuse to make it easy to light. 'Light the blue touch paper and retire'… The bangs were tremendous, a thunderclap resounding round the valley, echoing, re-echoing and slowly dying. The results were less impressive; usually just about six inches disturbed enough to be able to dig out before repeating the procedure. Guy Fawkes Night lost its appeal for Ian, somehow it just couldn't compete.

The finished silo and sheep sheds

The silo was ready for 'haytime' 1963, and Murphy's Law dictated that that was the first half-decent Summer, when they could have made hay. Still, Jim was relieved to have the silo full to overflowing. Noon Bank alone had half-filled it, the new crop of rye-grass proving its worth. The previous winter had severely tested the new tenants of Thorneythwaite, and everyone else around. The big freeze started on January 2nd and didn't slacken its grip till well into March. The pipes in the farmhouse froze first: with no heating other than the Aga and a coal fire the bedrooms and bathroom were sub-zero all night and all day. Only the tap in the kitchen kept going. Out in the byres the cattle's warmth managed to keep the water flowing in the troughs in their stalls, and they could just about wrest a living from the poor, blackened hay that was all they had been able to salvage the previous August. The sheep, on the other hand, refused to eat the stuff, and Jim was reduced to cutting down holly and ash branches, having noticed them chewing on some which had fallen. Betty opened the fell gate so as many as wanted could at least seek shelter in the intakes, and gnaw the moss that grew on the North side of every tree, but

19

those left on the fell must have suffered severely. She wanted to gather the fell, bringing them all into the intakes, and buy in some decent hay for them, but Jim would have none of it.

"All the other farmers around say you have to leave them out to keep them hardy; otherwise you'll be feeding them every year 'cos they'll come in even if it's a warmer winter." It was certainly 'survival of the fittest' – but there didn't seem to be many qualifying as fittest come lambing time.

About three weeks into the big freeze the underground pipe from the water tank on the fellside froze. Ian volunteered to try to thaw it out using the flame-thrower, a primitive bit of gear that heated up a tube of diesel as it neared the flame end, attempting to gasify it before it reached the flame. When it worked it did indeed throw out an impressive amount of heat, but more usually it sprayed liquid burning diesel all over the place. Needless to say, he failed to thaw any underground pipes, and the cattle and humans were without running water for the next six weeks. Ian escaped to school and the luxury of taps and flushing toilets; Betty and Jim had to fend for themselves as best they could, and had to let all the cattle out of the byres twice a day to go down to Black Syke for a drink. It takes a lot of water to sluice down mouldy old hay.

Ian didn't only escape to school. Derwentwater Lake froze over inches thick – some said the ice was two feet thick, and a lorry was driven from the boat landings to Nichol End to prove it. He and his girlfriend, Jen, spent at least an hour at the end of each school day out on the ice with friends, skating, playing ice hockey, and generally mucking about till darkness put an end to it.

It says a lot for Herdwick sheep that most of the flock did at least survive that harshest of winters, though lambing time showed how great the cost had been, with most having reabsorbed their foetus lambs in a bid for self-preservation. That winter at least they justified their reputation as the only breed capable of living on the high fells.

Chapter four

Freya's story 1000 AD

I knew when I eased from sleep to a drowsy awareness that something was wrong. It was just a feeling of impending doom that soon crystallised. Ragnar: the man beside me in our bed was gone. I knew it in my heart long before my mind would accept it, and my mind wouldn't let me turn over to check. Perhaps if I just lay here he would be alive, his usual jovial self. How long could I lie there? How long could I hold back cold reality? You won't believe this, but I lay there forever, refusing to confirm what still might not be true, but which once confirmed could no longer be denied. I lay there till Erica parted the skins which divided the room, to ask with a laugh if we were ever getting up. Her laugh died in her throat as she took it in.

Ragnar was dead, fallen away in the night sometime. He was stiff beside me, gnarled hands clenched tightly, his beard, long grown white, flecked with spittle. Someone gave out a long, drawn-out cry of pure anguish: I could scarcely believe it was my throat let loose that terrible sound, my distress that was itself so distressing. Erica held me close as the scream subsided and the sobs began. All the time my body was reacting so profoundly my mind was doing the strangest things. It hovered in the roof timbers, looking down detachedly on the sobbing old crone below, being cradled in the arms of her daughter-in-law. It dwelt on the solid construction Ragnar had made for us, the circular hut we found at first being far too mean for our use. As he had said, so many years ago now, with Borgar Dalr rain you really needed good stone walls – and an even better roof. My man had built in the manner of our fathers. Rectangular, rather than circular, thick walls, an arm's length of thickness and more, with close fitting big stones forming the inner and the outer leaf, and smaller stones packed tight in between so you couldn't see through from one side to another anywhere. Thick walls which would throw off the rain and, coated with mud on the inside, would hold heat in the house, for the winters were savage here. The roof was a living carpet of grass, where he had piled sod upon sod, on a framework of solid timbers, with a goodly pitch to throw off the rain. Everything was designed to keep out that terrible rain, for that first desperate winter it had nearly killed us all. But he built in that same enclosure we had found when we first came – partly because there was a lot of available stone from the ruins of the old huts, partly because it had been quite easy to restore the clearing, and partly because it was the one place I felt at ease, safe.

At the peak of the roof, where my mind busied itself, he had built a wooden vent to let out the smoke from the fire that burned continually in the hearth below, and set a cunning cowl on it, again to throw off the rain. The only opening was the doorway, and again Ragnar had made a solid wooden door on leather hinges that could keep the weather out and the heat in. It was dark inside, till your eyes got used to the gentle light of the fire and perhaps a candle, when we had got sorted, but it was warm, warm enough to allow my man and me a longer life than was usual. But now he was gone, and I wanted no more days to my life. How long had it been? Airily my mind escaped the house, where it had no wish to remain, and inspected the tall oak that he had left standing on the ridge behind the house. Every Spring Ragnar took his mighty axe and with two blows cut out a notch, one for every year we shared in this haven from the world. There were fifty notches – my roving mind didn't need to count them, for we had celebrated this Spring when he cut the fiftieth, drinking down the good sweet mead that Ingmar made from his bees' honey.

The house that Ragnar made for us.

Oh yes, fifty years saw huge changes in our valley. Suddenly my mind could support its flight no longer. My eyes focussed on my dead love and the tears began to flow. The crone ceased her sobbing, to Erica's relief and mine, and I became a grieving widow who knew that's what she was. With many a backward hesitant look Erica left me briefly to fetch Ingmar from whatever it was he was about this morning, and the task of mourning began in earnest. Are you surprised to hear me call it a task? All I can say is that I found it so: somehow I had to make sure all these incomers who had joined us these last fifty years knew what they owed my man. I knew they didn't really want to know, or knew already, but I must need rehearse it all, time after time, with this person and with that: anyone who would listen. And they did all listen, for there was respect both for Ragnar and for me. We had blazed the trail they had all followed to a new life, to the freedom of the valley – blazed it literally, too. Single handed, in those early years, before others came to join us, single-handedly we had made our clearing, Ragnar chopping down tree after tree, big gnarled oaks and the smaller birch and holly, till the earth could see the sky and I could grow some vegetables, a little oats. He had to steal back down the valley, many times, to gather seed from the cultivated plots on the outskirts of Cese-wic, while I lay coddling our boy, terrified he wouldn't return, that he would be caught. In time he made a sort of track through the forest, blazing occasional trees so he could easily find his way in the dense woodland.

Eventually, of course, others joined us, led by the track and the scarred trees. The first time we were wary, slipping away from the clearing when we heard an approaching footfall, but one glimpse of the bedraggled family standing at a loss at the door convinced us we were in better shape than the newcomers, and had nothing to fear. Clearly, they too were outcasts, fleeing from summary justice. Soon there were others, perhaps outcast, or maybe just following our Norse desire to explore, and soon there were established tracks through much of the forest, with marks blazed on many trees. The newcomers made their own clearings, and the clearings developed their own names. Stonethwaite, where the boulders lay in the woodland too big to move; Rose-thwaite where the briars blossomed each year. There weren't many families yet, but my Ragnar was their acknowledged leader, and I chief among the women, for we had blazed the trail. Perhaps for only the second time in history the upper end of Borgar Dalr was home to a people.

Then came the sheep, a motley flock of a dozen ewes and a tup. Dirty grey, individual animals, each one distinguishable from the rest, once you got to know them. Only the two yearlings were a different colour, a dark brown. The aptly named Walden, whose name means a forest valley, brought them from Cese-wic. Fortunately he had a big family, for these sheep weren't easy to handle, and preferred to go off in three different directions unless constrained. It must have been a tricky operation in the dense woodland – or perhaps the well-worn trail seemed the easier option to the sheep. Hard-wicks, Walden called them, and he maintained they had come all the way from their Norse homelands, brought in a longboat to

Whitoft-haven, the natural harbour on the coast where most Norsemen came in – though usually from Ireland these days.

Ragnar had cleared a couple of acres by then, right up to the raised boundary of the old enclosure we'd found that first few days we were here, and grass grew where previously there had been nothing but the scrub and undergrowth. This was perfect for the Hard-wicks, once we had made enough hazel hurdles to pen off an area for them to graze. Moving the hurdles was a twice-weekly job that the youngsters could do, and there were many youngsters now, with immigrants and burgeoning 'locals'. Thorneythwaite was a hamlet, self-sufficient in a very basic way.

The wolves were a problem, now we had sheep. Before they had left us alone, more frightened of us than we were of them, though we guarded our youngsters carefully. But a dozen sheep herded together were altogether too tempting, in the middle of the night. We woke to a great commotion, the sheep bleating and running, and Ragnar leapt to his feet clad only in his night-shirt and grabbed his axe, shouting at me to rouse the others. He leapt the hurdle, thundering like Thor on a bad day, swinging his axe at the pack of wolves that had the sheep trapped in a corner, three already ripped apart. Cowards that they are at heart the entire pack slunk away, tails fixed well between their legs, but not before Ragnar had stove in two of their skulls, and given another a mighty slice it wouldn't recover from. By the time the other men had risen and appeared it was all over, but our flock was sadly depleted, and the survivors badly shocked. Here was a new task: someone would have to keep guard each night, huddled over a fire, ready to raise the alarm.

Next came the cattle – a couple of sorry looking beasts, one of them in calf, the other already milking. Walden brought them too, stolen from Cese-wic one night. Ragnar was furious. Such an obvious theft was sure to bring a raiding party bent on revenge, and we spent many an anxious night on full alert, ready to defend ourselves. No-one came: perhaps they weren't sure where the thieves had come from, or perhaps they couldn't raise enough men brave enough to venture up the forest. Nevertheless, Ragnar was so incensed by Walden's thieving ways that he insisted he should make his own home, some distance from Thorneythwaite. He chose to go to the very head of the valley, the other side of the marsh to our South, and he made himself and his big family a timber house there. Because it was a clearing among the sedges and sieves of the marshland he called it Seathwaite, and so it has remained. Time will tell if it can survive, for there's hardly any valley land he can clear, just the far-reaching marsh between us. I'm told he lets his sheep run on the high fell, above the treeline, where there is grazing of a sort. Perhaps it will work, but he must be hard-pressed to keep them from the wolves.

We have our own sheep and a couple of cows, and I have to admit it's good to have the milk, the meat and particularly the wool to make new clothes each year. But my heart reaches out still to those early years when it was just Ragnar and me, Ingmar and our other children, when they were young. We were hunters, then, hunters and gatherers of the fruit that each autumn brought. The valley was ours, ours alone. Ah well, I'm an old woman now, and times change. Not for the better, though, not to my mind.

Chapter five

Jim Hall

We had a major problem at Thorneythwaite, in the early days: how to generate a cash flow. Yes, we had wether lambs to sell in the back end of the year, and store cattle at the same time, but neither brought in a huge amount, and it was a long time between income cheques – about eleven months. Most farms in the valley, indeed in the Lake District in general, could depend on tourism for cash-flow, a steady trickle in of money throughout the year. Billy Dixon and his wife, the tenants before us, had a useful Bed and Breakfast business going. So successful that there was a timber shed in Lamb Close that they and their son Ralph decamped to at the beginning of summer each year so as to allow all six bedrooms in the farmhouse to be used by guests. Ethel Dixon cooked up fried breakfasts on the four-oven Aga each morning, and there was a dining room and a separate sitting room for them all, leaving the Dixons their own sitting room and the old kitchen.

Our problem was that Betty refused point-blank to take in Bed and Breakfast guests, with all the cooking and laundry needed to maintain that throughput of people. As she said, forcefully, she wanted to be outside, farming, not inside skivvying all day. We compromised, as you do in marriage. There was a newish form of holiday being taken in the early sixties called 'self-catering', where a family would rent a house for a week or more and cater for themselves. This sounded much more sensible to Betty – she could cope with laundry and cleaning one day a week. There were teething troubles of course, mainly that we lived in the house too. So a family would have to rent the far end of the farmhouse, with the dining room as a kitchen/diner, their own living room, and four of the six bedrooms. But they would have to share the stairs with us, and more importantly the single bathroom and lavatory. Three of us and maybe nine or ten of them, still better odds than it was in the army. For the first three years there was also the lack of electricity to contend with, but they seemed to like the idea of candles and calor gas – at least for a week. It took us the first few months to get set up and put an advert in 'The Lady' but we were ready for our first guests by the summer holidays. A single family from the North-East took the whole month, five weeks at the princely sum of nine pounds a week. Well, we didn't want to set it too high.

We were more professional by year two, 1961, and it did go some way to providing year-round cash, just not enough of it. Some neighbouring farms had campsites, pretty ramshackle affairs with primitive facilities, but again a cash crop. Our landlord forbade any serious camping, but did say we could allow a particular Scout Troop from Millom to camp whenever they wanted. Well, one Scout Troop is very like another, don't you think? So we broadened the remit to allow any Scouts – or indeed organised groups of kids – to camp on Tup Close, where the grass never grew longer than a couple of inches in a year. The crunch came when he decided to visit the valley and walk over his domain. He thumped on the door and demanded to know what we thought we were doing allowing any old Scouts on his land. Only Millom Scouts were to be afforded the privilege! I told him where he could stuff his Millom Scouts, one by one if he fancied, and that was the end of camping and the sixpence a day per Scout. Not to his face, sadly.

And anyway, we wanted to make our living from agriculture, not tourism, so it was clear we needed an intensive unit or two, with regular sales. That narrows it down to pigs or poultry, and after five years of pigs at our previous small-holding I was pig-sick. Battery hens it would be. We already had two rooms of deep-litter hens, on the barn floors above the shippons in the smaller barn, and were retailing their eggs in the valley to the guest-houses and hotels, and I was confident we were only scratching the surface of the market. The problem was, where to install these battery cages. None of the buildings were suitable: we needed a purpose built unit that would be warm and easy to clean, or so Mr Ollerenshaw said. Fortunately he knew just the ticket. After the war the government had put up thousands of 'prefabs' – factory made asbestos walls and roofs that could be put together on site, originally for people to live in, and now, fifteen years on, for other people to take down and use elsewhere as sheds... and henhouses.

Betty, Ian and I piled into the ancient Land-Rover that served as car, lorry and trailer puller and had a day out in Dalkeith, the current source of prefabs. The site boss was a very helpful fellow – been in the Army Service Corps like me – and showed us what he said was his best example, but warned that we would need to make a timber skeleton to re-erect it if we weren't having internal walls, as they were integral to its construction. He promised to see personally to its taking down and loading on a lorry – 'bit rough, some of these lads, and you don't want things ripped apart'. Cash on delivery, in pound notes, please. Fair enough, at that price.

So we got our intensive egg production underway. It had better work, and work quickly, because the two banks of cages and the 700 hens took all the capital we had left, plus a sizeable loan from the Midland Bank, at 7% interest. The only problem was the cleaning and grading. If you're sending all the eggs to the Egg Marketing Board, for stamping with

27

the little Lion, there's no problem. If you're selling them yourself to every hotel in Borrowdale they need to be clean and graded small, medium or large. Betty and I spent a couple of hours every night with one little weighing machine between us, wiping and weighing. Talk about 'Go to work on an egg!'

The only other sources of precious income are the subsidies. Without them hill farming would be buggered. Let's face it, we produce skinny little Herdwick lambs, only fit to eat after some lowland farm has fattened them up, and likewise skinny little store cattle. If we had to live on the skinny little cheque they produce each year we'd soon be bankrupt. Through a quirk of history, Betty and I had our chance to influence subsidies – whether we managed or not I don't know. I knew Harold Wilson's wife when we were both learning clerical skills at the Gregg School in Carlisle. She was Gladys then! She's Mary now; I guess it sounds better for a Prime Minister's wife. They were due to stay overnight at the George Hotel, in Penrith, and damn me if we didn't get an invitation to join them for dinner that night in the hotel.

"Just how friendly were you two back in 1934?" asked Betty, dangerously demurely. Hell, I was eighteen, Gladys was seventeen… we were pretty friendly – friendly enough to elicit an invitation to dinner some thirty years later, and to have sent Christmas cards all those years.

"Oh, you know – long before your time, love."

The problem was Betty really can't stand Harold. She's Tory to her toenails, though she does always say "Labour? Best party ever for farmers; trouble is they wreck the rest of the country." I've stopped saying anything, it only leads to arguments. Still, she agreed to come – as long as she could have a new outfit.

"I'm not having Gladys showing me up." No contest! I'd back Betty every time. In the event it was a lovely evening, and Harold really did seem interested in what we had to say about fell farming, and he promised to have Fred Peart, his Minister of Agriculture and coincidentally MP for nearby Workington, come out to visit us to get a grass-roots picture of the problems of fell farms. We felt distinctly uncomfortable in a sense representing hill farmers' views to such an important figure as the Minister of Agriculture, since we had only recently become genuine hill farmers, but we gave it our best shot. I don't suppose we had the slightest effect on such a well-established figure as Fred – he'd been Workington's MP since the Labour landslide of 1945, and knew the region intimately. Still… Fred Peart's Annual Review that year (1964) made special mention of the social value of farmers, and for the first time since the war the value of Government guarantees on prices were bigger than our increased costs. For years the Tory Government had been trying to eliminate protection and support for agriculture by making us more competitive on the world markets, surely doomed to failure when most other countries were actively protecting their farmers. Fred introduced import controls, especially on imported New Zealand lamb, which could only help us.

As part of the programme for structural reform his subsequent White Papers also proposed mobilization in the special support for hill and upland farmers which had existed in varying forms since 1940. Livestock headage payments were put on a long-term basis and increased in value (1965), hill ploughing grants were introduced (1967) and further structural measures applied (1969). While assisting the achievement of productivity targets and especially the targets for beef, these measures were also in part stemming from the concern with regional problems and, within that, the peculiar problems of remote rural areas.

No doubt all this would have happened anyway, but I can't help a little private feeling of pride that something that started as a bit of a fling between a couple of teenagers in Carlisle might just have made a contribution to Lakeland fell-farmers viability, and that Peart's visit to Thorneythwaite might have helped.

Chapter Six

Alice de Rumilly, the elder, late 12th Century

One look at the falconer's face was enough to bring my world crashing down. He fought for words, and came out with the strangest of expressions. "My Lady, what is good for a bootless bene?" I knew just what he meant – my boy, my darling boy, was dead. What indeed the good of prayer now, for it could avail nothing. With infinite sadness I answered him, prophetically, "Endless sorrow!"

Between his gulps, both for air, for he had run far with his news, and because he sobbed so, he gave up his story. He was charged to take care of Will, my only son. They had been hunting alongside the River Wharfe, Will with his trusty wolf-hound Holdfast. I must have told Will a hundred times not to jump the river at The Strid, but I might as well have kept my peace. Boys turning into men have a lot to prove, to themselves as much as to anyone else. The falconer told how Will was in hot pursuit of a deer which cleared the Strid with ease. Will himself also easily leapt the chasm, but Holdfast – ill-named hound that he is – balked the leap, and being on a strong lead pulled my boy back, into that fearsome torrent that is so constrained there. I could not blame the falconer, but for all that I did: I beat upon his chest, I railed at him for his carelessness, I threatened him with death for his treason in losing my boy. But what is good for a bootless bene? Nothing would bring him back.

I would give all my estates, my Skipton Castle, our Egremont Castle, once more to gaze on his radiant face. My husband William and I had so much, yet now I have naught, for he is gone and I have lost our son. Will was to be so great, to inherit so much… when men called him, as they did, the Boy of Egremont, it meant so much to me. Yes, he was Lord Egremont's – my William's – boy, but he was so much more. He was the boy who would make Egremont great, complete the mighty castle, take in hand the Barony, subdue the truculent dales men who chafed at the few taxes we levied upon them. What point now in Baronies, in lands subdued to our rule?

I know what it is: it is God's retribution on my cruel husband's many callous acts. He was my Lord William, son of Duncan, who was King of Scotland, and he should have been King had not his Uncle David given him titles enough for him to relinquish the throne. He was but young then, when King Duncan died in 1094. He was a lot older when he married me, a seventeen-year-old girl in 1130. Of course I had no choice – mine was one of the titles King David gave him by insisting on our marriage.

With me he got what he wanted, a share in the Honour of Copeland and the Honour of Skipton. With me came Egremont Castle, Cockermouth Castle and Skipton Castle. And with me he got a son, now dead, and my beloved girls, Cecily, Alice and Amabel. But he was a hard, vicious man, who had butchered many both in battle and in battle's aftermath. I do not miss him.

My Skipton Castle in the snow.

And so history repeats itself. I am only the Lady of Skipton because my brothers, Matthew and Ranulph, died before they had children, just like my Will, my Boy of Egremont. And just like my three girls, there were three of us, Avice, me and Maud. Just as we three did, my three girls will inherit my estates, and three husbands will rub their grubby hands in delight at the lands they will take on. I shall leave my Honour of Copeland, with its blighted Egremont Castle, to Amabel, and that of Allerdale with Cockermouth Castle to Alice. Amabel is closest to Will, both in looks and temperament. Copeland has never meant as much to me as Skipton, for here was I brought up. Here have I made my bequests, setting up Bolton

31

Abbey for the monks of Embsay. That was the last thing we did together, Will, my Boy of Egremont, and I. We signed the charter, and I shall rejoice to see the Abbey completed in my Will's name. I shall leave Skipton to Cecily, who bears her grandmother's name – her grandmother who first owned Skipton.

I wish young Alice well of Allerdale, for its taxes have ever been hard to garner. The men of the valleys are but subsistence peasants, scratching a bare living on their few acres of land. Wool is their best crop, the only produce with a price, and after clipping time is the only time to send around the bailiffs. And some are so far from anywhere – wild Borrowdale for instance. It is impossible to get neither days labour nor monies in lieu from them, savage Norsemen as they be still.

I have lived long – longer than I would wish, since Alexander, my second husband died in the year of our Lord, 1178. He was mine only comfort that terrible time when young Will died. Twenty years we had, good years, but now they're gone, and I must to my Maker too. It is Anno Domini 1187; I do not think I will see the new year in.

Alice de Rumilly the younger

One might think we three, Mother's 'Trinity', could be grateful for our mother's sake for our inheritance, for it came at the price of her loss of 'The Boy', who would otherwise have inherited all. Perhaps we could, had we not married, but husbands bring dissent, and children all the more so. I could have none – I suppose I am barren, cursed by the blight that hovers over our family. The blight centres on Egremont Castle, and the men who claim to own it. Amabel married Reginald de Lucy, a most vexatious man, and had a son Richard de Lucy, if anything even more sorely vexing. He sued both myself and my sister Cecily for a larger share of Copeland and Allerdale, and because his uncle was Justiciar he won. It did him little good, the Egremont blight got both him and his father: Reginald died in 1200, and Richard a scant dozen years later.

Perhaps because I have no issue I can afford to be generous, but I find it gives me pleasure to support our religious houses. Besides, it keeps me close to Mama in memory. She was forever granting charters to the monasteries, even before Papa was dead. She founded Embsay and funded its move to Bolton Abbey, and she was generous to Fountains Abbey, the huge new Cistercian monastery on the banks of the Wharfe – dread river that took her boy, my brother. Fountains was founded the year she and Papa married, so it was especially dear to her. So it was my pleasure to re-build the church at Crosthwaite, near Keswick, in my lands of Allerdale.

The renewed church shall serve the valleys, and particularly lowly Borrowdale. And for the sake of my soul, and for that of my beloved Gilbert, my first husband, I gave that East part of the valley including Watendlath, Langstrath and part of Stonethwaite to Fountains Abbey, for the monks will farm it better than the surly serfs left over from a darker age.

I gave East Borrowdale to Fountains in 1195, just before I married Robert de Courtney, my second husband. I could not be sure he would approve, so the charter was signed before our marriage. By my time of life I feel it better to put down markers – and it has worked, for I find him as generous as I could wish. When he died in 1208 I had to find a lot of money, 250 marks, out of a total fine of 500 pounds (plus ten palfreys and ten fillies), so I sold the West part of Borrowdale, which was now cut off from the rest of my Allerdale holdings. Perhaps I should have sold to Fountains, giving them all the valley, but I felt our family had given them a fine start already, so I sold the West of the valley to Furness Abbey, their sister Cistercian foundation down on the very South-West of the land before the Bay. Founded in 1123 it is eight years older than Fountains: a little sibling rivalry in the valley will do no harm!

It has few vills therein, just Grangia in the North and Seathwaite, Longthwaite and Thorneythwaite in the South. They paid me £156:13s:4d; just short of the 250 marks I needed following Robert's death.

Radulf, great-great-great-great-grandson of Ragnar.

I'm the seventh generation of our family to farm Thorneythwaite, and I'm fiercely proud of what we have achieved here. We keep our history close, our family, telling and re-telling the old stories in the winter nights. Well, there's not a lot you can do by candle-light when it's dark for sixteen hours of every twenty-four. So I know the story of how Ragnar and Freya and those who followed took on this hard lump of God's earth, how they cleared fields, cut down trees, made a home to bring up a family – know it by heart.

And now I hear from a traveller from Cese-wic that we've been given away! Who the hell is Lady Alice to give us away? What right does she have to own us in the first place? The way I see it, Ragnar made this place, this farmstead, out of virgin ground, belonging to no-one, and having made it, it belonged to him, and so to us who have taken his name. So what made her and her like think we owed them taxes and fees and whatnot. French anyway, the lot of them. William the Conqueror! He never came here to conquer us, nor his fancy favourite son, William Rufus. 'Ah, Billy lad, here, you can have England when I'm gone.' Pah! Let him come here and try claiming Thorneythwaite. They've never had a mark from us, and they dursn't come through the jaws to try. Not that we'd have a mark to give, it's hand to mouth here. We eat what we produce, and we wear what the Herdwicks produce – and bloody scratchy wool it is.

So what will these monks do, would you suppose? If Norman overlords got nothing from us I can't see a bunch of holy men getting very far. Furness Abbey, they say, owns us now – and Fountains have owned the far side of the valley a dozen years or more. They can farm, I'll give them that, and of course they're not short of man-power. I would think any man worth his salt would rather work out here in the fresh air than scribble away in some Abbey. I hear they have to get up at three o'clock to pray – and that's just the first of six times. I'd rather work than pray, that's for sure.

Don't go thinking I'm a heathen, though. Thor and Odin lost out to Jesus Christ some time past, here. I suppose it was marrying lasses from Keswick that started the change. Our story is that great-grand-dad Eirikr was the first to stray, seeking new blood and tramping all the way to Cese-wic to get it. She was Christian, and in the way of these things, Eirikr was soon Christian too, and their children, and there we are. We still tell the stories of Thor and Balder, in the long winter nights, but they're just stories now. Me, I think the stories of Jesus and his God are the same, but I keep quiet, since my Mary doesn't. And now, thanks to Lady Muck, we have a fancy church at Cese-wic, St. Kentigern's at Crosthwaite. Now his is a story I can admire, one I like to tell the kids.

Mungo, as his family and friends called Kentigern, was the bastard son of a princess who was raped by the son of the king of Rheged – our country. The princess's father, the king of Scotland threw her from a pinnacle in his rage, thinking her a whore, but miraculously she survived and made her way across the water in a leaky coracle. That's the sort of start a Saint should have, worthy of one of the old gods, and he went on to convert all these Northern lands, with many a miracle.

I've been to Lady Alice's church, for my own wedding, for like great-grand-dad Eirikr I picked out a Cese-wic lass. And I've been for funerals, for we are good Christian folk now. The valley is not the same, not as it was in the stories we were told and tell on to our children. We still notch the oak for each successive year, just as good Ragnar did of old: but we are on the sixth tree now, for we move on every fifty notches, and there's two on the latest tree. For sure Thorneythwaite is not the same, for two hundred and fifty years of men's endeavours do change a place. We've burnt a lot of forest, we've cleared a lot of stone, and we have pasture and some ploughing. Sheep roam the fells now, descendants of those hardy few the stories tell of that first gave wool for comfort. Hefted, they are, content to stay on their own bit of fell; and hefted I am too, happy with my bit of land, with this sturdy new house, with my good Nell and our fine bairns.

Well, we've seen off the Normans – or at least Lady Alice has. Let's see what the monks of Furness will get up to, now they think they own the land.

Our new house, thatched with reeds from Overclose Bottom.

Chapter seven

Jim Hall

God, I wish I had said something to our landlord, when he read the Riot Act over a few scouts camping. Who does he think he is? Just because his father was rich enough to have bought Thorneythwaite long ago – does that give him a right to say how it's run? He doesn't have to feed a family on the bare living it produces. He's not the one hiding yet another dead ewe behind the wall, wondering if spring will ever come. He's not up at dawn just to save a lamb or two because that's all there is between us and bankruptcy.

But then, would we be any better off if the National Trust owned the farm? They own practically everything else in the valley, but there isn't a tenant with a good word to say for them. Funny, isn't it, once upon a time the King claimed all the land, and demanded taxes and rent from those they graciously allowed to do all the work. Now 'the nation' owns it all, or that's what the Trust claims, and still demands taxes and rent for the privilege of slaving your guts out to scratch some sort of a living from rock and bracken. And if there turns out to be something more worthwhile on the land – mineral rights, graphite mines, copper mines, gold mines even; or tourism and campsites – then Oh No! that's not for the likes of you miserable tenants. We'll have that, and thank you very much! It's all right for you, Beatrix Potter, selling all your little books to make a fortune so you can play at fell-farming. You try making a living here without your books, or your B&B, or your campsites.

Sorry, it's been a very fraught week. We need to make some hay each year for the sheep, as they won't eat the silage, and we cut the four-acre Nookem ten days ago. With all the hen muck we have to spread from the battery birds we get a thick crop and it takes some killing for hay. After several tries, all spoilt by yet another day's rain, we managed to get it dry enough to bale yesterday. The trouble is, here, the sun sets far too soon over Bayes Brown, and the dew soon starts falling, especially in early September as it is now. Well, we baled it, but it was going to get dark long before we could trailer it all into the barn, so we made smallish stacks on the field and hoped for a dry night and to be able to get it in today. What did we get? A typical bloody Borrowdale downpour, a couple of inches of rain I would say, and every bale soaked through. So we've spent today cutting them all open again, spreading them out by hand, and now we have to try to get it all dry again. I wouldn't care, but I know damned well it'll be rubbish by the time we get it, after days of work, with very little feeding value. Sometimes I think Thorneythwaite will crush us, Betty and me. But we've sunk all our capital in the place, so we need to make it work one way or another. Thank God Ian seems to love the work: any time he's not at school he wants to be out on the farm.

One way we're trying to make a bit more is to cut out the middle man with the fat lambs. The normal way on these fell farms is to take all the lambs off their mothers in early September – spayning it's called round here – and to send the gimmers (females) to winter on better land out to the coast, paying maybe six pounds apiece for the privilege. The wethers (males) are then usually sent to Cockermouth or Penrith auctions for those same down-country farmers to fatten up and sell for a lot more money than they paid us! We get less than the six pounds we have to pay for the gimmers, so where's the sense in that?

We filled in the space between the silo and the barn, and built another pole barn on the other side of the silo, and we've made slatted floors over the whole area; so now we can bring all the hoggs inside, male and female, and winter the gimmers ourselves, and fatten the wethers ourselves too, using hay and barley feed. We save on the gimmers, and we make money on the wethers as we sell them fat. BUT WE DO NEED HAY. So when we lose a field, after a fortnight of back-breaking work, I confess I do get a bit ratty when crossed.

I'm not sure how much longer we'll go on keeping beef cattle, either. Again it's traditional on these fell farms to mix cattle and sheep. It's always been understood that each cleans the pasture for the other. Too many sheep for too long and you get worms and other nasties: the cattle clean them off at no harm to them. So Pop would have said, anyway, and he was from a long line of farm labourers – so I suppose I must be too. But we have drenches now, to kill the worms, carbon tetrachloride to kill the liver fluke, so do we still need the cattle? Not only so, but Ollerenshaw is always keen to use us as guinea-pigs to test out new drugs. We make it easy with the slatted floors, he can sort through the flock in the dry! He makes me laugh; one month he's certain such-and-such a drench is the best on the market, then in six months' time he's backing another. It's a good job they're all free to us.

The Ministry of Agriculture (and Fisheries and Food, MAFF, to give them their full title), encourages us to run cattle on the fell in Summer, and we tried it for a year or so. But Thorneythwaite Fell is so poverty stricken they started to eat bracken, which Ollerenshaw says can cause cancer, so we soon stopped that daft idea. Anyway, Betty reckoned they came off the fell weighing less than they went on, so what was the good in that? It's all very well to make rules for an 'average' fell, as if such a thing existed, but all fells are different, and we reckon Thorneythwaite Fell and

Glaramara, our sheep run, must be nearly the worst in Cumberland. North-facing, narrow-backed, full of rock and bracken, there's hardly any half-way decent grazing; and in Winter it's likely to freeze solid and sustain nothing. No, the cattle will have to go, then there will be no point in silage and we'll have to make hay on all the fodder fields, come hell or high-water – as both will, inevitably.

The truth is the only things that keeps our head above the high-water are the grants and subsidies MAFF dole out to us, the little brown envelopes that come with a cheque. As Betty says, the only time farming really pays is in a war – and that was certainly true of both our wars this century. While there was rationing – right up to 1953 – and the government was buying farmers' produce, markets were good and steady. Since then it's been downhill all the way. So, thank God for a labour government and good old Fred Peart. Things can only get better.

Jim mowing with horses back in 1947, at Myreground, West Cumberland, before they had a tractor.

Chapter eight

Borrowdale under the Monks. 1232 AD.

Radulf, great-great-great-great-grandson of Ragnar, again.

I am getting old now, and I have added twenty more notches to our sixth oak, so my family have owned Thorneythwaite 272 years since Ragnar and Freya first set foot here. Not that we do own it, that much has been made clear to us by the abbot of Furness, Robert of Demon. Well-named for an abbot, don't you think? He may be a holy man, but he's got a sharp eye for business, and his business is making Furness Abbey grand. I was wrong to think monks would be easy overseers: they are far more grasping than the Lady Alice – and they're here, in the valley, everywhere. Setting up their own farms, and demanding days of labour from us, and tithes of what little we do produce.

Sheep: that's their speciality, and they've taken over the fells for Summer grazing. There's a new steading just across the River Derwent from us, over Nicol Dub. We call it a Saetre, and with all the alder trees growing in the wetlands there we know it now as Saetr'Alder. Because they take the sheep away to Winter pastures out on their lowlands they can stock the fellside fairly heavily in Summer, and every year they're eating away more of the upland woods, creating new sheep-walks. The woods never re-generate because the sheep nip off any new shoots, and the fell across the valley looks very different already from when I was born here.

Now they've done the same with Seathwaite, taking it over from Gawain and all his family and stocking the fells for miles around. You wouldn't believe the number of sheep they gather together in October to drive up the valley to their Wintering lands. Yes, I did say 'up' the valley, for the monks drive them up to Stockley Bridge , a mile up the valley from Seathwaite, then up Grains Gill to Esk Hause, and over the top to join their other big Saetre at the head of Eskdale; Bother-il-keld they call it. I suppose they join with all those hundreds of sheep too, and go on down Eskdale to the lands they have on the coast – a lot nearer Furness Abbey than we are. It's an astonishing sight and marks the end of Summer here, and the start of the long, dark, wet and miserable Winter that plagues those of us who are left. They know a thing or two, these monks!

As Spring begins, and the first shoots of green give hope we'll live another year, we see them streaming down Grain Gill on their way back to us. The ewes are heavy in lamb, and they must travel slowly, and no doubt they rested at Brother-il-keld a few days, while they sorted out each farm's quota for the Summer. Each Summer the quota seems bigger, as more and more fell woodland is taken over.

They can work, too, these monks, I must give them that. Each July they gather the sheep down to the steading for the clipping, and it takes a lot of labour to relieve these Herdwicks of their coats. Once clipped they are back on the fell for a couple of months, but the fleeces are all rolled up individually, and tied with a twine of the neck wool, and packed hard in wool sacks. They balance the wool sacks one each side of a pony, and soon the long caravan of pack horses sets off, each roped to the one in front, and led by a monk as they make their way to Kendal, the wool centre of the North, as it's called.

They go by a different route, of course. The Seathwaite horses come right past us at Thorneythwaite, and Mary shyly puts in a request for a trinket or two to be brought back from Kendal when the horses return. The Saetr'Alder train goes down the West side of the river, through Johnny Wood, and over the Rosthwaite pack horse bridge to meet up with the Seathwaite train. Then it's a long haul up past the vaccary at Stonethwaite and away up the long miles of Langstrath, over Stake Pass, into Langdale and so on to Kendal. They go with a strong guard of monks, armed with hefty sticks which they generally use to assist their long walk; but this wool is valuable stuff, and these monks very ready to guard their hard-won sacksful.

They haven't bothered us at Thorneythwaite yet, not for sheep walks, what we call herd-wicks, up on Glaramara. I suspect it's just too rough, too poverty-stricken, to be worth their while. The few sheep we have we keep on our in-bye land, and we stock just for our own use. I want none of this pack horse business. If we made money the Abbey would only want it off us in taxes. So we pay a few tithes, and they leave us alone. We clip thirty sheep, and they must needs have three fleeces – but that leaves enough for Mary and the lasses to spin for our clothing. We grow a few acres of oats for our daily bread, and just enough barley to brew some ale, but the weather and the soil make a mockery of the job. The barley never ripens properly, but it does for beer.

The monks from Fountains Abbey own the whole of the East of the valley, with Watendlath up in its little valley of its own, and Stonethwaite and Langstrath. The grazing for the sheep in Langstrath is a lot better than Saetr'Alder and Seathwaite and they keep their sheep there all year. Again they've removed a lot of fell woodland, and in Summer the sheep roam the high fells, but there's enough valley bottom in Langstrath for them to winter there, and have their lambs before they go back to the fells in May. The Fountains monks have built a string of shielings where the shepherd monks live for months on end, looking after the sheep. There's a set of three up on Greenup Edge where the monks live in Summer to tend the flocks, keep an eye out for wolves, and clip out any fly-strike. Down in the valley bottom there's another set of three where the monks spend at least some of the winter and more importantly lambing-time. I suppose they joined the Cistercian Order to have the opportunity of prayer and meditation: there will be plenty of time for that alone up on the fells all Summer.

Sheep are only part of the Furness Abbey farms, though. They've gone in for cattle too and have what they call a vaccary at Stonethwaite which produces enough milk for all their brothers in the valley, and cheese to send back to Furness. There's some good land on the valley floor at Stonethwaite, with deep soil the same as we have at Thorneythwaite to the South of the farmstead, where the lake must have been back in the old days. But where ours is still very marshy, full of sieves and sedges, the Furness monks have dug drains and ditches in their marshland and produced good dairy land. Easy enough when you have lots of manpower – and can press us peasants into service as part of our fees to the Abbey. I just wish we had the same manpower to drain around Black Syke, then we could grow some decent crops.

The other big thing the monks can do with all the men they can call on is to build walls. And now there are so many sheep in the valley, there's a strong need for walls, I can tell you. Up at Seathwaite they've built a combination of stone wall and a hawthorn hedgerow to keep the sheep out of the valley bottom, and up on the fellside and tops. It needs a goodly barrier to keep these little Herdwicks out of good grazing – they know full well that the grass is greener on the valley side of the wall, and if they can find a way through they will. Funny how the sheep have taken on the name of their pastures – perhaps the monks didn't understand what we meant when we spoke of herd-wicks as sheep walks.

We look on, we who have lived so long on these few acres that we call our own; this Thorneythwaite that has nourished the sons of Ragnar over two centuries. My sons want us to copy the monks, burn the woodland on the fellside above our few tiny fields, and run a flock of sheep there. I counsel caution, and for now I prevail, and I do so for two reasons. Firstly, I don't believe Glaramara will support sheep in Winter – hardly in Summer, even, and we certainly have nowhere for them to go, not like the Furness sheep. And secondly, if we did manage, I'm sure the Abbey would soon want to take the enterprise over, and there is no way to gainsay them. No, I tell the boys, we have ten acres cleared, cleared of the trees that were here when Ragnar first set foot here, and cleared of the stones that littered the fields when we plough a little for oats. Ten acres

41

keep us very well – why make more work just to give the results of our toil to the grasping Robert of Demon?

But I feel change in the air. I shall not hear our cuckoo many more times, for the cold and wet is seeping into my bones. We have five sons, Mary and I, and they will fight when I am gone. Three are married, and I fear their wives more than the boys themselves. We have three houses here, all stone built and sturdily roofed like Ragnar's original which has been reroofed so many times it can hardly be called Ragnar's any longer. Some boys will have to go, to make their own clearings and houses, as we have for generations. But it gets harder, for there is not that much woodland left, and the monks' sheep press in all around. Foreby, the Abbeys claim all the land and would want a hefty rent for any new steading. So I fear some of my sons must take their wives, and my grandchildren, and make a life in Cese-wic, or beyond. It will break my Mary's heart, for she loves the little ones fiercely, but the truth is Borcherdale is getting crowded. Once we were the only clearing in the valley; now there must be fifty and more. For a hundred years it was our valley, we who vaunted our Viking blood. Then for a hundred years the Normans said it was their valley, and we must need pay our dues and our taxes. Now the Abbeys say it is theirs, and we little more than serfs and villeins to work for the glory of God – well, for the Abbots who are His body on earth, and their Abbeys which are His house.

I do not like these changes that I see. Before the Abbeys got their fat fingers on the valley we were kings of our own midden. The Norman barons demanded their fees, but they left us alone. Now the Cistercian brotherhood is changing things, and changing them quickly. The flocks of sheep they bring in nibble their way down into the upper woodland, removing any undergrowth, and like an old man's receding hairline each year the woodland edge creeps ever downwards. It won't be long till the Furness sheep stay all Winter, then we'll see the valley's woods go the same way. I'm glad I'm old and will not see the destruction they bring, but I fear for my children, and my children's children.

Chapter nine

Jane Edmondson

Seathwaite, 13th August and 4th September 1966.

Jane Edmondson and her brother John got dressed up in full rain gear – wellies, macs, and each with one of those yellow sailor hats with the string that came round your chin to hold it on in the wind – and went out the door of Rain Gauge Farm to shut the ducks in for their Dad, Joe. Tonight the farm seemed particularly well-named. The rain gauge up in its little enclosure would be gurgling merrily to itself, little knowing that tonight it would measure five full inches of Summer downpour. Jane was nine, her brother John nearly two years older, and this was their nightly job.

Rain Gauge was the only property at Seathwaite not owned by the National Trust, and Joe made a slightly precarious living raising poultry for sale to farms all over Cumberland, and by rearing turkeys for the Christmas trade. A living supplemented, as was the case on almost every farm, by Ruth taking in Bed and Breakfast guests. Just as Billy Dixon and his wife at Thorneythwaite before Jim and Betty went there, Joe and Ruth spent the Summer months sleeping in a small shed across the yard, to free another bedroom for the visitors. Jane, John and their younger brother Joe were allowed to share a bedroom in the house.

The main farm at Seathwaite was owned by the National Trust and tenanted by Joe's older brother Stan and his wife Nancy. Being the dale head farm it had sheep rights on all the fells round three sides of the valley, from Glaramara to the East, round Allen Crags, Esk Hause, Sprinkling and Styhead Tarns in the South, across the face of Gable and through to Gillercombe and Bayes Brown to the West. They ran thousands of sheep, all clipped by now, with the fleeces all wrapped and ready for packing in the barn.

The little beck that ran through Joe's duck field had grown in the rain, and was in a hurry to get through the field and down to the main river. Jane could hear the river from here, a growling sort of noise, like a bull getting himself in a lather. A waterfall had developed in the middle of the field, where the beck had washed stones into a little dam, and the kids spent a few minutes kicking the pebbles away so the water could rush on unimpeded. Darkness was almost on them by the time they shut all the pop-holes to keep the ducks safe from foxes for the night, and by the time they were back in the house they were cold and very wet.

Meanwhile, Joe had been over to the turkey house to fill the feeders and make sure all was secure for the night. He arrived back not long after the kids, and as he stood by the outside door, watching the torrential rain hammering down, he became aware of a change in the noise. There was still the clatter of the rain on the tin roof of the coal-house, but above that there was the sound of a steam train approaching fast. A moment later the door burst in, throwing him off balance, followed by a wall of water that swept him down the corridor and hard up against the bookcase at the end of the passage. The bookcase with all Ruth's precious books fell over, consigning them all to the floods. The water poured on past him, filling the passage a yard deep, and into all the rooms on the ground floor. The kids! Where were the kids? Water like this could drown them in no time. Anxiously he yelled for Ruth, and was relieved to hear her shout back from the bathroom, where she had them all in the bath to warm up.

His next thought was for the visitors, but he needn't have worried. They were all in their bedrooms, dinner being over and the time well past nine o'clock. The hens! Oh God, the hens, the turkeys, the ducks – they were all trapped in their sheds, and if the water was three feet deep in the house it would be the same in the sheds. Ruth was just in time to catch him and tell him not to be so bloody daft, if he went out in that flood he would be swept away. There was nothing for it but to sit it out. They couldn't even go to bed, as their own shed would be in the same state. They sat upstairs on the landing for long hours, in a state of shock, as the waters rushed by outside, and a steady stream ran through the house itself. It was pitch black by now, the electricity long ago fused and useless. Ruth knocked quietly on each bedroom door to reassure all the guests that the house was safe, but breakfast tomorrow might be a bit difficult.

Jane woke early next morning and threw open the curtains. She could hardly believe her eyes. The yard was never the tidiest of places, but now it was a complete shambles. The river was running deep and strong right through it. Sheds, feeding troughs, even a Ford Cortina, lay tumbled over each other. And the stones! Everything from pebbles to great boulders lay at the edge of the water. Her father came shambling out from the turkey house, his shoulders down, his old mac tied with a bit of baler twine sagging round his knees, and he looked as if he was crying. Jane had never seen her father cry, and the sight seemed more shocking even than the desolation all around. Of course, all the poultry were dead, some still trapped in the sheds, hundreds more swept away on the current, to be discovered for days later littering the fields down the valley even as far as Mountain View, a couple of miles away.

*The flood waters on Sept 4ᵗʰ 1966, behind Rainguage Farm
showing the poultry sheds afloat and the Ferguson
tractor almost under water.
Photo courtesy of Jane Sutton.*

Behind Rain Gauge, over in Seathwaite Farm, Stan and Nancy were likewise stunned at the devastation all around. The river had torn through their house, and old Stan's next door, soaking the ground floor, the carpets, the sofas, the new electric cooker. But worse, somehow, those thousand fleeces in the barn, the mews of hay ready for fodder that winter – they were all soaked and useless too. The houses would dry out, but the hay was gone, and the Wool Marketing Board surely wouldn't buy sodden fleeces. The entire summer output was wasted, and Stan, like his brother Joe, seemed over-whelmed, as if the river had gone over their own heads too, drowning out the vital spark that keeps us going. The only ones apparently unaffected were Joe and Ruth's kids: they sat on the lowest stair still above water and skimmed digestive biscuits along the water in the corridor, till Ruth caught them and chased them out into the watery world outside. A photographer from the local paper pictured Jane and Joe rafting on the still rapid waters in an old feeding trough.

Further down the valley others were coping with their own results of the wanton destructive power of nature. Seatoller was a boulder field, the normally placid beck having brought down hundreds of tons of stone scoured out from the banks, which were now yards wider than before. The stone was piled against the backs of the houses; the bridge over the beck to the top row of quarry-men's cottages was but a memory, even its abutments obliterated; and the gardens at the back of the main row of cottages looked more like a giant shingle beach. There was less sheer earth movement further down the valley, where the water had been able to spread out over the flood plain. For a while, till the waters receded, it looked much as it must have several thousand years ago, with a great lake covering the fields and roads. When the lake drained out through the jaws of Borrowdale it left, not the silt of ages past, but the wrecks of cars at impossible angles on wall tops, the carcases of sheep caught out in the open fields unable to find respite from the rising waters, and the debris from the farmyards and back gardens caught in the torrent.

And what of Thorneythwaite? Here we slept on through that torrential night, aware only of the rain hammering on the windows – nothing unusual in that. Here we got up next morning to find puddles here and there, but nothing to worry about. Till Betty tried to drive down to Keswick for some groceries. She was back in five minutes, round-eyed in surprise. "The lane's gone!"

Jim was his usual bluff self. "What do you mean, 'the lane's gone'? How can a lane go?" We all trooped off to see how a lane could go. The first hundred yards hadn't gone anywhere, but as we turned the corner to where the lane should have been constrained by field walls it had indeed 'gone'. There must have been a raging river tearing down it all night, for it was gouged out to a depth of two to three feet right down the walled section, a good two hundred yards. Keswick shopping was off, but when we walked out to hear the news of how the rest of the valley had fared we realised just how well-sited Thorneythwaite was. We had huddled in the shelter of the rising moraine behind the house, the pine trees breaking the force of the wind. Fifty feet above the river and valley floor and well away from the fellside we were safe from any flooding, and most of our fields were also well above the flood plain. As so often, Noon Bank and Nookem were still under water, but they had had no stock in, and the hay crop was safely off. Jim breathed a sigh of relief, and rang the landlord's agent to ask them to see about repairing the lane.

Valley folk are resilient, and up at Seathwaite Stan and Nancy, and Joe and Ruth at Rain Gauge, were soon beginning the drying out process. Carpets and rugs, sofas and chairs were soon out in the slightly apologetic sunshine, steaming out their unwanted wetness. Joe wandered disconsolately through his sheds, piling poultry bodies into a barrow for burial in one of the holes the flood had left behind. Ruth was bidding farewell to the visitors who could all leave for dry homes and beds, with a story to last a lot of dinner parties. Wryly she surveyed the wasteland of the yard. They had had it tarmacked no more than a month ago, and very smart it had looked after the rough gravel that had served a thousand years. It didn't look so smart now, torn up and chewed over like one of the dogs' old blankets. Grimly she wrote, in capital letters, in her visitors book – only damp, having been on the kitchen table, just above water level – 15th AUGUST: CLOSED DUE TO FLOODING. The next entry, a mere fortnight later, records her re-opening, and her first guests after the deluge.

Across the yard in Seathwaite Farm Stan and his sons, 'Young Stan' and Peter, began the huge task of unwrapping well over a thousand fleeces and laying them out in the sunshine all over the back field to dry out – before laboriously re-wrapping them and refilling the wool sacks, with a very nervous eye on the weather. Fortunately nature seemed ready to accept that five inches of rain in one night was enough for the present.

The day that Ruth re-opened, 29th August, Joe re-stocked his poultry sheds, having straightened them out and dried them as best he could. He picked up a van-load of day-old chicks from Keswick Station and popped them in the incubators. The contractors came back and re-laid the tarmac in the yard. The river had gone back to its proper course, though the bank it had poured so much water over looked worryingly vulnerable. Stan and his lads had re-packed the wool sacks and were doing their best with the sodden hay mews. All four houses were dried out, the furniture, with a few tide marks to show for its adventures, back in place, and life was beginning to return to normal.

On the night of the 4th September the rains returned. The Seathwaite families lay in their beds, wide awake, only too mindful of that low river bank. Somewhere in the small hours of the morning they heard the dreaded sound of the water rushing through the farmyards, as the Derwent tried out its new route for the second time in three weeks. They didn't get up: what was the point? The devastation next morning was greater than the first, the stoop on their shoulders the more marked. The brand-new tarmac in the yard was ripped up again. The furniture and carpets were all to take out again. The wool was once again soaked through. The week-old chicks lay drowned in their prison. Ruth wrote in her visitors' book, the capitals underscored this time: <u>CLOSED FOR ANOTHER FLOOD. FOR GOOD.</u>

This time the government stepped in, sending the army to help sort things out. Squaddies with diggers, a crane, heating equipment and dozens of calor gas cylinders to power them took over from the overwhelmed inhabitants, bringing with them some humour, some encouragement, and best of all the promise to sort that river bank out for good. They loaded all the tons of boulders and loose tarmac onto the dumper truck and used it to fill huge wire gabions that began to line the river bank. They dried out the tractors and cars, long stranded where the force had thrown them. They put heaters in the houses to dry them the more thoroughly. They re-laid the ill-fated tarmac. They were there for three weeks: three weeks in which shoulders slowly returned to their usual jaunty angle, smiles erased the creases on foreheads that had felt the end of the world was nigh. Three weeks to restore an ancient hamlet to some sort of normality, and the spirits of its people to their normal equanimity. October was a blessedly balmy month.

Chapter ten

Stonethwaite and Langstrath Around 1301

Ralph, grandson of Radulf.

Almost no-one around the valley remembers the old ones now, our forefathers and ancestors who first cut a home in the oak woods. There are so many newcomers, both the Abbey monks and merchants and iron workers that the old ways are forgotten, except here at Thorneythwaite. Here we still trace our roots back to Ragnar and Freya, and bless them for finding this favoured spot above the many floods, and away from the prying eyes of the monks. My parents sort of compromised with my name, I guess. I think of it as the same as grand-dad, Radulf, but this form, Ralph, is fairly common around here. The monks have added to it, and we all sound a bit grand now. They needed to define us tenants better than just Ralf or John or whatever, so we've all been given an extra name. Here at the head of the valley they've added 'de Borcherdale Head'. I think it has a nice ring – Ralf de Borcherdale Head – but my brother Randel says it just makes us into serfs, vassals of Furness. Well, it's only on official documents. Sadly, there isn't enough work or food at Thorneythwaite for all our family, so Randel and I work the bloomery on Smithymire Island round in Stonethwaite, just up the Langstrath valley. Richard, who owns it, is now Richard Langstrath, according to the monks. We stay there all week in the little shieling we have on the island, but we get back home every Sunday to see Ma – and for a decent meal, if I'm honest.

Iron men, we call ourselves; it makes the lasses blush and laugh. And iron men we are, turning the red ore into good workable iron to make tools. It's hard work – we need a hell of a lot of wood to make the charcoal for the furnace to melt the iron ore, and a hell of a lot of muscle power to blow the bellows when we do fire up. Langstrath is a great place for the job, though, with a great forest of trees to go at. And the more trees we cut down the happier the monks are, as they get more grazing for their dairy cattle. We're slowly working our way up the valley from the vaccary at Stonethwaite. There are woods for ever, enough to see generations of us if I ever have the time to get a family. I have a fancy for young Astrid – another good old name that's being taken over now. She works among the monks in the vaccary. You'd think that would be a safe place for a woman, but the tales she tells of these Furness monks give the lie to that thought. Celibacy? Don't make me laugh, they're as red-blooded as the rest of us, some of them at any rate.

It takes Randel and me a couple of weeks to get a bloom of iron completed. We have to spend at least three days going up to Ore Gap, near Angle Tarn, just below Esk Hause and quarrying out enough red ore to sled back down Langstrath to Smithymire. Perhaps we'd be better having the bloomery further up the valley, so there'd be less sledding, but for one thing the monks count our clearing the woods near Stonethwaite as our tithes – not just us, but enough for our folks at Thorneythwaite too. For another thing, it's a lot nearer Astrid! And the monks' alehouse. Oh yes, they're not abstainers from alcohol either, believe me.

It's every man for himself up at Ore Gap, if you bring your own pick and shovel and you find a decent vein you can take as much as you can carry on the sled. It's heavy, dirty work to get a sled-full: we throw away a lot more rubbish than we get ore, as you might expect. Sledding it downhill is fairly easy, but when we get to the valley bottom we have to carry the sled between us, and Langstrath is well named: it's miles down to Smithymire.

But in some ways, getting the ore is the easy part, it's making enough charcoal to fire the bloomery that takes the time. I sometimes wish these lazy monks would do the job, but I suppose I mustn't grumble, at least it's a living. Having said that, it was them who taught us the skills – and then left us to it. The whole art of it is to burn a lot of wood without the air getting to it. We build a great bonfire of poles of wood that we have to cut and trim – ash and hazel are best we find, and birch. Oak makes great charcoal, but takes forever to fire, so you have to have either an oak burn entirely, or the mix of the others. I said 'without air', but that's not quite true. We have a four-inch post upright in the middle of the heap, with all the poles leaning into it, and another four-inch pole on the ground. When the heap is built we pile sods all over it to keep the air out, then pull out the centre post to make a chimney, and the ground post to let a tiny amount of air in – and to feed burning tinder in to start the process.

We keep a wary eye on the top of the chimney hole. There always has to be a wisp of smoke, and some heat coming out or the fire has died and the process is ruined. On the other hand, too much smoke or heat means there is too much air in, and the charcoal will be poor. You need to wet the sods just enough to keep the balance right, and it takes us about three days and nights before the whole heap is reduced to charcoal, so we take it in turns, Randel and me, to watch the fire while the other gets some sleep – or slopes off into Stonethwaite to see if Astrid is around. When the fire is out, because all the wood has burned to charcoal, we carefully take off the sods and collect up our precious black cargo. I don't know why, but when you burn the charcoal again, this time with loads of air, it burns a lot hotter and brighter than wood, and that's what we want.

Sketch of a charcoal-burning stack by Alfred Heaton-Cooper, 1908

We cart the charcoal onto Smithymire Island and make a big pile: we'll need a lot once the bloomery starts to work. First we have to make the kiln where we'll smelt the iron, and this is partly why we chose Smithymire. There's loads of clay on the banks of the island, clay we use to build up a stone kiln, maybe two feet diameter inside, and three feet high, with a wide chimney at the top, and a hole at the bottom. The stones need a thick layer of clay outside and in, or they would shatter in the heat we're going to make in there. By the time we've finished the walls are at least a foot thick, with the clay smoothed off as best we can with our hands. We stick the nose of a big set of bellows into the bottom hole, and set to. Randel gets a fire going and pours the burning wood in through the top, followed by the first of the charcoal, while I pump the bellows to get it burning fiercely, till we reckon the clay has set well and will stand more heat. It would be a complete disaster if the kiln broke before the job was done – and it has, on more than one occasion.

The next few hours are back-breaking torture, pumping the bellows for all we're worth, ten minutes each, turn on turn. If you're not pumping you're feeding more charcoal and ore mixed in through the chimney, with the heat blasting out at you. It took us a while to get the hang of it, but now we seem to get the heat just right each time, so that after we've shoved enough into its maw there is a lovely bloom of iron settling in the bottom of the kiln. We can see it by peering in past the

51

bellows, and when it's big enough – about the size of a man's head, we can stop pumping and smash up our carefully built kiln to get the bloom out with a pair of tongs the blacksmith made from some previous burn! And hit it like mad with a big hammer he also made, on a big flat rock on the island, perfect for the job. If we've got it right, and we usually have these days, all the slag flies off as we hammer the bloom, and we're left with a lovely lump of iron, maybe five to ten pounds in weight.

It's a hell of a lot of effort for not a lot of iron, but we turn out enough to keep the blacksmith in Stonethwaite happy, and as I said, it counts as Thorneythwaite's tithes and feeds Randel and me, so we aren't complaining. Except when it's raining, of course. None of those jobs, except the charcoal making, are much pleasure in the rain, and it does rain a lot in Langstrath.

Astrid has just told me some bad news. It looks as if Furness Abbey will no longer have the vaccary and the smithy, or any need for our services. I suppose it all depends how it works out, and maybe the new owners will keep us on, but there won't be the connection with Thorneythwaite any longer, so I'm not sure how it will work. There's been rumblings for a few years now: Furness Abbey have always claimed the Stonethwaite dairy farm as theirs, even though it's in Eastern Borcherdale, where all the rest of the land was given to Fountains by Alice de Rumilly. Now, apparently, Fountains are going to be successful in claiming it back. They came up with a detailed description of which abbey owned which bits of Borrowdale drawn up a hundred years ago, but it's a bit ambiguous about Stonethwaite, and Furness always said it was theirs, even though it eats into Fountain's land. Fountains took it to court – and lost! We all thought that was that, but they kept on trying higher courts till King Edward Longshanks got involved, and he solved it in a Solomon fashion by confiscating the vaccary. Seems you can do anything if you're king. Then, since it was no good to him, he put it up for auction, and Astrid says Fountains have just bought it for forty shillings. All legal and above board, or so they say.

I suppose Randel and I will go on working for the other abbey, as long as they'll have us, but we'd got to know the Furness monks, and how they worked, and their blacksmith. I don't like change, but change seems to happen anyway, no matter how you try to stop it. The only good thing is that Astrid doesn't, either. She'd got the Furness monks tamed. They flirted with her, but it went no further than that, but she's afraid of a whole new group of brothers coming in, and she wants us to marry, to make her a wife, and off limits. It's time, though it's a queer life being a charcoal burner's wife. She'll have to get used to the shieling – and Randel! He snores louder than a wild boar.

Chapter eleven

1964: Jim

I swear this lad of ours will be the death of me. He reminds me so often of my older brother, Tom. Keen as mustard, but rough and thoughtless, charging in without thinking about the consequences. Tom farmed with Betty and me on our first farm, Myreground, down in West Cumberland, and I would say he broke more gear every week than I did in a year. If he was forking hay he wouldn't take any notice of how it was mewed, just stick his fork in anywhere and pull like hell till he managed to tear some out from where he was standing on the natural lie. A moment's thought would have made his life easier, but no, not Tom. And when it came to handling the horses he was worse than useless. I could see our father looking on perplexed as to how any son of his could fail to understand a horse as badly. Of course, Father was a horseman, born to it at a time before tractors, so he'd grown up all his life handling them.

After Myreground Tom went off to theological college and got himself made into a vicar for the Church of England, though Betty reckons his heart is really with the Catholics. Now he has a parish outside Penrith, Milburn is his vicarage – a great rambling Victorian house made for a priest with a big family – and now with just him in it. It was good of him to come and help at Thorneythwaite at clipping time, especially in our early years when there was no electricity. But it was hard on any sheep he clipped, they generally needed a dab of Stockholm Tar on the odd wound he inflicted.

And now Ian is growing and becoming useful, he's just the same. It's a bit like having Tom back again – you never know what he's going to break next. He loves tractor work, but you can do a lot of damage with a tractor when you drive as fast as he does. He's worst with a buck-rake on the back: I don't think he realises how much it sticks out the sides. Last week he sidled up to me – always a sure sign he's done something wrong – and said he'd knocked a stone out of the corner of the loose box beside the gate into the farmyard. Would I come and give him a hand to put it back in? When we got there I might have laughed if it hadn't been so serious. A stone, he said. Well, it was just one stone, but one of the lower quoins – the huge stones that form the corner of a building, and weigh a couple of hundred-weight. Eventually we had to build up a wooden base to keep the quoin at the right height and then force it back into place with crow-bars and a ten-pound hammer. Of course, it wouldn't go back snugly, and now it offends my eye every time I drive in past it.

I really lost my temper with him last week, though. It was the end of silage time and he'd been hard work all the way through. He loves tractor-work, which causes tensions straight away, since Betty always thought the tractor was her province. She takes badly to forking round the outside of a field while he charges about on the tractor, and I get it in the ear all the time. Ian mowed the field – part of Great Field it was – and finished in a filthy temper. He'd been off and on the tractor a hundred times he said, because the cutter-bar kept blocking and breaking back on him, so he had to reverse, and every time he reversed the mown grass wrapped up on the drive shaft, so he had to cut it off with a knife. If he'd gone at the job more quietly, in a lower gear, he would have had time to see the blockage before break-back, but no, speed, speed, speed; even though it's slower in the end.

He was bringing the silage in on the buck-rake, Betty helping fork it on when the tines wouldn't slip under, cursing under her breath at his impatience, and I was forking each load out on the silage pit, trying to get a decent layer. I wasn't in the best of tempers either, as England were losing the third Test match badly. He said the next load would be the last in the field, and I was looking forward to tea and a break from this back-breaking job. I heard him tearing along the track, jolting over the rough terrain, when suddenly there was a loud bang, the sort you know is going to be expensive. I ran out, hoping at least that he hadn't damaged himself, to see the buck-rake lying forlornly on the ground, the tractor come to a dead halt, and Ian looking very sorry for himself sitting on the seat looking back at the damage.

Damage it was, of the most expensive and unnecessary kind. He'd loaded the buck-rake far too high, obviously trying to make good his promise it was the last load, and at the last jolt on the track the hydraulic arms had broken clean in two, dropping the load like a stone. Once again – how many times? – I told him he needed a bloody nursemaid, and why the hell had he tried to put so much on? He just looked mulish and sheepish at the same time, if that's possible, and stared at the ground saying nothing. Just then Betty returned from the field, ready for her tea too, and took the scene in with a long appraising look. She told Ian to go and make the tea, while we saw what could be done. He scuttled off, tail between his legs, while she began the delicate job of trying to placate me.

"He's only trying to help, love. I know he's a bit too keen, but surely that's better than a surly kid who wants nothing to do with the place." I made a huge effort to suppress all the invective I really wanted to let loose. It wouldn't help, and of course she was right.

"But why does he have to be so rough? It's just like having Tom back again, though I think Ian's even worse!"

Betty with a big load of silage on the buckrake. 1963

"I know, love, but look on the positive side. Both Tom and Ian work for no pay, just for the love of it. How else could we afford to make a living on this place – or Myreground in Tom's day?"

"Well, getting those hydraulic arms fixed will cost a month's pay anyway, so he's not much of a saving."

Of course, I calmed down, and I could see that it was good that Ian wanted to help so badly – if only he didn't 'help so badly' sometimes. After all, what would be the point in putting so much effort and heart into Thorneythwaite if it meant nothing to him. Ted Dexter and Ken Barrington put on a tremendous third wicket partnership to save the test match at Manchester, after Australia's first innings total of 656 had looked unbeatable, and life returned to normal.

Ian was sixteen that Summer, and I was coming up to forty-nine. Towards the end of August he got his O-level results, and I must admit he did well, though I'd never let him know I thought so, of course. Three A's, three B's and three C's: the A's in Maths, Physics and English. He'll go into the sixth form at Keswick School... and what then? I know I complain how much of a liability he can be, but what will life be like here for Betty and me if he goes off to University and we get left trying to look after Thorneythwaite on our own? Betty's right: he is a tremendous help when he's not breaking things, and he does work for nothing.

We gathered the lower fell last week, just him and me – Betty was busy cleaning the end of the house for the next lot of visitors, and the two of us can manage Coombe Ghyll without her. I got the bit between my teeth and thought 'Right, you bugger, let's see just how much you are growing up.' So I went up the track up the second intake like a bat out of hell, absolutely fast as I could go, to see if I could leave him behind. He looked a bit startled at first, but I suspect he realised what I was doing pretty quickly, and soon we were practically running up the fell. He did keep up with me, but he was gey red in the face and sweating like a horse by the time we got to the top. I was completely out of breath, air rasping into my lungs, and we collapsed laughing on the fell just outside the fell gate.

"What the hell was that all about, then?" he spluttered. After a minute or two I could answer: "Oh, just seeing if my post-prime equals your sub-prime! I think we can say it does!" The trouble is, post-primes go downhill, sub-primes go up. I don't think I'll try that experiment again next year.

Gathering's another of those times when I wonder if I know my son at all – but in this case he's nothing like my brother Tom. Tom never swore, that I can remember. Ian, well, I don't know what to say about him. We've hardly got into the job before he starts, and his language is appalling. Somehow it's so bad neither Betty or I find we can say anything about it. If it was just the odd curse you might bring it up, but it seems to be fundamental to the lad, a way of blowing off steam. It's queer, he's as polite as you could wish for ordinarily, but when he's working he seems pent-up and explosive – so much so neither of us mentions it, it seems off-limits somehow.

Coombe Ghyll is a bit of a non-gather. It is easy, with such steep sides all round stopping any sheep getting away from us, but there are always very few of our sheep anyway. Mostly Joe Weir's Chapel House sheep take over the bottom of the Ghyll, and ours are high up on the Coombe Door end of the hanging valley. After our race up the fell I sent Ian up high under Coombe Door, while I took my time gathering the sides down towards Raven Crag. Perhaps he was trying to prove something, but he went far too far up the end prising sheep out that should come in the high fell gather, and bringing them back ended up at the top of Raven Crag, not the bottom as he should have been. I guess he'd put a lot of effort in by then, and his language towards his dog Fly was ripe to say the least.

Fly started life as Flash, when Ian was still a kid, but by now he would have been embarrassed to shout that, so he'd elided the name.

Standing where I was I got a grandstand view of what happened next. One sheep split away from the little flock he was bringing across Raven Crag and jumped down onto a ledge near the top. He should just have left it – it wasn't crag-fast, and we would have got it in the main gather later. But no, stubborn man/boy that he was he must try to get it back up to the rest, cursing and swearing as he did. Frightened, the ewe jumped for the next ledge and missed its footing. It scrabbled on the bare rock to get itself safe, but it was to no avail, and it dropped from the ledge into the void. Raven Crag at that point is sheer, in fact slightly overhanging, and the sheep must have fallen unimpeded seventy feet at least. It hit the rocks at the bottom with a sickening, liquid crunch, twitched just once, and lay dead. I heard Ian swear again, a different kind of curse, and move off along the top with Fly and the rest of his flock, coming round the end of the crag to join with those I had gathered.

Neither of us mentioned the incident. Nor did I tell Betty, some things are best left unsaid.

Chapter twelve

Ralph de Borcherdale Head again

1315 – 1318

Things are bad at Thorneythwaite, in fact things are bad throughout the valley. Our father died in 1312, and Randel and I have come back to the farm to help Mother keep things together, but it all seems to be going wrong. I don't think it's our fault, but I do wonder if Father would have been able to ride out these terrible years better than we seem to. It's the weather at the bottom of all our troubles; such rain and floods in summer, and so cold and snowy in winter. The stock hardly get a chance to dry out before it hits them again, and up on the high fells the monks' sheep are suffering badly. On the tops the snow hasn't melted since the year father died, almost as if the weather itself were mourning him. Nothing grows: we've sown oats and a little barley just as father did, but it is so cold, and so wet, everything just rots in the ground.

There's nothing to feed the sheep and cattle on in winter, and we've taken to pollarding ash trees for the feeding value in their bark. The sheep at least like it, though whether it does much good I don't know. I suspect it's why they seem to be losing their teeth early, but that might be down to their poor condition. We've had hardly any lambs these last three years, and no calves at all. What stock is still alive are all getting old: if things don't get any better soon there won't be any farming left in the valley, even the monks' sheep are wasted and barren. Many a little farm has gone to the wall, with people simply not having enough to eat and so making for Cese-wic – as if there's likely to be anything there for them. I tell you, the old and the weak have died off like leaves off a tree, shrivelling before your eyes and dropping, desiccated.

We hang on at Thorneythwaite, killing and eating the weakest of the stock before they die of hunger, but we've precious little left. Astrid and I have a son, Reifr, but we'll have no more unless the times heal. Poor Astrid is gaunt and starving, as we all are, and like the ewes I think is barren now. Just as well, I don't know how we would fill another belly, and I can't imagine Astrid producing milk from her poor shrivelled teats. She would have been better staying at the vaccary, though I doubt any cows are milking now, either. Randel, thank God, hasn't married, so there are only the four of us adults, with Mother, and young Reifr.

1319 – 1321& onwards

I look back on our Iron days, Randel's and mine, with a strange, sick sort of longing. The work was hard, but we were strong, the food was good, and Astrid was a beauty; smooth, silky skin drawn tight over full breasts, promising so much. Now times have been hard for so long there is no beauty left, in her or in any of us, nor in Nature, nor in the seasons, nor in the valley. There are no promises left, only the threat of starvation come the next winter. As if the appalling weather of these last five years wasn't enough, now what sheep and cattle there are left in the valley – and there are few indeed compared to father's times – have all started to go down with the Murrain, a terrible wasting sickness that kills them after only a few days. We are back to my ancestors' days, Ragnar and Freya, coming to a valley not knowing how they would live from one day to the next.

No, it's much worse now. Then, according to the stories, there were fruits, deer to kill and eat, and, importantly, no neighbours. It sounds bad I know, but there is so little food now that neighbour is set against neighbour, stealing, rustling, hoarding. Then, if you needed more land, you could clear a bit more of the forest and make another strip to plant with what you needed, and watch it grow. Now there is no more to clear, not that's any good, and in any case unless the weather improves there would be little point anyway. The clearings and fields we have produce virtually nothing, and now the sheep and cattle are dying in droves. If things don't get better very soon I fear there will be no more Thorneythwaite – just as there is no more Seathwaite since the last flood.

The Furness monks had done a good job there, clearing the trees, draining the swamp, building walls and fences to pen the hundreds of sheep they ran on the fells – and ran all year round, now. The days of summer grazing only have gone, with enough land cleared to make hay for winter feeding. In any case, they have bred the sheep to be hardy enough to survive on the high fell even through the winter – or they had till the Murrain got to them. Then, two winters ago, disaster hit. In mid-April, after a month of nearly continuous rain, we had two days when it never stopped. The saturated ground could hold no more water, and the river rose almost like a tide, sweeping over its bank, through the huts and farmyard where the monks were living, carrying rocks and mud and flooding into the land they had so carefully drained, filling the ditches and the dykes, covering everything with a thick layer of glutinous mud. Their walls and fences were no more, pushed over, flattened, and covered feet deep, never to be seen again.

Many monks were lost, drowned in the fury of the deluge which had swept through without warning. Some were never found, buried who knew where under the new ground, the new marsh that quickly grew its own new quota of sieves and sedges. Seathwaite, the clearing in the sieves, went back to sieves again for a generation, till there was new heart, new resolve by Furness to start again, as the Murrain finally exhausted its grip on the livestock, and the few left could start new flocks. Once again, we at Thorneythwaite gave thanks to God for our position, high on our own little moraine, out of the waters. We were starving, practically with no stock, but we survived.

And slowly, month by month and year by year, the weather improved. The high snows melted in June, the oats produced some heads, the hay crop grew and we got it safely dried and under cover. We had but two cows left, and a bull calf that would have to serve his mother and his aunt, and a few gaunt sheep, escapees somehow from the pestilence that had struck down so many in the valley.

Twenty years later we heard of a similar pestilence, this time among the people. There was a terrible plague that caused black boils to erupt all over their bodies, followed almost always by death. Perhaps we were lucky that the hardships of previous decades had decimated the valley's population. With so few neighbours we escaped the Black Death entirely, though I did hear of many cases in Cese-wic, where the people lived cheek by jowl.

All things pass, and there always seem to be some left to carry on. Now at last, as the Earth moves into the second half of this dreadful century new hope comes to Thorneythwaite. Reifr has married, another girl from Stonethwaite, and they have three bairns, two girls and a boy, and their childish laughter warms my old heart. We have re-built the house, with higher walls than the old house. And we have a new roof! Not only have we rebuilt, but we have moved its place too. There is a place no more than a hundred paces to the West where the moraine rises much higher, offering more shelter, and we have built there. The awful rains of the early part of the century played havoc with the old turf roof, seeping through to begin with, and then washing soil and mud down on anyone below. Once breached it was impossible to stop, and we spent a miserable winter till we could renew the turf. Now there's a new way that some are trying. There are outcrops of slate up on Honister fell that we can split with a chisel to produce slabs of slate that can make a better roof than the turfs could manage. The rain runs down one slate, and as long as the one below reaches up under it, it carries on running down the roof, till eventually it runs off. Of course there are a few drips, but at least they are clean, not sodden mud.

The new house is square, with a decent space inside for all we need. The walls are thick, just as Ragnar's were, but we have left an opening for a window, so there is a bit of light inside. I made a wooden casement that fits snugly in the hole when it's too cold or wet, but in summer we leave it open, that and the door. The door is on the East wall, for the wind and rain very rarely come from there, and the window on the North wall, strangely, for the same reason. Nearly all our weather comes from the West or the South, and the moraine shelters us well from those quarters.

All in all, Borcherdale has come through these trying times more or less intact. Some of the poorer hovels have gone, either abandoned or washed away. Some of the lower-lying steadings have succumbed to the floods, overwhelmed and abandoned, but most of the clearings still support their families. There are not many of us left who remember the harshness of the early 1300s, for life is short and has been all the shorter for most who lived through those times. I don't know how, or even why, I have lived so long, and I would to God I had not. I lost my beloved Astrid twenty years and more since, and Randel too. Reifr and his family are good to me, and I like to think that like my own father I have some wisdom born of the hardships to pass on – but I doubt they see it that way.

The two abbeys tightened their hold on the valley, of course, in the aftermath of the blights we suffered. We valley men, born and raised here, died in our dozens from hunger and cold – as did the poor monks themselves. But there are always new monks to take their place, and to take over abandoned steadings. It wasn't long before they had built again at Seathwaite; it was far too good a sheep-farm to let it go to waste. I don't suppose the new breed of monk living there gives the river a second glance, but you wouldn't catch me living on its flood plain. I have seen too much of that river's destructive power.

Chapter thirteen

1967. Ian begins to spread his wings.

I was eighteen when Richard, Mark and I set off for our modern version of 'the Grand Tour', though I was nineteen by the time we returned. It was the 5th August,1967, and I had been nervous that I wouldn't make it. In my mind I was integral to hay time at Thorneythwaite, obviously my parents couldn't manage it without me to do all the tractor-work, mowing, tedding, rowing up and baling. Then all that labour of loading the bales onto the trailer and off again into the Bank Barn. How could they do that without me? After all, Dad would soon be fifty-one, and Ma just five years behind him. But... I had done my A-levels, and I deserved this break. Anxiously I nagged them to let me cut more than one field at a time. By the skin of our teeth we made it, sheep clipped, hay baled and into the barn – all bar Nookem, the four-acre field nearest Seathwaite.. It had been a good Summer, with a lot more sun and less rain than usual.

Actually, it had been a great Summer, my first as a man, not a schoolboy. I did my A-levels the previous year, with good results – but just not good enough for Cambridge. I could have gone to Imperial College, London, or Manchester, but Fitzwilliam College, Cambridge wanted a bit more maturity. And so did I. It suited me very well to have most of the next year off school, not for a Gap Year, as a few of my more enterprising fellow students were, but to farm properly as an integral part of Thorneythwaite. I had to spend a couple of months back at school to sit entrance exams for both Oxford and Cambridge, and was accepted into Mansfield College, Oxford, to read Maths. No-one told me I would be the only mathematician in the college, nor how hard that would make it.

But from Christmas 1966 onwards I could spend my entire time on the farm, and I relished it. Dad and I put up a second prefab, doubling the battery hen output. This time the site was more difficult, needing a lot of building up and concreting before we had a floor capable of taking another of the Dalkeith cast-offs. Building, constructing, I loved, and the farm gave many excuses to indulge my pleasure. On the other hand, livestock management perhaps wasn't my strongest suit.

Ma and Dad went on holiday in June, off to Donegal and their beloved Ring of Kerry where they had met back in 1939, just before the war. Leaving me in sole control, with many a list, many an admonition. The sheep and lambs were back on the fell, dipped, smitted and ear-marked, and the cattle had all been sold, so in truth there were only the hens to be looked after – the two battery houses and two lofts full of deep litter hens. This was well over 1500 birds, and of course it was my job to collect the eggs, clean and grade them, feed all the hens and clean out the battery cages daily; no small task in itself.

All went well for the first four days; then I noticed one of the deep-litter lofts weren't laying as many eggs as they had been. Were there rats, eating eggs in the nest-boxes? I could see no sign of broken eggs, as there surely would be. Ah well, Dad would be back in a couple of days, he could sort it out. They returned very happy with their holiday, and with photos of themselves on horseback 'doing the Ring of Kerry'.

"So, how's things been? No disasters I trust?"

"Well, I've put up that big wall gap in Horse Close, and got some muck out onto Field How. Oh, the hens in the second loft seem to have gone off lay. Are they getting old?" He was out of the kitchen still in his best clothes and up into the loft before I could say more, so I stayed to hear Ma's stories of their holiday. She had loved it – made her feel young again she said. And it hadn't changed a bit in the thirty years since they met there in '39.

"A few more cars, I suppose, but there are still horses and carts. It's like going back to when I was a girl in Bristol."

Dad came back in, with a face like thunder. Oh hell, what had I done?

"You need a bloody nursemaid! Eighteen, going to Oxford. Reading Maths? You haven't the brains of a five-year-old!" Ma looked crestfallen, all the delights of her holiday crumbling on the floor. I too was floored: I'd expected praise and gratitude for holding the fort while they had time off.

"Did you not think to check their water when they started going off lay, you great lummox? Did you think they would all just decide to go on strike? Honest to God, you might be a bright bugger in some ways, but you haven't the sense you were born with!"

No, I hadn't thought to check the water. Apparently the float had got stuck up, so the trough wasn't filling, and I hadn't noticed. Ma twitched her eyebrows at me, our long-understood signal to make myself scarce. She would mollify Dad somehow, and in any case there was absolutely nothing I could say. I gathered a week or so later she had gone on about how lucky it was that it was just the loft, with only fifty hens in, not a battery bank of three hundred and fifty. I began to look forward avidly to the Grand Tour… five weeks away seemed a good idea. Pity I had to get through two more months before it. Two months of the hardest work of the year, which perhaps was a good thing.

Early in July we gathered the fell – the only occasions when its narrow back seemed a good thing. The three of us could make a decent job of gathering the four or five hundred ewes and their lambs down the wedge-shaped hill, starting at the top of Glaramara. We were gloriously unaware of its ancient history, and of the outcrop of tuff rock, still visible, which had been the source of so many stone axes some five thousand years before. We'd long ago learnt to leave the fell gate open, and the gate into Tup Close, so they could stream right down into the fields unimpeded. If there was any bottleneck ewes and lambs got separated, then it was hell on wheels trying to get everything through, with ewes turning back bleating for their lambs, and lost lambs darting off in all directions. Everything was to clip, except the lambs of course. Most of our neighbours clipped the hoggs – last year's lambs – first, but it seemed like unnecessary work to gather twice, risking mismatching ewes and lambs.

The slatted floor in the sheep shed.

We clipped on the slatted floor, which was perfect for the job, staying clean throughout. And with a roof over it we could pen a hundred sheep in for the next day's clipping if it looked like rain – and in Borrowdale it usually looked like rain. We only had one electric clipping machine, and as with most of our machinery, I commandeered it, while Dad used a pair of hand-shears, as he had all his farming life. Occasionally Ma clipped a few hoggs by hand as well, but more usually she smitted the clipped sheep and wrapped up the wool. We weren't very fast, and on a good day only got through maybe a hundred and twenty between us, so the job went on all week. Dad was happy that there was a Test Match on the radio; except that the West Indies hammered us regularly that year, with Gary Sobers running amok.

The other annual stress was hay time, of course, but this year was kinder than most, and as I said, only Nookem was left for them to do when the time came for the great adventure.

Dad was adamant: "Get off with you, of course we can manage Nookem. What do you think we're going to do when you go to Oxford?"

Good question: did I want to go to University? The truth was, I loved Thorneythwaite and farming. And how would the two of them manage alone? Gathering would be a nightmare, and the last nine months had shown there was plenty of work here for them and me. Why exactly was I going to leave them to it?

"Because you're a lot better at Maths than you are with animals." Dad could be a bit blunt at times, but put like that I didn't feel like staying: only later did I realise how astute he was.

So off we went, the Three Musketeers: Paris – must get here; Rome – must get here; Vienna – must get here. It was that sort of holiday. So I missed Dad's horrendous accident – which of course only happened because I wasn't there to look after them. Because I wasn't there to help, when they had successfully got Nookem baled Ma and Dad decided to bring the bales in the easy way – loading them onto the buck-rake and transporting them twenty at a time back to the barn. The buck-rake lowers to the ground on the hydraulic arms of the Little Grey Fergie, so loading is easy, then you lift the hydraulics and off you go. It takes a bit longer because Nookem is the furthest field from Thorneythwaite's bank barn, and there were twenty-odd bales left for the last load. Rather than come all that way back, Dad insisted on loading the lot, which made the tractor a bit light on the steering – almost overbalancing backwards, in fact. Ma protested, but Dad was having none of it. He would sit on the bonnet as they went up the hill out of the field, to keep the front wheels on the ground.

All went well as they came through the gate, but as the slope increased his weight wasn't enough, and Ma lost steerage. The tractor veered to the left, towards the edge of the built-up ramp that led up the hill. As it reared up, Dad fell off the bonnet, right in front of the careering tractor, which now lurched uncontrollably and inevitably plunged off the ramp, running over his stomach and ribs with the back right wheel. Now, the weight of the tractor and the load of hay was well over a ton, and as she came to a stop against the field wall Ma was certain she must have killed him, and sure enough, when she shakily dismounted and ran back to him he wasn't breathing and had gone blue in the face. Panic-stricken she pummelled his chest and was rewarded by him giving a great shuddering gasp, as his flattened lungs tried to re-assert themselves.

Now what to do? The farmhouse and telephone were five hundred yards away, and her beloved Jamie might be about to die. Fortunately Noble Bland, their neighbour over at Seatoller Farm, had been turning his own hay in the field next to Nookem, and looked up when he heard Dad's shout as he was thrown from the bonnet. He saw the tractor plunge over the edge of the ramp and realised what had happened. Noble ran to help. Noble didn't make a habit of running, and was out of breath when he arrived, certain in his own mind that Dad must be dead. Quickly taking in the situation he told a nearly hysterical Betty to keep Dad warm and talk to him and keep him conscious, while he ran to Thorneythwaite to phone for an ambulance.

Between gasps for breath he asked for 'Ambulance', and managed eventually to explain what had happened and where – including the need for the ambulance to drive along to the field. Fortunately there was someone in the self-catering end of the house, who promised to direct the ambulance when it came. More slowly, now that it was out of his hands, Noble made his way back to Betty, more than half afraid he would find Jim dead. All that time Betty sat there, nursing his head, still afraid to move him at all, with all their life together playing in her head, soothing him and his laboured breathing, saying God knows what – anything to keep him with her.

It was two hours before they caught the longed-for sound of a motor coming along the track; two hours in which he was unable to say anything, needing all his inner resources just to keep breathing. Each breath cost him dear, sending a searing pain through his chest. The ambulance men took one look at the scene and shook their heads in astonishment that he lived, and carefully slid him onto a stretcher and into the vehicle. Ma climbed in beside him; there was no way she was letting him out of her sight now. Mightily relieved, Noble wandered off back to his hay. He had sat tongue-tied beside the pair of them all that time, excluded from their intimacy, yet unable to leave.

The surgeons at Carlisle Hospital were amazed when they examined Dad, after Ma told them what had happened. There were a couple of broken ribs, and his lungs were still struggling, but nothing like the massive damage a ton of tractor should inflict on a fragile human form.

They kept him in for a couple of days, sedated to help the pain of breathing, till he was clearly fit to return home.

When he was up to it, he and Ma strolled along to the ramp to try to work out how it was he was still alive. They decided he must have fallen right in beside the ramp, giving him a tight, but just big enough, space so that the wheel compressed his chest but didn't completely flatten it, as it surely would on flat ground. Noble had long since taken the bales into the barn for them, and parked the tractor on level ground. At Dad's insistence, Ma got back on, started up, and shakily drove it home. Dad limped along behind her – she wouldn't let him ride on anywhere!

Jim, restored to health, clipping with hand shears.

Chapter fourteen

Agatha Borkerhead: Reifr's great-grand-daughter. 15th Century.

I only just remember my great-grand father, Reifr, and his stories of the terrible famines they suffered at Thorneythwaite when he was a boy. It sounds a dreadful time: I'm glad things are so much more settled now. Furness Abbey are good landlords, on the whole, keen to improve the land and the state of our farms. I like to think Thorneythwaite is a cut above most of the scruffy little holdings around us. We hold the middle of the valley here, as we have from time immemorial, whereas all the other clearings are more recent. We have some ploughed land – ridge and furrow, turned over by our two fell ponies with a single furrow plough. Most of the little farms down in Rosthwaite share a town field, where each has a strip of the ploughable land, and of course Stonethwaite is a bigger operation altogether with the vaccary there. I know one of the lay canons there: he's not a monk, but he is part of the Fountains Abbey set-up and keeps the accounts of the vaccary – Desmond. It's quite important to me that he's not a monk!

Desmond had to do a survey of the Fountains side of Borrowdale – from Watendlath to the head of Langstrath, all the East side of the valley. He found no fewer than 41 little farmsteads on that side, and there must be at least as many on our side of the valley. Of course, most of them are a lot smaller that our Thorneythwaite, and we have all the fell to ourselves; not that it's very good, but we do have a fair number of sheep up there. Nothing compared to Stonethwaite of course, but they can call on novice monks for labour, and they do! They make more hay than the rest of the valley put together, Desmond says, and they sell quite a lot of it off. Would you believe it? He says they took £17 6s 8d for hay sales last year. The vaccary tenants have to buy it from the Abbey, even though they've grown it and made it. It seems a daft system to me, but Desmond says every part of the Abbey's books have to be kept separately.

They have their own grange up at Watendlath where they store hay and oats and barley – and the beer and wine for the monks' table. Our side, the Furness Abbey lands have a grange near the head of the lake, and that seems to have changed the aspect of the valley. Grand-dad used to say there hardly was a track to Kese-wic in his day; everything came and went either to the sea over Sty Head, to Kendal over Stake Pass at the top of Langstrath, or out to Castlerigg along the top of Walla Crag. There was nothing in Kese-wic but St Mungo's church at Crosthwaite, where they went for funerals. Now, though, there are a few easy tracks down the valley to the grange, for the mules to take their loads, and there's a half-decent track down the East side of the lake to Kese-wic. It stays close to the lakeside, partly because the trees thin out there, and partly because it's so steep and rocky anywhere inland from there. There are no farmsteads from the grange till nearly Kese-wic, the ground is so useless. However, once you get to the village things improve. There are some really good farms, ploughing the good deep soil between the two lakes, and much more importantly as far as I'm concerned there is a Saturday market in the middle of the village, where people meet to sell and buy and chat and gossip. I love it – the chance to get out of the valley for a day and to buy and sell and find out what's going on out in the world. Of course, I do get Desmond to tell me what news he has, but it's all a bit distant – Fountains Abbey is so far away. I want to hear scandalous tales of valley people, and you hear a lot more out of the valley than folk will tell in it!

I have to get up in the dark in winter to get our eggs and cheese in a pack on my back to carry to the market so I'm there early enough for customers still to be wanting my stuff, but it's well worth it for the chance of a gossip and maybe a little bargain to take home. One thing I have noticed: it's often raining when I set out but dry before Kese-wic, and yet still raining when I get home. This is a terrible valley for rain, I sometimes think we'll have children with webbed feet to compensate.

Let me tell you about last Saturday; you have to laugh! Seemingly, one of the monks up at the grange had been seeing more than he should have of Mary Jopson – in both ways, if you take my meaning. Her brothers, big strong valley lads, espied the two of them sneaking off into one of the storage barns, and they gave them a few minutes to get down to it, like, then burst in on them. The story goes that one of the lads held the monk down while the other got out the razor they'd brought along and shaved his arse in a tonsure to match his head!

I hope my brothers don't catch me and Desmond. He doesn't have a tonsure on his head, and I don't want him having one on his backside, either. We're careful, though, Desmond and me. You wouldn't catch us in a barn, we like to walk. No, really, we like exploring what there is left of the valley that hasn't been cleared for this or that poky little farm. There isn't much woodland left on the valley bottom, but there's still a lot on the fellsides. It's all getting old, though: the sheep nibble off all the new saplings and shoots before they get a chance, and slowly the old trees are rotting and falling. We had a big storm last night, with the wind ripping up the valley with a huge roaring sound, and this morning we had seven old trees down at Thorneythwaite, and goodness knows how many more up and down the valley.

Johnny Wood's our favourite, and we meet there on a Sunday. It's about halfway between Thorneythwaite and Stonethwaite, and it must be just like all the woodland was before there was so much cleared. I don't know why the sheep seem to leave it alone, unless it's just too overgrown for them to bother it. It's full of fallen trees and moss and bramble and rock, so it's hard even for us to make tracks through it – but that's half its attraction! Such a mix of trees. Oak and elm, of course, and the birch that seems to spring up everywhere. Here and there there's a holly tree, and the berries have been superb this autumn – a hard winter to come, no doubt. Ash saplings seem to generate anywhere there is light. In the wetter hollow in the lower part of the wood there's willow and, of course, alder. Alder seems best placed to take advantage of the wetter ground, and let's face it there's a lot of wetter ground in Borrowdale, and in Johnny Wood.

The ancient yew trees at Seathwaite.

The most famous trees in Borrowdale must be the mighty yews up at Seathwaite. Desmond and I walked up the valley last Sunday to have a look. People say they're over a thousand years old – some say they sprang up miraculously when Jesus was born. They are certainly immense enough to be that old. Desmond wanted to measure the girth of the biggest of the four yews, which might just have been an excuse to get me to hug the trunk. I felt a bit silly with my arms round it, fingers on both hands just and so managing to touch his as he hugged the other side. Then we had to lie on the ground arms stretched out while he marked how far we reached. Then he paced it out and reckoned it was just over ten feet in girth! We have a yew at Thorneythwaite, but I can hug all the way round that one on my own, easily. Our family stories say it was planted by Freya and Ragnar when they first came to the valley, and even that is nearly five hundred years ago now.

All those years of lasses like me finding a man like Desmond, or the men of Thorneythwaite finding a woman to take to wife and to bed. That must be twenty generations, and we carry all the stories in our hearts and tell them round the fire of a night, so each generation learns about all who went before. Of course there's a lot missed out, just the highlights keep on being told. Ragnar and Freya – well, they're guaranteed a place, and we still tell where they came from, such a cold land, away across the sea. And the stories of great grandfather Reifr, I'm sure they will go on for ever, with the times being so hard. But so many of us just pass our days here quietly, there isn't much to tell. What might they say about me? Just another Thorneythwaite girl, born here, brought up here, but destined to leave and find my own home, with Desmond I hope.

In the meantime, I'm a spinster. A lot of farms sell their wool, and make a good price, but here at Thorneythwaite we prefer to spin a proportion of our clip. It all adds value, and we can sell what yarn we don't use ourselves in Kese-wic. Father says he just does it to keep us girls out of mischief, and give us something to do, but he'd be hard put to make ends meet without our little industry. Not that Herdwick wool makes great cloth, but it's all we've got, so we make the best of it. First job is to wash all the fleeces we'll use, and a messy, cold job it is. At least it's in what passes for summer here, but the beck is still freezing. I have to stand up to my knees in Nichol Dub for hours on end, sluicing through fleece by fleece, soaking, pummelling on the stones at the side, wringing out and then doing it all again. And again. And again. We lie them out on the field to dry, and hope to God it doesn't rain. By the end of the day my legs look like rough pastry, but my hands are all smooth from the lanolin.

Gathered up into a great pile and stored in one of the barns the wool can bide a while till winter, when there's more time, as long as it's good and dry and the mice kept away. When it's quieter I gather up a fleece and take it into the light and pick it apart. After the washing it's a very tight mat that I have to tease out and get ready for carding. I'm very proud of my cards – bought for two shillings in Kese-wic – for they make the job of lining the fibres up much easier than fingers. Then I make a roll of what I've carded, and it's ready to wrap onto the distaff. It's a tricky job to hold and turn the distaff in the crook of your arm, pulling the roll off slowly with your left hand while spinning the spindle to take up the yarn

71

with your right. That's why I get the job! Father had a go once. Once only. We don't have a loom, so Mother spends a lot of the Winter knitting, as do I. Without us women the men would go naked in the Borrowdale rain.

Thorneythwaite will be Ralf's; as first-born boy it's his right, and he is a good farmer, so I'm sure the old place will breathe a sigh of relief to be left in safe hands for a generation.

It hasn't always been so. There have been times we nearly lost it, and not just in those desperate days of the murrain and the plagues last century. Reifr's son, my grandfather, is held up in the family stories as 'The One Who Lost The Farm'. They called him Randal, after his unmarried uncle, and he should have had it reasonably easy, when Thorneythwaite was back on its feet after the near Ice Age they had when Reifr was born. Perhaps that was the trouble, but for whatever reason this Randal failed to pay the tithe due to Furness Abbey for three years running. Some of the stories say he was too proud, and refused to accept that he was just a tenant, not king of his own midden. And some say he was a wastrel, a poor farmer who couldn't make a living on a farm that's kept our family for so many generations. A lazy drunkard. Whatever the truth, and it depends on who's telling the story, the family were evicted by the Abbot and the farm stood empty for two years. It was his sisters who turned things round, my great-aunts.

Neither married, or had children, but they had the nous to go begging to the Abbot of Furness Abbey – the stories say they actually made the journey on pack mules, over Sty Head and all the way down the coast to Furness. They petitioned him, pleaded with him, and pointed out that Thorneythwaite was standing empty, tenantless and therefore useless to the Abbey. Randal had died, proud to the end, they say, and they had inherited his young son, my father, and what little there was in the way of possessions – the mules they had travelled on. Maybe the Abbot took pity on them, or maybe he thought any tenant was better than none. For whatever reason he agreed to their taking the farm on again, and they managed to keep going till my father was of an age to take over.

I admire them, those two maiden aunts, and I confess to a secret jealousy that Thorneythwaite will be Ralf's, with no question. I could manage it, I know, and I know a lot more about it than Ralf ever will. But it's no good to kick against the pricks, tenancies are men's business – till they make a mess of it.

Chapter fifteen

Betty Hall: 1962 – 1967

She intrigued me from the start, this slip of a girl my young son wanted to bring home: Jennifer, or more usually Jen. They were so young, both of them, only just teenagers. I was glad he did want to bring her, though, much better than boys' usual furtive little affairs. Glad and surprised, for Ian is habitually secretive – perhaps it's because Jim and I tease him too readily, and he is easy to tease. He should have had a brother, but after my still birth I couldn't face carrying another to full term only to be so disappointed. Or a sister – I would have liked that. In fact he was meant to be a girl himself, Jacqueline I'd named her in my heart. And the second one. Perhaps that's why I find I like his girl so much. I suppose it's ridiculous, with them both thirteen, but I would like to see him marry her someday. I daydream of them carrying Thorneythwaite on after our day. Some days I need that daydream. The wireless forecast speaks of the low pressure systems that bring us so much rain as 'depressions'. An unintended allusion I'm sure, but this rain gets under my skin sometimes. With the cloud lowering down and the hills all around there are days I feel so claustrophobic I have to get in the car and invent a need to shop in Keswick just to remind myself there is a way out of this dead-end valley.

She lightens it, Jen, that's what it is. She brings a ray of sunshine on the cloudiest day and I feel my mood lift just to know she'll be here today. Nearly every weekend she's up for Sunday afternoon. That's about all the time they get off from Keswick School. With it being part boarding they have Saturday morning school, sport or music in the afternoon, and she's a Methodist and at church on Sunday morning. I was a Methodist – or perhaps I am a Methodist? I don't bother with church now, but Jim takes Ian to St Andrews at Stonethwaite most Sundays. Quite a surprise, somehow, I thought Tom had all the religious genes in the Hall family.

Perhaps it's because she reminds me of myself when I was younger. Always keen to be outside, helping, working with Jim and Ian, though she'll need to put on a bit of weight and muscle before she's a farmer's wife! She helped gathering the fell last week, with her dog Judy. Funny little ginger mongrel with absolutely no idea about sheep, but she will bark, so if it's just a case of driving them down the fell Judy has her uses. Actually, my bitch Nip isn't much better, it's as well Jim has Beaut and Moss. I wonder what Jen makes of Ian's language on a gather? I notice he started off a lot more guarded than usual, but it wasn't long before he got up steam. Not nice for a well-brought-up Methodist girl.

Betty, Ian, Jennifer and Jim. Hay-time 1963

She'd been coming up for well over a year when she completely sealed my hope that they would stay together. One of the jobs they always did together was collecting all the eggs in the battery house, often over six hundred, collected straight onto trays of two and a half dozen. Occasionally we get one without an outer shell, just the soft inner membrane holding it all together. She ran giggling like a minx into the house with Ian in roaring pursuit and hid behind me, begging me to save her from him. He had egg yolk dripping down his face and in his hair. Bit by bit the story came out, how she'd puckered up those pretty lips and sidled up to him for a kiss, then scrunched the shell-less egg on his head and run like hell. I was so proud of her! I would love to do that to Jim sometimes, but I never will now. We get too old, and it's such a pity. I should have had a daughter – now, perhaps, I have, and it's lovely.

They shock me, sometimes, and I'm not sure why I'm shocked. It's their open affection that undoes me. After dinner we all tend to sit for a while, and when Jen is with us Ian commandeers the big old chair in the corner of the kitchen, by the Aga. Definitely the master's chair. And Jen snuggles down on his knee as if to the manner born. They don't kiss, or anything blatant, yet it unsettles me, and I never know quite how to react. Jim seems completely at ease with it, though when she's not there he teases

Ian relentlessly about his girl. And they spend a long time up in the barn, and I'm never quite comfortable. Jim insists it's harmless, and I'm sure it is, but I feel a bit 'in loco parentis' for Marjorie and Norman's girl. Again, she's completely natural about it all and never turns a hair when I pick bits of hay off her jumper before letting her get on the bus to go home.

They do go out together in Keswick, too, Ian biking down the valley if it's an evening do, because there is no bus after six o'clock. It's quite strange to me to watch the interaction between him and Jim – it's a bit old bull and young bull. Jim turned fifty this September, as Ian turned seventeen. It would be in 1932 that Jim was seventeen: school behind him and a secretarial course at the Gregg School – and a motor-bike to roar around Carlisle on, with this girl or that clinging on the back. Lord, it seems so long ago, before that bloody war – pardon my French. Now we sit together every evening at the kitchen table weighing eggs, hundreds of eggs, watching a grainy television. BBC is all we can get, and even that is on a long cable out onto the intake. He'd been needling Ian about his generation, sex and drugs and rock and roll, as he put it. Suddenly Ian snapped, the first and only time that I can remember, and railed at him about television as a drug. How we spent every night in front of it, 'hooked' as Ian put it. How we'd let ourselves drift into limbo, never going out, never having fun, just watching 'the bloody Horse of the Year show'.

Jim really lost his temper. All the justifications about the need to work, to provide for an ungrateful son, to try to make ends meet. All the usual stuff, but I could hear underneath it how stung he was, how he recognised that sly bit of truth in the accusation. We have grown middle-aged too soon, lost the friends we had before Thorneythwaite. There are dances in the Institute at Rosthwaite, but somehow we never go now. Of course we do still have old friends, mainly mine from down South, who visit us and we make the effort then. Even so…Ian stormed out: he was going to the pictures in Keswick with Jen, on his bike. Goodnight!

An hour later the rain started, one of those filthy pitch-black Borrowdale nights with the wind whistling round the house and the rain driving down at 45°. Two hours later the phone rang: Ian, out from the pictures, Jen taken home by her father. "Do you think you could come and pick me up, Dad? It's absolutely chucking it down."

"You're always talking about adventure. Have an adventure – bike home." And he put the phone down.

Betty and Jennifer – happy days!

So I was devastated when it slowly became clear it was all over between the youngsters, five years down the line. Not that I was told, of course, I had to ask when Jen hadn't been up to the farm for weeks. Young men! They can make me so angry, when they're being stupid and stubborn and arrogant. I remember them in the war, and before, so keen to be right, unbending, certain. I know he's wrong, throwing away the best and making do with the rest. Now he can drive, out with his mates, out with the girls, out with God knows whom. He doesn't bring them home – ashamed of them I suspect; knowing they'll be judged against Jennifer and found wanting.

It's a strange year, this, Ian's 'gap year' that isn't really. He's working full-time with us, and it's lovely, but it feels ephemeral, out of time. This is how it could be, from now on, if he'd settle down with Jennifer and slowly take over the farm as we get older. That's how it is on most farms, sons taking on from their fathers, arguing like mad, the young wanting to try new things, the old digging their heels in and pointing out all the dangers and pitfalls. I know there are confrontations all over the place, but at least there's a continuity, and the old can get older with dignity, doing what they can, what they feel happy with, while the next generation finds its feet. I would like that, especially if he had Jennifer with him, to keep him from getting too serious. I could grow old with them in charge... Still, it's not going to be. He has his place at Oxford, reading Maths! Of course I'm proud of him, and of course I want the best for him, but it would have been lovely if he could just have been a little bit less clever, a little bit less ambitious, because he does love this place, and the work, and it could have been so good. And, Oh God, this year out just turns the screw.

How will we manage, when he's gone? He laughs and says terms are only eight weeks long, and he'll be home as much as he's away, and I suppose that's true. But when his three years are done Jim will be fifty-five, and I'll be fifty, and how will we manage gathering then? I can't imagine he'll want to just farm Thorneythwaite after three years of Oxford. I can see how it could all be good, but I can't make it happen, and it's killing me, slowly.

Chapter sixteen

Ralf Borkhead 1537

So, Sir, you are the King's evaluator, come to view fair Thorneythwaite before you double my rent. What's that you say? 'New brooms sweep clean'. Aye, your master Henry's all of that, if what I hear is true. Swept away our abbey, swept away our monks, swept away our landlords after all these years. And now he'd have you sweep me away less I pay doubly for the improvements I have made. No Sir, I will not hold my tongue. You may have the power to throw me out, you'll not stop my mouth as well. You say I am a useless farmer, that the Duchy of Lancaster deserves better. You shall see that the opposite is true, that in my forty years as yeoman here I have made huge improvements. What's that? You cavil at my use of the word yeoman, Sir? All right, I am a tenant, not an owner, but only because rich landowners from Alice de Rumilly onwards stole the land that should rightfully have been ours for ever. So yes, I call myself yeoman, and if ye know what's good for thee thou'll not disagree.

Right, then. My father died at the start of the year of our Lord 1500 – died of an apoplexy brought on by too hearty a celebration of the new century on Lady Day, March 25th. He left me a farm and a house nigh in ruins. Let's start with the house, and you'll allow I'm sure that what you see before you now is as fine a dwelling as is in all Borrowdale? Two storeys, each a goodly room some sixteen feet square, with a stone staircase outside to the upper storey. A fine, new roof, covered with slate riven by mine own hand and fetched by cart frae Honister. Let me tell thee, Mister, that upper storey was built by these two hands when I had to rip off the old, leaky rough slate roof bequeathed me by my father. Not by those lazy good-for-nowt abbey-crawlers who've got what they deserved. By mine own hands, Mister.

You see this fine barn, wherein we stored the season's oats? That new threshing floor is mine, Sir, riven and sawn by these same two hands, hands that flailed for forty seasons, and would fain flail the blackguard that calls me too lazy to continue. Those oats were sown by these same hands, in ground turned over by faithful Nell there. Faithful Nell who has borne me North more than once to fight the bloody Scots Reivers who rape fair Cumberland. Oh yes, Sir, I have fought, and will fight again if called on e'en at my age. That's why I call myself yeoman.

Will't look on these fine Herdwick yows, brought down frae Glaramara for thee to value – as if thou'd know the value of a good heafed yow. Over a hundred we run – now is that not good husbandry? Aye, and twenty head of cattle, good milkers all with a fine bit of beef in the arse. What will't say is their value, Mister? Perhaps thou'll walk with me, inspect the walls I've made? Aye, Sir, walls that I have built, me and my lads. Walls that shut off fields, la'al bits of a few acres where oats may grow, where hay may be had, safe frae the mouths of these hungry Herdwicks. I'd have thee know what it is thou's charged to do, to charge me double for the work that I have wrought, or throw me and mine off what is rightfully ours.

Bird How, Eskdale.
The same pattern as the 16th century Thorneythwaite.

Hold your tongue, Ralf Burkhead, if ye know what's good for thee. Give me no more lip, or thou shalt feel the weight of the King's displeasure, meted out by these fine bailiffs. Knowest thou what is happening these two years past? How that thy former landlords, that accursed Abbey of Furness is taken down, the abbot run, tail between his legs to be vicar of Dalston, leaving his monks destitute, thrown out,

80

dispossessed of their ill-gotten gains. Speak not again to me in that proud vein, or you shall feel the same weight upon thy shoulders Abbot Roger Pyle could not contain. Shall I tell thee how it went, so you can at least earn your keep in the alehouses of Borrowdale regaling your neighbours with the tale?

List then, while I tell it, and mind, no more of your bluster or I'll loose the bailiffs on thee. Let me acquaint thee of a word I'd guess ye ken not: Attainder. Mark it well, Ralf Burkhead, for 'tis the word whereby thou'll lose this Thorneythwaite if ye hold not thy tongue, as 'tis the word that has stripped many an abbey of its gold, its silver, and its lead; if so be thou pay not willingly. Attainder is the forfeiture of land and all rights when th'art found guilty of treason. And thou will be found guilty of treason if thou pay not quietly. I'll swear to it, if it's needed.

My Lord, the Earl of Sussex, Robert Radclyffe, has a neat way with abbots. Some of the bastard sons of Rome were clearly guilty of high treason, opining openly that good King Henry had no rights over them – that they were subject solely to Rome and the Devil's spawn who rules there. Even here, in lowly Borrowdale, I'd guess ye've heard of the damned Pilgrimage of Grace in Yorkshire, and its bastard child the Bigod's Rebellion here in Cumberland. No? then let me tell you, so ye begin to respect the power that bids thee shift. Robert Aske was a nobleman who should have known better than to join in the uprising that started in Lincolnshire, complaining that good Henry did wrongly to behead the siren Ann Boleyn, but he led this ill-fated Pilgrimage of Grace. Was ever a movement more artfully titled – what say you, Ralf Burkhead?

Oh, you say nought, perhaps you would pretend such affairs of state have no resonance in Borrowdale? I trow ye know more of Bigod's Rebellion, seeing as Michael Fisher has heard you speak in glowing terms of its aims. Treason, Mr Burkhead, if I could be bothered to follow it up. But no, you will meekly pay, or surrender Thorneythwaite, will you not, even as Abbot Pyle surrendered Furness.

I was telling thee of Sussex, and his way with abbots. There was many an abbot caught up in the Pilgrimage of Grace – Fountains' William Thirsk among them. Ah, I see ye know of his fate – I suppose it is common knowledge in the inns about. Hanged, drawn and quartered, 'tis not a pretty fate, Mr Burkhead. To lie there, half dead already, while the executioner slices you from groin to chest, cuts off your genitals, then wraps your entrails on a windlass and slowly draws them from your belly. Twenty-two feet, they say, that's the length that's slowly drawn from you as you die.

But come, Mr Burkhead, were you not telling me how you are master of Thorneythwaite, and I could hold my tongue? Not so cock-sure now, Ralf? If you want to be sure of your own cock, ye do well to hold your peace.

I was telling you of my Lord Sussex, and his way with abbots. Another involved with Bigod's foolishness was the Abbot Paslew of Whalley, down in Lancashire. Ah, I see by your face you know that he too was hanged – but then, he got off lightly, did he not? He held on to his entrails, but he was, I confess, a somewhat grisly sight hanging, stinking, in chains outside his gates. It was there that my Lord Sussex brought your own good abbot, Roger Pyle, to see would he surrender Furness quietly or face prosecution for his well-known treachery to King Henry. Perhaps it was the sight of John Paslew, swinging gently in the breeze outside the room that persuaded Abbot Roger, or perhaps it was the promise of the incumbency of Dalston – who knows?

The point is, Mr Yeoman Burkhead, Furness Abbey is gone. The King's Commissioners took its fine gold and silver plate, and their labourers removed the lead from its roof – all to be melted down, none to remain as idolatry. The labourers removed, too, the fine Popish arches with their pretensions. Do you know who is carrying on the work, now the King's men have gone? Shall I tell thee, Ralf? It is thine own servile neighbours, no, not here in Borrowdale, but around the abbey. There are pig-sties with carved angels in the walls, Ralfie, there are stables whose glory far outshines Bethlehem, let me tell you.

And what of its canting monks, with their feigned piety. Your masters, your landlords past. What of them Burkhead? What do ye think they are doing now? I'll tell thee, and again thou can recount it in the alehouses. Thirty-three there were, cloistered there in great comfort, living off the fruits of thy labours, Burkhead. They are gone, Burkhead, just as ye too must pay, or soon be gone. Forty shillings they were given, forty shillings each – save for half a dozen too old and impotent to fend for themselves. Good King Hal, in his great generosity, afforded them sixty shillings each, to serve them till they die.

And now, thy farm is forfeit, forasmuch as Michael Fisher has let it be known what thou hast blethered of in the alehouse. Pay up, or go quickly, Burkhead, ere my Lord Sussex hear of it, for then I fear thou'll not escape with thine life. Think hard on that windlass, Ralf, think hard on it. Thorneythwaite, and all of Borrowdale that erstwhile belonged to Furness Abbey is now part of the Duchy of Lancaster, and the king himself its landlord.

82

Chapter seventeen

Betty Hall

I sometimes think we'd have no friends if we hadn't held on to those we made when we were young. Jim has two in particular, from his Scotby days. Len and Nance Doran, who were our witnesses when we married, and our only guests! And May and Bill Taylor – May Richardson as was in Scotby days. Let me tell you a little about both sets, before I introduce you to mine.

Jim and Len grew up together in Scotby – as indeed did Nance. September 3rd, 1939, the very day war was declared, they enlisted, together, thinking to fight together, to watch out for each other. Each was twenty-three; in their prime. Little did they know the ways of the military. They were separated from day one, Jim destined to continue his clerking work as a sergeant in the Royal Army Service Corps; Len to join what would become the Desert Rats, eventually seeing action in El Alamein and fighting his way up Italy towards the end of the war, while Lucky Jim sunned himself in post-blitz Malta.

Len was with Jim when we first met, each on walking holidays in the West of Ireland. My friend was Kathleen, at 5'10" considerably taller than poor Len, who nevertheless had to do his best with her while Jim tried out his chat-up line with me. It went like this... "Well, how lovely to meet you, what's your name then?" "I'm Doreen, Doreen Draper".... "Hmm, em, do you have a middle name?" I should have gone straight back to Kathleen, but I never could resist a challenge. "Elizabeth: Doreen Elizabeth Draper." "Right then, Betty, would you and your friend fancy a drink perhaps." From then on I was Doreen to everyone in Bristol, but Betty to anyone further North.

Well, they both survived, thank God, Jim as I have said eager to make a new life on the land. Len went back to Teddy Coleman's building firm in Carlisle, taking up where he left off. He and Nance were married during the war, but never had children, and they took to Ian as a valued godson. We didn't see that much of them in the Myreground days, but when we moved nearer to Carlisle we met frequently, for dances, drinks and walks. I suppose Thorneythwaite is forty miles from Carlisle, but easy enough for them to come for a day, a weekend or to look after Ian when Jim and I manage to get away for a week's holiday – for all Ian protests he can look after himself!

I've never dared ask, quite, but I suspect May comes in the Gladys Mary Wilson category of young ladies Jim knew in his bachelor days. However, she married Bill before the war, though they say they only saw each other a very few times between '39 and '45. They have one son too, Robin, a year to the day older than Ian. Bill is night-editor of the Manchester Guardian, which must be a monumentally stressful job I'd think, but they love to get away to the Lake Hotel in Keswick, and always spend a day at least with us when they're up. Very fond of cricket, is Bill, just as Jim is, and there's always a game in the yard here at Thorneythwaite when they visit, for all the gravel and stones. It's lovely to see Ian and Jim enjoying playing together – there's precious little time for play on the farm.

We generally get a walk in when Len and Nance are here, often up in Langstrath. Jim and Len are both ardent pipe-smokers, so we've never been quite sure which one was to blame for 'the great conflagration'. I'd made up a picnic and we sat in the old dead bracken at the bottom of Sergeant's Crag taking our tea. It was a beautiful day in early June, often the best time of the year here in Borrowdale. We'd dipped all the ewes and lambs, smit them up and ear-marked them, and got them back to the fell. If there ever is a quiet week in our farming year this is probably it, though of course there are a million maintenance jobs we could be doing. But enough of that, this day was made for walking, talking, and making the most of old friends. Nance and I lay back in the warm, crisp bracken, talking of this and that, with a skylark high above us twittering her song.

As we peered up trying to pinpoint the tiny bird we became aware of a drift of smoke, and the whiff of something burning. Jim, Len and Ian had wandered down to the bridge over the gin-clear waters of Langstrath Beck, and the picnic area was burning fiercely at our side. We leapt up and started to try to beat out the flames with our boots, looking, Jim said later, 'like a pair of banshees doing some primitive fire dance'. We yelled to them to come and help, but it was no good. The fellside was well alight and the fire racing up the hill, fanned by what had seemed a friendly breeze just a few minutes earlier. Ian of course thought it great fun, leaping about stamping out what he could – as were we all. There was no question, the fire was winning, and very soon we just had to stand below it on the blackened ground and watch it tear up the hill.

"There's no real danger" said Jim, perhaps a little optimistically, "once it's gone through the bracken it'll run out of fuel in the higher crags." Other groups had stopped on their route by now and were standing gawping just as we were. With a bit of a jaunty whistle Jim gathered up the picnic leftovers into his rucksack, and suggested we 'sort of mosey on?' It was one thing to suffer the silent criticism of a few tourists, but it would have been mortifying if any neighbouring farmers were to see us. We moseyed on, up to Blackmoor Pot, glancing back with increasing relief as the flames vanished and soon after the smoke too.

Blackmoor Pot is both a lovely but a sad place for us. The beck has cut deep into what must have been soft earth or rock between two high rocky sides. The water itself looks to be twenty feet deep, coursing maybe thirty yards along its cut; and the surface is at least fifteen feet below those jaws through which it flows. Many's the lad who has leapt in to impress lasses in the party: and they deserve to impress, for it's a fearsome jump, with the stream so narrow. Jackson Weir was Joe's son, from Chapel Farm, now a man in his own right with a wife, Kathleen Harrison from Brotherilkeld, and children. Stonethwaite Fell is one of their sheepwalks, and they gather it down to Langstrath and walk the sheep back from there. Often on a hot day's gathering Jackson would take off his boots and his jeans, being shirtless already, and leap in to cool off. This time last year he did it for the last time, for his friends looked on in increasing panic for him to surface. One of his tricks was to swim with the current under water, emerging well downstream. This time they looked in vain, scouring the clear water for a sight of him. Much later the Police divers recovered his body from under an underwater overhanging rock face. So much to live for, but a life blown out like the thoughtless swatting of a horse-fly. Just thirty-two.

My old friends go right back to our schooldays in Bristol – Colston Girls' School. I have two who've kept in touch, both of whom married late – well into their thirties. Hilda, now married to Ted Beckett and therefore stepmother to his two children, Christine and George; and Gwen, who married Dougie Houlden and surprised everyone, including herself, by giving birth to Marinda when she was forty. It would be hard to imagine two more different men – three, I suppose, if we include my Jim. Ted is a brute of a man, a countryman with hands the size of dinner plates and banana fingers. He's deeply involved in fishing, with rods on the Test and a stocked pool at their home near Southampton. And yet he's also a musician, often entertaining us on the cottage piano I keep in the sitting room, more in hope than expectation that Ian might be musical.

Dougie, on the other hand, is a city boy to the tips of his delicate fingers. Immensely dextrous, he is a member of the Magic Circle and delights in astounding us with odd tricks at odd times. I vividly remember him opening a new pack of cards and shuffling them vigorously, when we were to spend an evening playing whist. He divided the pack in two, curved the halves and with a flourish slotted them together and dealt the four hands. To my private delight I found I was holding a full hand of spades – every one, dealt in order, from two up to ace. Of course, one look at the others' faces soon told me we each had a complete suit... and

Dougie had the hearts, the trumps on a first hand. "Oh, that's no good" he cried, and taking them up shuffled them again and dealt. This time he showed us his hand: four aces, four kings, four queens and a jack!

These two, Gwen and Hilda, are my connection to my homeland. I have come up here, to this dark and sodden valley, following my star, and I love it. But I need these friends, these gentler breezes of a Southern clime, when I'm out in the teeth of a Northern gale, with the rain battering down. I need to be reminded of our childhood, when we three were the Three Graces. I should not have said that: there was only one Grace, my mother, and I would rather not remember, but cannot forget, that earlier childhood, before Colston School, before Hilda and Gwen, when my mother Grace was all that stood between the rancour of my father and me.

My father was a bastard, both literally and metaphorically. A mean-spirited, manipulative, philandering bastard, who loved to dominate his only child. Mother saw to it that I spent most of my childhood with her parents or sister. My beloved Grampy was a carpenter, and I spent happy hours in his workshop helping him with his jobs. Mother's sister Eva was married to another gentle toiler, Reg, who was an upholsterer, and had been stone-deaf since contacting meningitis aged seventeen. He spoke quietly, and in answering I didn't need to make a sound, just mouth the words carefully. Such a contrast to my loud-mouthed, foul-mouthed father.

Colston was a blessed relief as I grew older, and I spent less and less time at home. Looking back now I see that while Mother made such a good job of protecting me it was at great personal cost, as she bore the brunt of his excesses. I was delighted to get a job in the Tax Office, and all the more so when we were moved on the outbreak of war to Colwyn Bay. I was nineteen, and shot of my father for good. It never occurred to me that my mother was only thirty-nine and stuck with him for life.

Life wasn't to be that much longer. Thirteen years later, sick of his over-bearing, sick of his philandering, of his meanness, of his total hold over her, she took a bottle full of sleeping pills and never woke up. A few months later he moved in with the woman next door, neatly taking over her house, her life, and freeing the assets tied up in our family home.

So Hilda and Gwen are very important to me, the only link with my birth-place and childhood that I care to recognise. Of the three of us, Hilda is undoubtedly the beauty. A 24 inch waist, gorgeous thick, curly dark hair, and a friendly laughing demeanour that attracts all around. I can't imagine how she managed to stay unmarried for so long before falling for Ted and his two children. Perhaps she wasn't prepared to sacrifice that figure bearing children of her own. The first time she visited us with husband and step-children in tow I scented trouble, God knows how. Normally I'm a late-riser – an owl, not a lark – but this day I came down early to the kitchen, to find Jim with his back to the Aga and his front to Hilda's back, hands fondling those pert breasts.

Hilda

Black bile rose in my throat, almost making me throw up. Visions of my hated father blotted out the real sight before my eyes. Had I married a man cut from the same coarse cloth? Was my long-time friend nothing but a traitor at base? I turned on my heel and ran from the room, ran from the two of them, ran from my father, from my dead mother, ran from the putrid reality of a world gone rotten at its core. For an hour I locked myself in our bedroom while the world spun wildly around me. I must leave, but where would I go? For the first time I truly understood my mother's dilemma. Where do you go when the world has turned to quicksand?

I heard a timid knock on the door, and Hilda's voice. 'Doreen, let me in, please, we need to talk'. What is there to say when everything's gone? 'Fuck off, Hilda.' I've never used that word, never before. She wouldn't go, and somehow the indignity of having her outside where anyone, Ian, Ted, his children, might come across her got through to me and I relented. I couldn't look her in the eye, and she certainly couldn't hold mine. She swore it was the first time, that Jim had simply grabbed her, unprovoked. She swore ever-lasting friendship, and begged me not to let this spoil it all. Somehow I believed her, and through her protestations a little of my father sparked into life in me. God help me, but I saw how this gave me a hold, an upper hand, an ace I could play when I needed to. I struggled hard to hold my man during the war. I got engaged to another simply to make him jealous – and it worked. I gave up my former life, I followed him on his strange choice of lifestyle when that war was over. I'm not giving up now, and I'm certainly not giving up my friends.

Am I shallow, too rational and unemotional? Yes, I am. But I am what I am, and from now on, I'm in control. We don't make new friends. I know where I am with the old ones, and I know where Jim is, too.

Chapter eighteen

Richard Birkhead. The latter half of the 16th Century.

Ordinarily I probably would hardly have known the German miners had arrived in Keswick. I don't get out much – far too much to do on this farm to be gallivanting off to Keswick, and they're far too keen on parting you from your money anyway. Can't say the same for our lasses though, they're off at any excuse. Our Alice is very thick with the Fisher girls across the beck at Seatoller, Janet and Elizabeth, and every Thursday Market Day the three of them are off early with whatever bits and pieces they have to sell, and never back till dark usually. Willie Fisher's lad, John, takes Willie's old mare to carry the stuff, and generally looks after them – or so she says.

She goes over t'bridge at Nicol Dub. It was early in '64 she came back full of excitement because 'Town's full of Dutchmen, Dick! They're looking for gold!' Lambing time it was; I could have done with her at home to help out, now our Father's died.

She doesn't seem to care about the la'al feud our family's had with them Fishers, ever since Willie's father let on to the King's men that our Father had been shouting his mouth off about yon Boleyn girl and her bastard daughter. Now I'm doing t'same, and her our Queen. We never speak about it anyway, better pass sleeping bulls quietly, is my motto. Still an' all, there's a vicious streak in them Fishers, and I'd rather she stopped at home. Thorneythwaite's been good enough for generations of its lads and lasses, why do these young buggers need to be abroad? Any road, she kept on week after week with the news of what these Almains were getting up to, and every time I wandered down to Rosthwaite to the alehouse it was all the talk there an' all. After a bit it caught my imagination too, and I started to be glad of the bits of gossip she'd picked up – meant I could match rumour with fact when old Tommy Jopson started on his tales.

Turns out there's this feller called Hechstetter – Daniel Hechstetter, queer sort of name – and he's brought a dozen miners over from Germany to prospect for copper in Borradell and Newlands. Tommy says he has letters from Queen Elizabeth herself giving him permission, on account of the country needs this copper stuff to make the warships stronger. Some talk of a Spanish Armada, whatever that is. Alice says the word in Keswick is that this Hechstetter's a clever, subtle sort of feller, but the Englishman who's supposed to be showing him the ropes is nowt but a wastrel. Thomas Thurland's his name, already black in Keswick for the debts he's run up. Our landlord in the alehouse says he owes the George in

Keswick over five pounds, and now he's high-tailed it back to London. What a life these fellers must live, always on the road! At least a four-day journey, so they tell me, in a rattling, clattering, shattering stage coach. And Germany? How long must that take?

Hechstetter's prospecting up the valley here and in Newlands, and they say he's found a promising vein at what the German's call Gott's Gab – God's Gift, so they must think it's going to make their fortunes. What a way to work, though, coming hundreds of miles from home, leaving your wife and kids, to slave away underground here. At least it keeps them out of the rain I suppose. Me, I've never been further than Keswick, and that only for the church at Crosthwaite for special occasions, and I'll bet none of our neighbours have either. Our Alice, now, God knows who she's seeing in Keswick, but I'll bet she's up to no good. Not with that fly pair Janet and Lizzie Fisher. Just as long as she keeps herself from their brother, at least.

She came back last week with a terrible story of what he'd done, and I fear it's nowt but the truth, for it was all the gossip in Rosthwaite last night. Seems young Johnnie Fisher gets a bit of ale in him on these Thursday trips to Keswick. If I'd known that I might have had a better go at stopping Alice going with them, but she's nobbut my sister and teks little notice of owt I say. Last Thursday he and a gang of his Keswick mates came across one of these German miners on his own out the back of the alehouse, likely having a piss agen the wall. Johnnie whips the lads up, demanding to know what the hell this Almain thinks he's doing, pissing agen a good English wall. Poor bugger's standing there with his prick in his hand, facing mebbe a dozen of them, and Fisher punches him on t'side of his face, 'to teach him some manners' he says. T'Almain goes down and then they all pile in, kicking and shouting and telling him to piss off back to Duchland if he wants a job, not come tekkin' Cumberland work.

I don't suppose they meant to kill him, but the fact is they did. Kicked him senseless and left him in the alley. Whether he died from the kicking or froze to death I don't know, but I do know his death is down to Johnnie Fisher at the finish. It was gey late when Alice got back that night, white as a sheet and trembling all over. It took my Lizzie a lang time to get the story out of her, she was shaking that bad. Course, she didn't know the Almain was dead then, we only heard a few days later when the news filtered up the valley. By then young John was nowhere to be found – buggered off over Sty Head into Wasdale for a few months till it all died down.

Hechstetter knew his name, though, at least that he was a Fisher. A good job he didn't know where he was from – though why I should care I don't know. Like I said, there's a vicious streak in them Fishers. Still, they're neighbours, and the last thing you want is bad neighbours, so nobody said owt to Herr Hechstetter, and after a bit everything went quiet. Mebbe there was some good came out of it. I think that savage little gang were a bit frightened of what they'd done, and mebbe with Fisher off the scene they settled down. Mebbe Keswick folk had realised just how much money the Almains were bringing in as well, and put a bit of pressure on the daft lads. Whativver, there was no more baiting and battling, and soon it was like they'd always been around, and they were marrying Keswick lasses and having babbies with queer names.

The arms of the Company of Mines Royal
granted 26th August 1568
by the College of Heralds

  I don't know whether Hechstetter thowt to put a bit of watter between his men and the Keswick roughnecks, but his company bought

Vicar's Island on Derwentwater as a sort of headquarters. It's only mebbe a hundred yards off-shore but that's enough to stop the drunks I'd guess. It was grand for our Robert – my youngest brother. There isn't enough work at Thorneythwaite to keep us all, so Robert got work with the Germans carting stuff around for them. All last winter he was tekkin stone and wood and muck from 'Milady Muck' as he calls her when he's had a pint or two, to Vicar's Island for the building. 'Milady Muck' is the Lord of the Manor's wife, though Robert reckons she wears the trousers and calls the shots. Lady Katherine Radcliffe to give her her proper title, and she and her husband (that way round) own most of the land and the woods around the lake and in Keswick itself. 'By God', says Robert, 'but she knows how to screw them Germans.' She let them build a smelter to get the copper out of the ore at Brigham, on her land, for practically nowt – a shilling a year. So that's where they put all that capital to make the bellows, build a water culvert and so on – then she charges them a fortune for the thousands of trees they must needs have to make the thing work! Naewhere else they can get them, so she has them over a barrel.

You might wonder how you cart stone and wood and muck to an island? Easy in winter, 'cos the lake freezes over solid for about three months and it's just a short haul from Milady Muck's lands. When it came to it, the Almains didn't really use the island to live on, more as a storage and produce plot, and no doubt it was a lot easier to guard from the Keswick pilferers than anywhere else would have been. I told you yon Hechstetter was a wily feller. I don't think he ever bested Lady Katherine, though, and however much copper they took out of our fells they were hard pressed to make a profit till they started using coal instead of wood for the smelter at Brigham Forge. She didn't own any coal mines. Before that they were trying to bring wood from Ireland, of all places, by ship to Workington. Hell, it must have been a costly business.

Any road, the Almains – The Company of Mines Royal as they called themselves, on account of Queen Elizabeth was behind it all – opened up a mine in Borradell as well as Gott's Gab in Newlands, this side of Manesty, and they called it Copperplate 'cos they reckoned the quality of the copper they were getting out was t'best in Europe. Nae doubt the Queen wad be pleased about that, but it didn't all go her way. The fight was the talk of the whole district for nigh on a year, the Earl of Northumberland tekkin on Her Majesty in a fight for who's copper it was anyway. The Earl reckoned all mineral rights except gold and silver belonged to him as he owned the land. It was well-established – says Robert, who thinks he knows it all now he's working for the Company – that the Crown owns all gold and silver but the landowner owns any other minerals. I would say you should know better than to tek on the Queen, and sure enough Earl Percy lost his case. The court decided that seeing as how there was some gold and silver in among all the copper the mines were Crown property and had never belonged to him in the first place. What a surprise!

Sorting the ore: the two masters on the left are trying the 'streak' on a touchstone. From Munster's Cosmographia, Basel, 1552, a copy of which was among the books in Keswick at this time.

He was a slow learner, the Earl. Instead of accepting his fate he thought to bring the Queen down in revenge, and backed Mary Queen of Scots in her bid to oust Elizabeth from the throne, and tried to bring her into England through his Workington port in '68, and when Fleming of

Cockermouth scotched that scheme he was one of the leaders of another Northern attempted coup, the Rising of the North. After what happened in King Henry's time you would think folk would learn, but no... so he lost his head in 1572, and his mines, and his lands. I might be a simple yeoman, but after Father's run-in with the Kings man back in 1537 when Furness was dissolved I reckon the further from London and the Crown you are, the better for your health.

I've drifted a lang way from telling you what was going on at Thorneythwaite when all this was happening down the valley, but, man, they were exciting times. Borradell and Keswick must have changed more in those thirty odd years that Hechstetter and his German miners were here than ever before. I doubt there'll ever be sec a time again, but I'm an old man now, and mebbe that's just old man's talk. And Thorneythwaite was caught up in it all, just like everywhere else in the valley. I misdoubt there was a single la'al farm that didn't send one or two of its sons to work for the Company one way or another. Keswick must have doubled in size, with all that money coming in and Alice said it got so you could buy anything either in the shops there or on the market. Fabric, clothes, fancy food, even tobacco, newly fetched from the New World. A far cry from when it was just 'Cheese-town', which is what they tell me the name Keswick means.

Here on the farm Gawine and Edward and I all married and had families and of course they had to move out when the house got too small for us all. I would say the men could have all got on – we were outside any daylight hours anyway, but Gawine's wife Esaybell Williamson as was couldn't abide the close quarters, so they moved across to Seatoller, though Gawine kept on working for me. And there was plenty of work, I can tell you. The bracken was beginning to get a hold on the intakes as the trees fell. No new trees ever grew, the little nodding Herdwick heads saw to that, and as the intakes cleared so the bracken took on, though we tried every year to cut it back. There's so much rock up there though that it's hard to take a sickle to it, and I fear we're losing the battle. We're not alone there; across the valley above Seatoller it's getting really bad, but if the Fishers spent a bit more time with a scythe they could do more on their smoother ground.

Chapter nineteen

Frances Hudson-Birkhead, late 1500s – early 1600s

Lord, but it's funny to look back on it all – how important it all seemed at the time, but now Pouf! Nothing but pollen carried on the wind. Memory: what is it? Vague stirrings in the back of my mind, all that's left of what once burned so bright, so shameful, sometimes. But I'll tell you my memories, or some of them, then maybe they'll have a substance. Do you wonder at my words – think perhaps the valley girl's got above herself? Ah, but we women were all getting above ourselves, when the realm had a woman as Queen. And what a woman, what a realm, what a century! I count myself lucky beyond words to have been born in the Sixties, into the flowering of this fair England, with Elizabeth our Queen, Shakespeare our bard, Raleigh our explorer and Drake our defence. And at Keswick, where my father found fortune and success in his dealings with the Company of Mines Royal. Father had a carting business: any other time of century he'd have been no more than his father before him, a man with a horse, but suddenly there was need for carting on a scale as never before nor since. Stone and slate and lead and iron for the building of the Smelter at Brigham, then, when it was done timber by the ton, by the hundreds of tons, timber till you'd think the whole of Cumberland must be denuded. Timber from my Lady Katherine's estates, timber from Mr Phillipson's estate at Calgarth, on the shores of Windermere, timber from the docks at Workington. 'Heavy stuff, is timber' I remember Papa saying fondly, 'deuced pricy to transport!'

And after the timber, the coal from Caldbeck, from St Bees – again, heavy stuff, and deuced pricy to transport. And of course the copper ore to bring from Newlands and from Borrowdale – heavy stuff, ore... Papa grew rich and well-connected. Many a time he and Mama dined with Daniel Hechstetter and his wife, Radagunda, and they in our house in Keswick. Mr Hechstetter's' son Daniel Junior was the same age as I, and Mr Hechstetter kindly allowed me to attend, at a price, many of the lessons he had with his tutor, along with his younger sisters Veronica and Susanna. The Germans I think had a more liberal attitude to the schooling of girls than is common in England. And so, as you see, I can read and write. I even have a little Latin and Greek, though much good might that do me here at Thorneythwaite.

For I fell from grace, and from my parents' good esteem. I fell the way most girls fall, from chamber-maid to countess. I fell for the charms of young John Birkhead, though not so young, at twenty-two, and me a maid of twenty-three. 'Old enough to know better', chid Mama. 'All that education, that expense!' bemoaned Papa. They would have me marry, and marry soon ere disgrace fell upon their hearth, but I would not. Call it hubris, if you like, call it foolhardiness: I think now it was perhaps a feeble attempt to hold onto some vestige of self-respect. If they would have me marry I would not, and indeed I never married John though we lived together here forty years and six fine children more – though I could not keep them safe.

So I moved in to Thorneythwaite. John's father, Richard, had died the year before, 1587, but Elizabeth welcomed me warmly. It mattered little to her whether we were wed or no, she was happy that her first-born son would be a father, and happier still when I produced a boy, my William, to follow on the family line. In any case, she soon confessed she and Richard had never married themselves, and she was proud of my determination. I discovered soon enough just how important that line was to them, for she could proudly recite their forefathers back many generations. She told me tales of Viking ancestry, the very first to settle in Borradell so she said. I've no reason to doubt her, and I confess it gives me a prickling sensation at the back of my neck to think the bloodline I've contributed to has been on this piece of ground for centuries. Not that the farm itself is anything special, not to look at anyway. Papa and Mama came up the valley to see us when Will was born, and I could see by their faces and that peculiar puckering of Papa's upper lip that they felt I'd fallen a long, long way.

True enough, the house offers little to admire, just two rooms downstairs and two above, with an outside rough stairway. One bedroom for Elizabeth, one for John and me and young Will; and John's brothers, Christopher, Thomas and Robert had to make do downstairs. They grumbled a bit about being evicted from our room where all three lads had hunkered down, but it wasn't long till they had wives of their own and we were adding to the old house. With four sons at home Richard had made many improvements to the old place. Even the barn and cattle shippons were stone-built with good slate roofs. There are quarries up at Honister, just a couple of miles up Seatoller Fell where anyone can take a cart and hack out enough slate, with time and fortitude. When they weren't cutting slate they must have been building walls, for there were new fields made in the boggy ground to the South of the knoll Thorneythwaite stands on. Ironically, all that stone had to be carted in, as the ground there is deep soil, though very wet. What with building, slating and draining there was work for everyone, and enough sheep and cattle to feed us all.

I blush to tell you the next part of my tale, for if I brought a level of disgrace to Papa and Mama, my brother John lowered our name to common criminality. He was a bit younger than me, and came to live with us at Thorneythwaite in 1595 to make his fortune at the Wad Mine, as he said. It was a funny old mine, up above Seathwaite. A bit like the slate at Honister, folk had been poking about on the top for years, just taking what little they needed for marking sheep, mainly. Then suddenly it started to be valuable. Just as it was good for marking sheep, so it was good for marking paper, drawing and writing – not that that needed a great deal of the graphite, as John told me it was properly called. But it was easily carved to make moulds for making coins (and counterfeits!), and smeared on cart axles it eased the turning of the wheels marvellously. And of course it wasn't long before the quacks 'discovered' it had amazing healing properties, anything from rheumatism to the pox, or so they said. The first man to start mining it commercially was Matthew Buck, who took on a twenty-one year lease from the Crown in 1594. My brother John started work for Buck, and they amassed seven tons of dressed wad in Willy Braithwaite's barn at Seathwaite. At something like £13 a ton young John was riding high, as he frequently told us, labouring for nothing but our keep at Thorneythwaite. Piqued, I told him it was time he paid us rent and something for his keep – two bob a week! Well, it was just the price of less than half a stone of wad.

John hadn't been there a year when Buck died – pneumonia, I wouldn't be surprised. They were picking and digging in the Upper Wadhole, often up to their waists in water, and John would arrive back shivering some days in Winter. Well, whose wad was it now, said John, that seven tons nicely stored away? He got together with Richard Tolson, under-sheriff for Borrowdale, and they hatched a plan to draw up a writ claiming all that wad as theirs. A learned man, Tolson, but not a wise one, for of course Buck's widow – rather quickly re-married to William Gale – brought a petition against them. Now John might have had a legitimate claim on a ton or so that you could say he'd mined personally, but Tolson hadn't a leg to stand on. The court fined them both £5, plus £3 6s 8d costs to Mrs Gale, and awarded the wad to the Crown!

Apparently, when the court looked into all the paperwork, it turned out Matthew Buck was a crook as well: he'd added an 's' to the singular 'wadhole' in the lease, so he could work the better Upper Hole, not the pretty poor Lower Hole. Nearly all the seven tons had come from the top mine, so the court argued it wasn't his either. That was the end of our John's mining career, for then, and probably just as well. He went back to carting for Papa – at least it's out in the open, and an honest day's work. The wad mines more or less closed for the next eight years, but the memory of what wad could be worth lingered on...

As I said, brother John went back to carting, and I'd like to think it was him who put the idea of the wad mine into the head of my erstwhile school friend Daniel Hechstetter (the younger). Old Mr Hechstetter died back in 1581, but he left ten children and Radagunda living in the Master's House in Keswick, and two of them, Edward and my friend Daniel, were as interested in mining, and as knowledgeable, as their father had been. These two took over from their father in the running of the Company of Mines Royal, still churning out copper in Newlands and several mines in Borrowdale. I'm not sure when the Company finally folded – it was early in the century, that I do know, about when the Old Queen died and King James came to our throne. Certainly by 1607 Daniel and Edward were free to turn their attention elsewhere, and where better than Seathwaite Wad Mines?

And, wouldn't you know it, Daniel persuaded brother John to go back to the wad mine. He said that since John had already some experience of the mine he would be 'invaluable'! So John came back to Thorneythwaite, taking precious space and still not paying any rent – or for the amount of food he ate. As he explained to me, patiently, 'It's hellish hard work, Sister, chipping away at rock. A feller needs a decent breakfast and an even better supper.' My responses were less patient, but no more productive. But at least we got to hear how things fared up on the fellside, and one thing I do say about John, he tells a good story. You'll remember that when John first worked there, with Matthew Buck, they were often up to their waists in water. The Hechstetter men realised there was no future for the mine unless it could be drained, and they had the money, knowledge and manpower to do it. Poor John was part of the manpower, and I don't know why he stood it. 'Great worker, your brother, Frances,' Daniel said to me once – in John's hearing. Papa had never said anything nice to him.

Daniel provided the small sharp picks, and a blacksmith to keep them sharp, and John and his mates took it in turn to pick a drain into the hill, right through to what John called the Grand Pipe, a great store of graphite. As he said, the problem is that maybe a foot deep drain would do the job, but how the hell can a man pick a one-foot high hole eighty yards into a fellside? No, they had to pick a tunnel 5'7" high – tall enough to swing the pick in – and 2 feet wide at their shoulders. 'Mind you' he added ' it's only wide enough at the bottom to get two feet in. We call it two foot by two feet!. It looks like an endless coffin as you walk along it, and sometimes it feels like that too.'

The adit, as John called it, worked of course. 'Nothing if not efficient, these Almains' John said, almost proudly. He took me up one day to see their handiwork, and he had a right to be proud. He had his lantern and led me in. We'd not gone ten yards till I started sweating – though it was as cold as the grave in there. I wish he hadn't called it a coffin level. I gritted my teeth, as much to stop them chattering as anything, I wasn't going to let John know how frightened I was. Frightened? Not quite the right word… it felt as if the walls of the coffin were narrowing in on me as I trailed along in John's shadow. He had the lantern in front of him, of course, and there was precious little light where I stumbled along in the beck that was running out of the mine. I concentrated on that beck: it was coming from somewhere and soon I would be there. 'Hold my hand, John… I can't see a bloody thing back here'. I don't think that fooled him, but he took my hand, and eventually we emerged into a wider chamber, wider and higher, much higher.

There were three men in there, all with sharp picks, filling barrows with lumps of rock they were picking out above their heads. 'Won't the whole roof come in?' I couldn't help asking. 'Ach, nein, this vad iss solid schtuff' replied a short, hairy, squat miner John called Hans. 'But look how gut it iss.' 'Nearly pure' explained John, 'and look, the vein is eight feet wide! We don't know how far up it goes, or how far down, but there's enough wad in here to keep us going for ever!' 'Enough for you to pay for your keep, then' I replied gruffly, fear adding asperity to my tongue. Hans laughed 'Caught you out zere, Johannes, I tink'.

I started my little account saying what a wonderful time we've lived in, we who were born in and around Keswick in the last third of the old century. In my life I've seen the town and the valleys, Borrowdale and Newlands, transformed. When I was born there was hardly a cart track up the valley, now there are good roads North, South, East and West. Roads to Seathwaite, roads along the back of the lake, roads up behind Grange. There are shops selling everything in Keswick, a self-important, prosperous little market town. The money has trickled down to the farms, and like Thorneythwaite many are vastly improved on the hovels folks lived in not fifty years ago. We owe a great debt to our German friends, many of them now neighbours too.

What I haven't told you is of the heartache of burying babies and children. No-one talks about it much, or the pain would be too heavy to bear. There's not a family in the valley but has lost as many bairns as they've raised, and it's worse the nearer the head of the valley you get. I blame the rain, for there are times when nothing in the house is dry, and the wee ones start with a cough and just go downhill. We lost our first-born, my beautiful William, when he was just four months old – and these were Summer months, but such a wet Summer. That dreadful cough, and the poor mite trying desperately for air with great whoops that tore my heart out. My parents said it was God's judgement on our state of sin – that only made me the more determined never to marry in such a vengeful God's church.

Our next two boys fared no better. When John was born in '91 I thanked that same jealous God for such a strong boy – truly his father's son, and when he had his second birthday I started to relax. I should have known better; that same bloody cough carried him to his tiny grave in October'93, and my grief brought forward Henry's birth a couple of days later. The poor premature bairn had scarce a chance, though he fought through that cold, hard Winter, only to die before the Spring. It was no surprise: as old Elizabeth grimly predicted 'That one will never hear the cuckoo.' Being right isn't the same as helping.

What a start! Three boys, all cold and dead, and no heir yet for Thorneythwaite. My girls were made of stronger stuff, but they took their time in coming. I think the grief of burying all three of my boys shut my body down. Certainly for years I could hardly bear John to come to me, and him grieving just as I was. Perhaps it needed old Elizabeth's death to free us from the glacier that bound us separate, but the year after I conceived again, and our lovely Elizabeth saw out the old century for us, just as Janet was the new century's present to us both, born New Year's Day, 25th March, 1600. With Anne a couple of years later, and finally Robert soon after, all of whom – praise God! – lived, it seemed we had a family and an heir.

It was not to be. Our only surviving son, of four that I brought in pain into this world, died in 1619, just sixteen years old. Of all the things to die of in this rain-sodden valley, Robert died crushed under the wheel of the cart, bringing a load of slate down from Honister, his father in control. The wheel that crushed Robert finally crushed John and me too. I was past child-bearing, and past caring. I will not live much longer, my soul has already died.

100

Chapter twenty

John Birkhead: Yeoman. Born 1566

My Frances has told you all that's of interest about Thorney'waite, there's varra little I can add – leastways of human interest. I suppose I've allus been more concerned with the Valley, the Farm, the stock, the state of the fell, so thou'll hear little from me of how folk fared. Yan thing I must tell thee about though is t'Great Deed, as they call it. Biggest thing that's happened in Borradell since the Abbeys was destroyed, or so they say. Ye'll know that Henry VIII took our bit of t'valley intill t'Duchy of Lancaster, an' of course it passed to Good Queen Bess and aw was weel enough till she died – at least we knew where we were, what the rent, or fine as they called it, would be. King James, though, he was a different kettle of fish. Wanted a load o' money sharpish, did James, so he sellt the valley! Just like that – to a pair of fly-by-night ne'er-do-wells frae London, yan William Whitmore and Jonas Verdon.

I suppose I should be grateful, 'cos we got the chance to buy t'farm, lock, stock and barrel. Leastways, that's what I thought we was buying, till Sir Wilfred Lawson got his grubby paws on aw the fells an' common ground, though God knows he had nae right. Sharp buggers, Whitmore and Verdon – far too fly for us folk who'd nivver even been out of t'dale. First of aw they sellt what farms Sir Wilfrid hadn't already got his hands on, and nearly broke us aw finding t'coinage to buy. Then if they didn't sell us aw t'woods and commons an' aw that. Well, we thowt that's what we paid out mair good money for, but it seems Sir Wilfred got the better part of the deal – or mebbe just the better lawyer. Any road, it was nae time at aw till Sir Wilfred's bailiffs were round every farm reminding us that he was 'Lord of the Manor', and we owed him fines for any grasses on t'fell that our Herdwicks grazed.

You'll know that every farm has sheep rights on their own fell – grasses we call them. Every grass can carry ten yows. We've twenty grasses on Thorney'waite Fell up to Glaramara, and a further nine on Stonethwaite Fell. And t'bailiffs say they want a penny ha'pence per grass per year – on pain of lossing t'grasses if we diven't pay. Thou can imagine how much grumbling went on in t'inn at Resthwaite ower this, but there isn't yan of us can read this 'Great Deed', 'cept for my Frances. She's tellt us we're being done, but naebody can afford a lawyer to tek Sir Wilfrid on, so we're stuck with it.

Yan good thing, though, that makes us laugh, is that bloody Lawson didn't get his fingers intill t'wad mines. I tell't you they were sharp, this Whitmore and Verdon. Well, seemingly the Great Deed hods the wad back, specific, like. Whitmore and Verdon still own it – and pretty soon we started to see it was the most valuable thing in Borradell, worth more than aw t'farms put together, if you ask me. It's about the only bit of foreign news I've ever heard tell't of, but it was aw the talk in the inn. T'only other spot with wad mines was in Germany – Bavaria – and the Germans weren't letting any of it out of t'country. So if thou wants a bit of wad, and a hell of a lot of folk seem to, Borradell Wad Mine is the only place thou'll get it. Young Daniel Hechstetter was t'main miner, but he had to pay the company Verdon set up a pretty penny every year for the right to mine and sell. But if I tell thou they were making forty pounds a ton soon after 28th November, 1614 – the date of our Great Deed – thou'll see what I mean about its value. And in 1620, they sell't forty tons of best quality, and thirty tons of poorer stuff. Poorer stuff! Father could remember when aw it was good for was marking sheep. Can thou even imagine that? Nigh on a couple of thousand pounds worth of wad coming out of Sea'waite. Makes a penny ha'pence a sheep grass look a bit daft, so he didn't do that well, Sir Wilfrid.

Ye'll mebbe be thinking I'm hard on Sir Wilfrid. Happen you're right, but we have history, yon bugger and me, and it goes reet back till 1605, nigh on a decade afore t'Great Deed. That was back in the last days o' the Border Reivers, the murdering buggers from up in Canonbie who made life sae hard for Cumberland folk. They nivver bothered us in Borradell, but you don't have to go far out of the valley afore you start to see the piel towers folk had to build to keep their cattle and their womenfolk safe. T'worst of them all were the Grahams – murderers, blackmailers, kidnappers – you name it, the Grahams got up to it. Well, finally they went too far, or mebbe it was the change of the times. Old Queen Bess nivver really took them on – happen it was ower far frae London for her to care. But when the new King, James I as we call him, was on his way down frae Scotland he was varra keen to mek sure his new kingdom really was united, and he was holed up in Berwick for a night or two.

Happen thinking to see what was his mettle, the Graham's chose that very day to drive deeper into Cumberland than they'd been for years, murdering and raping their way right down to Penrith. James was livid, the story goes, and there and then he sets up a royal commission to govern Cumberland and the Borders as a Crown colony. Led by…Sir Wilfrid Lawson, Knight!

What's that got to do with me, and Borradell? I'll tell you, if you give me time. One of the ancient duties folk like Sir Wilfrid can levy on us poor yeomen is a right to demand we ride out as part of his army to defend the borders. He demanded it, and with a few other farmers frae t'top of the valley – John Jopson, Will Braithwaite, John Fisher – I had to saddle up Titch and go help round up a load of these Grahams. What do I know of fighting? Just enough to stay at the back while Sir Wilfrid's regulars took Grahams one by one and set them on boats bound for Ireland. But I got to see his cruelty, and his arrogance, this bold Sir Wilfrid. Yan o' the Graham's put up a bit of a fight, flailing about with his sword, and he cut yan o't'soldiers deep on the shoulder. Course they quickly ower-powered him, and Sir Wilfrid orders him back in his la'al but-and-ben, with his wife and childer with him, nails up the door and sets fire to the lot.

Ah'll nivver forget those screams, the wife and bairns burnt to death, and Sir Wilfrid sitting on his fine horse and laughing. "That'll teach them not to resist us" he says to his lackeys. I was sick behind a wall – that set him off laughing again. "No belly for men's work, then, Birkhead?" he says "we'll find work you do like then. Women's work." I had to scrub out the latrines for the next week. Like I said, we have history.

Well, it was nae surprise to me when the crack in the Inn was of how Sir Wilfrid was buying up tenements all ower Borradell – buying them off the man who'd owned them for years: Walter Graham. Walter's grandfather Richard had bought all the Fountains Abbey holdings in Borradell from Henry VIII back in1546 – all the tenements in Watendlath and Stonethwaite. When I was doing my service on the Borders bold Sir Wilfrid could hardly contain himself.

"I have him, Birkhead, I have him by the balls."

One of the main Grahams we were after, to exile off till Ireland, was Richard Graham, probably t'worst of all the murderous Reivers that ivver breathed. Richard was Walter's son. Richard should have hanged … but what happened? Richard had to go into exile, but he went armed with letters of introduction signed by good Sir Wilfrid guaranteeing him safe passage. A year later, Good Sir Wilfrid buys every tenement and bit o' land Walter owned in Borradell – and Richard lands back from 'exile'. I tell't ye we farmers stood nae chance agen the likes of gentry sec as these.

Frances died November 16th, 1625. The date is burnt on my heart with a branding iron. Thirty-seven years we had together – more than most folk. And she left three lovely lasses, Elizabeth, Janet and Anne, in their twenties now and pretty as pictures if I do say so myself. But no son, left alive.

Chapter twenty-one

Betty Hall. 1963-66

Visitors, visitors, visitors... I feel beset by visitors. I don't mind the paying kind too much, at least they pay the rent, and generally keep out of my hair; though it's disconcerting having to book a bath for a time that suits them rather than me. No, it's the never-ending troupe of friends who fancy a few days in the Lake District that gets to me now and then. Once you live in the heart of the Lakes all sort of old acquaintances want to re-establish moribund friendships and drop in for tea. Don't get me wrong, it's usually lovely to see them, but there is just so much work to be done each day that losing a few hours completely messes up my schedules. Most difficult of all, of course, are those who come and never want to leave – and I'm not even sure who some of them are. Jim's mother, Lizzie, I get on well with, and it's good to have her stay, but she comes with an assortment of elderly hangers-on who mean nothing to me, nor to Jim, he says. I blame his brother, Tom, who farmed with us at Myreground getting on for a decade ago. He's a full-time priest now, with a parish beyond Penrith – Milburn – and a vicarage built for a Victorian parson with a wife and a family of twelve. Tom's single and rattles around like a tanner in a money-box.

Take Mary Scott, for instance. Tom claims her as some sort of relation, and brings her with Lizzie each time she comes. They nitter and fratch on at each other till it nearly sends me up the wall, but each time Lizzie comes for a break Mary Scott comes too. Then there's Ned. Tom says he used to work on the farm their father worked on, as if that's reason enough for us to be landed with him. Ned's a good enough sort, though only eleven-pence-halfpenny to the shilling, but Jim has to find him things to do, and I have to feed him. And they come for a month at a time. Sometimes it feels as if I'm never out of the kitchen – a long way from those carefree days at Myreground when I was needed outside, in the byre, milking, ploughing, dosing sheep. Ian had to come too, wrapped up warm in his portable cot. I used to leave him at one end of a row of turnips, snig right along it, back along the next row, then he'd be ready for his next feed. Feed him, wind him, put him back down, and do the next two rows. Gawd, but I miss those days, when I felt so needed. Now it's Ian gets to do the tractor-work, Ian who takes the harder part of the fell when we gather, Ian who flexes his muscles and mucks out a hull after Winter: and I begin to feel un-needed, an extra in what used to be my story.

He came back from school one day last week, when I'd asked him to pick up a dress I'd left to be dry cleaned. I knew he wasn't really listening when I told him which shop it was. He came back without it, and when I berated him for his negligence he said he had gone in and asked for it, but when the shopkeeper said it was an oldish lady who'd left it he'd said that couldn't be the right one then. Jim tried to tell me he was being gallant, and that didn't help either!

Just when you think things can only get better, they get worse. Lizzie is starting to get forgetful, or downright confused, and Tom feels she can hardly manage at Rookery Square in Scotby on her own any longer. Her husband Tom, Pop as we've always called him, died just before Ian was born, and she's been fine on her own ever since, but she's what, eighty-six now, and I guess Tom's right. Obviously he can't have her; the vicarage is empty all day when he's out on his parish rounds, so here she came again… just for a month or so, she says, but Jim and I know it's for good. And Mary Scott came too! Tom's a lovely, kind-hearted vicar and all that, but Jim had to have a quiet word to say enough was enough. Mary could stay for a week or so, but then it was back to Scotby for her. Occasional visits to see Lizzie would be fine ('No they're not', I screamed inwardly) but please could Tom come back for her next week.

I wasn't the only one to take some time to adjust to Lizzie's rapidly diminishing abilities. I could see Ian quickly becoming irritated at the carousel questions and comments. She'd hop on one hobby horse and ride for a moment before switching to another, and in a couple of minutes be back at the first, and round and round she'd go. By now Jennifer was a regular visitor, coming to the farm every Sunday afternoon in term time and more often in the holidays. One of their pleasures was to carry in the half-size snooker table onto the kitchen table – no mean feat with its slate bottom – and challenge each other to a game. Lizzie would watch fascinated as the balls flew around the table, regularly and interminably muttering to herself and anyone who would listen 'Just like tomatoes, just like tomatoes'. There are only so many times you can agree that they are indeed just like tomatoes, about four in Ian's case and well over twenty for Jennifer, who definitely won that game in my eyes.

Jim, perhaps, among us all found it the most distressing. He had known his mother as a youngish woman, well, young middle-aged anyway, and it pained him terribly as she deteriorated both mentally and physically. Then again, I was the one who got the job of wiping up the various messes, and I found her continual presence increasingly stressful. One night she gave me the excuse I needed, wandering off into the darkness in the rain, with none of us noticing she had gone. Ian came into the kitchen, homework over. "Where's Nana?"

"Not like you to worry" Jim said sharply, "Is she not in the sitting room with you?" He realised the folly of the question before he'd finished, and rushed out to check the visitors' sitting room, hesitantly asking if they'd seen the old lady, and could he check their bedrooms, please? Drawing a blank in the house we all three grabbed raincoats and torches and set off into the night in the main three different directions she might have gone, shouting lustily. Lizzie from me, Ma from Jim, and Nana from Ian. No matter what name we gave the darkness gave back no answer. Jim it was who found her, well down the lane towards the valley road, refusing to come home with him as she had to get back home to make Pop his tea. Pop, who'd been dead these twenty years nearly.

"What if she does that in the middle of the night. When we're all asleep? She could be lying out in the rain all night, stone-dead by morning." Jim had to agree – "Well, then, what do you suggest?" I swallowed hard, but this was surely my only chance of a bit of time to myself. "We'll have to lock her bedroom door, it's the only way to be sure where she is at night."

"How will she go to the loo?"

"Same way you all went when you were in Rookery Square! I don't suppose anybody ventured out to the privy in their nightgowns?"

It was agreed. For now I was content with minimal custody, but I could surely stretch 'letting-out' time till I'd had my morning coffee. I'm no good to anyone till I've had that first cup. The next morning – Ian off to school, Jim out in the henhouses, I heard a terrible racket and shouting from her bedroom, right above the kitchen, and hurried up flustered to let her out. I turned the key as quietly as I could, and tried to assure her the door must have stuck. I expected a blistering response, but one of the advantages of dementia is that she forgets so quickly she couldn't remember what had happened. Almost the only time I've been grateful for her condition. Something must have gone in, though, because she never repeated that harrowing performance, but waited meekly till I went up to let her out – sooner than I might have if she'd complained.

This went on for three long, wearying years, with Mary the dear friend coming for her week nearly every month. I suppose I was grateful in a way, at least it gave the old lady someone else to plague with the ever-circling story she'd woken up with. Mary, who thought it dreadful we should lock Lizzie away at night, and wasn't afraid to tell us so.

In the meantime, of course, my Southern friends came for their week's visits, Gwen, Hilda, even my cousin Len and his wife Fran, though I'd little time for Len, who I thought treated my Aunt Eva badly when her husband died, putting her in some sort of home. They were a selfish pair, Len and Fran, never had kids and thought only of their pleasures. Fran said she thought I was a saint, 'putting up with your mother-in-law'. I doubt she said that in private, and it's a bloody good job she didn't say it in front of Jim, or they'd have been back on the road before you could say Jack Robinson.

I still kept a close eye on Jim when Hilda was around, but as far as I could see he behaved himself. Mary Scott was with us that week – fortunately there were no paying guests, or we would have run out of bedrooms. We really only get visitors in the main season, school holidays, half-terms, that sort of thing, which makes it easy to have 'the Southerners' here for a week in June, which is really one of the best months, and not too busy on the farm. I didn't want her, knowing Hilda was coming, but Tom would hear none of it. "She looks forward to it so, Betty, I can't disappoint her." I could, but I've never been able to stand my corner very well. I suppose it salves Tom's conscience over his mother's care to be able to think he's providing her with a friend.

It was a fraught week, no point in pretending otherwise, what with feeding everybody, clearing up after Lizzie's 'little accidents', coping with Mary's pettiness and trying to get out and about with my friends for a trip or two. At least we felt we could leave Jim's mother with Mary, she was well able to entertain her and make her cups of tea. Otherwise someone would have had to stay at home, you wouldn't dare leave Lizzie alone too long, or you wouldn't know where to find her, and she'd be completely lost once out of the house, though no doubt she could still find her way round Scotby blindfold.

Hilda and Ted left at the end of their week, promising letters and a return next year. I always feel a curious mixture of emotions when they go: relief that I can stop providing mountains of food; relief that don't need to keep an eye on Jim; but a sadness that I'm back alone in the cold, wet North – Hilda always brings a breath of Bristol air which lifts my spirits. And it's nice being 'Doreen' for a week!

The end of their week signalled the end of Mary's week, too, and I put on a cheery air and asked her if she'd enjoyed her time. She turned childishly sulky.

"Not going!"

"What do you mean, not going, Mary? Tom will be arriving for you any time now".

"Not going. You need me here." What did she mean? To help with Lizzie? Well, yes, she did take some of the never-ending roundabout of comment.

"What do you mean, Mary? Why do we need you? You're always welcome, of course…" Here I go again, why do I say these things. She's not welcome, why do I say she is? Guilt over Lizzie I suppose.

"Not 'we', you. You need me, to keep an eye on him." The emphasis was heavy, and my heart sank as I guessed what was coming. Suddenly, all my dams burst at once. I didn't want to hear what this viperous old woman wanted – was bursting – to tell me.

"Oh no you don't, madam, one more word from you and it will be the last time you come." The petulant child in her welled up in tears, tears of rage.

"He's no good, you know. He never was, even from a boy. Always after the lasses, and he still is." She hissed, I swear it, she was hissing. And Jim was standing behind her – I suppose he heard what was going on from the sitting room. Was there substance in her venom? I had kept careful watch, and I'd swear Hilda had been far too badly frightened last time to allow anything else to happen. Had Mary been here last time, and was this a harking back, or had I been blind yet again?

She saw her barb had hit its mark, saw my hesitation, and triumph flashed in her eyes. That was her undoing. In a voice so low you couldn't mistake the threat beneath it Jim said simply "Get your coat, Mary, and go say goodbye to my mother. You won't see her again." She crumpled, there is no other word. God help me, I felt sorry for her, but her words had done their job, opened up old wounds, wounds I would have to scratch, tear at, inspect, and finally try to salve once again.

I lie awake at nights, sometimes, in this ancient house, in our bedroom in the oldest part, going back – how long, three, four, five hundred years – and wonder at all the lives, all the relationships, all the fights, the making-up, the tragedies and the triumphs this bedroom must have witnessed. I try to count my blessings. We're healthy, we live a long time – though with Lizzie, is that such a good thing? We have entertainment, lights at night, a car to go places. All things they couldn't even dream about, those who have lain here before me. But like them, I have to fight for my man, my place in this rain-sodden valley. Like them I've lost a still-born baby. Underneath, we're not so different, them and us. In fact, perhaps they were better off, with big families, lots of bustle and a small world where you didn't even know what was going on in the next valley, never mind between America and Russia.

Lizzie died not far short of her ninetieth birthday, about three years after her poor mind had already died. Tom took the service in the crematorium in Carlisle, and I sat between my men, Jim and Ian, and, not for the first time, wished my girl, Jennifer, for so I thought of her, was with me: some feminine presence to protect me from the male. Sadly, she and Ian had parted a few months before. I will not let them remain apart. The stupid boy needs a bloody nursemaid, as his father has often said!

108

Thorneythwaite in Jim & Betty's time

Chapter twenty-two

Thomas Birkett. The story from 1628 - 1670.

It was perhaps the best day of the Summer, when Elizabeth and I got married at St Kentigern's Church, Crosthwaite: 19th July 1628. Certainly it was the best day of my life. Elizabeth is the daughter of old John and Frances Birkett, from Thorneythwaite, and John turned out in his finest Herdwick suit he'd had specially made for the occasion. Sadly Frances died three years earlier, and part of our wedding service was conducted round her grave in the churchyard. The vicar, Isaac Singleton, is very accommodating – but then, I did pay a handsome 'donation' to the church funds. I suppose I'm marrying into money, in a way. John was able to buy Thorneythwaite back in 1614 when those two scoundrels Whitmore and Verdun bought all Borrowdale and then sold individual farms to whoever could buy them.

I'd guess John had a fair pile stacked away, with the family having been at Thorneythwaite ever since Adam walked the earth. It wasn't the same for my father, Christopher Birkett, John's younger brother. Just like John he was born there, but first sons get it all, second sons get nowt. So we rented Yew Tree Farm, in Rosthwaite, firstly from the Duchy of Lancaster, then from King James himself – till he sold the lot to Whitmore and Verdun. With nothing behind him, father couldn't buy when they sold all the farms, so it was bought, as so many were, by Sir Wilfrid Lawson, of Isel Hall. And yes, all right, I did think that in marrying cousin Elizabeth I could reverse father's fortunes. Old John had no sons surviving – or so I thought. Four lads he and Frances had buried – so surely Elizabeth would be first in line to inherit?

Well, we got moved in to the old house across the yard from the main hearth at Thorneythwaite, and I started work for my father-in-law, and we settled in to wait for Elizabeth's inheritance. You never think about miscarriages till you have one – then it seems to be happening to so many women around. Three, Elizabeth had, before at last she carried John to full term and we could go back to Crosthwaite Church for his baptism, nearly five years after we got married. We named him for old John, no harm staking your claim. Six months later we were back again – this time for William and Elizabeth's marriage. We're a hell of a family for reinforcing the Birkett name and characteristics. Elizabeth and I are both Birketts, cousins, as you know, and William is one of the Chapel Farm Birketts – marrying Lizzie, one of the Seathwaite branch of the family. To be honest, I'm not sure it's that good an idea, you wouldn't use a Herdwick tup more than a couple of years running. We all look a bit like a Herdwick, now I come to think of it. Broad-browed, with a thick mop of curly black hair, that slowly turns grey, just like an old tup or yow.

Will's father, Nicholas Birkett, of Chapel Farm, had died back in 1627, just a year before Lizzie and I got married, and his older brother John took on the tenancy from old Sir Wilfrid and Will worked for him. Older brothers – the same the world over, no surprise there. What happened next was, though, a hell of a surprise, and of the worst sort as far as Lizzie and I were concerned. When Will and Elizabeth got married, old John invited them to come and live with him, in the main hearth at Thorneythwaite, and to work with him too. I didn't need much encouragement from Lizzie to go and beard the old man in his den, sitting in the ingle nook by the fire. He didn't move a great deal now, and hardly ever in Winter; I guess he must have been nigh on seventy.

He knew why I'd come, I could see it in his face, somehow shifty but determined at the same time.

"Thou'll be wondering what's ga'an on, then?" That took the wind out of my sails a bit, but at least it meant he was prepared to discuss it.

"Well, Grand-dad" – I'd taken to calling him that since young John was born – "What the hell is going on? Here's Lizzie your eldest lass, stuck out in t'old house that's hardly fit to live in, and thou's gone and put a pair of cuckoos in her nest. You're right, I am wondering what's ga'an on."

Grand-dad sighed, a long, heavy sigh, a thirty-year-old sigh, it turned out.

"Will's my lad, Thomas, my only lad left living. Where else does he belong but in my heart and in my hearth?" Dumb-struck, I stared at him for what felt like an age, as what he'd said slowly sank in.

"Bloody hell, John… you and Agnes? All those years ago, and nobody knowing? Did Nicholas not know? – No, he can't have, or he'd have killed thee. Frances?"

John nodded, a bit shame-faced.

"Aye, Frances knew. Seems a man can never hide that sort of thing, but a woman has no bother." He sounded bitter. I was glad – if Lizzie and I were going to lose her inheritance I hoped he'd suffered long and hard for it.

"I'm sorry, lad, I really am. But Will's my flesh and bone, the only son I have left, and he gets this farm when I'm gone. It's all in my will."

God forgive me, I laughed: indeed it was, all in his Will.

Old John moved out soon after this – down to Chapel, with Agnes. A pair of old lovers re-united thirty years too late. I never asked young John, Agnes's son, tenant of Chapel, what he made of it, but I knew all too well what the neighbours did. It took a long time before I could walk into the Inn at Rosthwaite without the bawdy comments and hoots of laughter starting up, but I bore it with a grin. It doesn't do to let this lot know how you really feel.

They had a few years together, till John died in 1641. We reckoned he was seventy-five, born a bastard and left all he had to a bastard. What more can I say? Agnes survived him another five years, and as luck would have it their graves lie head to toe in Crosthwaite churchyard.

Will soon made it clear I wasn't needed on the farm, and that suited me. To tell the truth, I could hardly bear to be with him. It seemed so hard, Lizzie being cheated of her rightful inheritance by some hole-in-the-corner carrying on so long ago. How the hell could John be sure Will was his anyway. Surely to God Nicholas was tupping Agnes as well? Well, it didn't matter. John was sure, and that was that. I got a job up at the Wad mine, working for Sir John Bankes. I'm no miner, God knows, but Sir John needed someone he could trust to oversee the mine. In 1641 it was turning out graphite as if there was no tomorrow, and we stored it on Vicar's Island in Derwentwater, which was easily defended. Wad was so expensive then folk would go to any lengths to steal it.

Sir John had a customer for twenty tons, which we had stored, ready to transport to Newcastle for shipping. Robert Ellison and Ralph Lomax if memory serves me, as slippery a pair of rogues as you're likely to meet. Two days before the contract was due to be signed, Sir John had a letter from them saying "we beg to inform we have another supplier prepared to ship to us at £15 per ton. Please advise whether you are prepared to meet this new price." Sir John had negotiated £20 per ton, and he was livid. Called me into his office in Keswick. "Birkett, what do you make of this, then? Can it be true? Is there wad out there they could lay their grubby little hands on?"

I knew this was one of those moments. Get it right and you're made for life; get it wrong and you're as good as dead. But I knew my wad, too. Seathwaite wad was the only one around, unless they were going for inferior grade produce from Bavaria, and I was pretty sure there was none to be had. I took a deep breath. "They're bluffing, Sir John, we might have lost a ton or so over the years, stolen away and hawked in the George and Dragon in Keswick. But never twenty tons."

Sir John laughed, a deep, mellow laugh honed in the Inns of Court in London where he was more at home. "You're right, Birkett, I'm sure of it. We'll charge them £25 per ton for their impudence, and see what they make of that!" And, by God, he did, and the rogues had to pay, because of course there was no more wad to be had anywhere. We made damned sure there was a limited supply: we'd work a couple of years, stockpiling maybe a hundred tons of wad on the island, then we'd shut the mine for seven years or so, just to keep the price up. Plus, of course, there was no telling just how much wad there was in Seatoller Common – there was no need to rip it all out too early and depress the market. I went back to being a sort of spy, I suppose. Living at Thorneythwaite and being local, I would soon get to hear of any vagabonds helping themselves to wad by night, and the company paid me a retainer for any snippet I could pass on.

Sir John Bankes, Justice of the Common Pleas, Keswick, 1640 – 44. Unknown artist, 1641 in the National Portrait Gallery

Sir John Bankes didn't really live to see the fruits of his investment in the wad mine, for he died on Christmas Eve, 1644. However, he was certainly not short of a bob or two, and he was good to Keswick. As Chief Justice of the Common Pleas for the area he knew better than most the lot of the paupers, begging or stealing just to keep body and soul together. Many didn't manage, and ended in unmarked graves. Just before he died Sir John bought George Brown's old orchard and tenement in the middle of Keswick, and in his will directed it be pulled down and a Poor House erected on the site. Gave £200 for its construction, and £30 per year in perpetuity for its upkeep, and that of the poor folk lodged there. I was there for the opening ceremony, in 1646, when the Civil War was really getting under way. It was good, in such uncertain times, to see paupers given a home to live and work in. But as I say, the times were uncertain indeed, as we were finding out. One other benefit he brought to Keswick and the sheep farmers around was to set up a fulling mill on the banks of the Greta – well, he didn't set it up himself, but he left £30 a year in that same will for its construction. It was the first of many, and meant all that Herdwick wool could be turned into coarse cloth in the town, and then sold for a much better price. He was a good man, Sir John. I doubt we'll see his like again.

As you know, I'm an educated man, unusual in this valley, and it wasn't long after William got himself ensconced in the main farmhouse that he invited me over to his hearth. Not a common event as you may imagine. This would be back in '32 I'd say, and he'd just come back from the first ever 'Manorial Court', presided over by old Sir Wilfrid Lawson – very old, by then. He was ever forthright, was Will.

"Thomas, thou's an educated man. T'lads in t'inn hev asked me if thou can read this bloody Deed Lizzie's father John and aw t'rest signed back in 1614. Yon Sir Wilfrid is calling hissel Lord o' t'Manor, but we aw think t'Great Deed made it everybody's manor. Will't have a look for us?"

There's a perverse delight in helping someone who's bested you, God knows why. I suppose it's rubbing it in that you have skills they can't even pretend to: and besides, he'd piqued my interest. There was John's copy, kept in a big iron box, in the farmhouse – I suppose all the signatories got a copy. It's a hell of a document, full of legal terms and hard to pick apart, but the more I read the more I could see Will's point. Whitmore and Verdon had sold off all the simple assets, the tenanted farms still owned by the Duchy of Lancaster – indeed, that's when John had bought Thorneythwaite. I knew Sir Wilfrid had bought a lot, but the sitting tenants had customary rights – they were assured their children had security of tenure. This deed, in effect, was selling off the Manor, and it was selling it to the whole thirty-six farmers named, plus Sir Wilfrid and John Lamplugh. There was a price paid, £25 10s, and I suppose it was paid pro rata by all the named parties, so they should all hold the Manor in some fashion. I know this is unusual, but it's what the deed seems to say.

So what should they have got, these tenants and yeomen? The key sentence, as I told Will, read:

'The said parties purchasers before named are concluded and agreed that the said Manor, wastes, woods, stinted pastures, courts, perquisites, and other casualties, royalties, and hereditaments which cannot be apportioned, divided and conveyed in such strict manner as the same requireth shall be conveyed unto them for the apportionable benefit of themselves and of the rest of the tenants of the said Manor according to the rate aforesaid.'

Will nearly exploded on the spot.

"Why the hell are we paying bloody Sir Wilfrid rent for our stints and grasses, then, if it says we own them ourselves?" Good question... I suspect partly because nobody's quite sure what the deed says anymore, but mostly because they're just a bit frightened of both old Sir Wilfrid, and more particularly his heir-apparent, young Sir Wilfrid. Young Sir Wilfrid has just taken on the role of Commissioner for the Crown Colony that the old man used to have. Young Sir Wilfrid is not a man to be trifled with, as we all found out a few years later.

William Birkett. The story from 1645 -1670

By God, but the Inn at Rosthwaite was alive with rumour and counter-rumour that night! As best as I could tell, Sir Wilfrid Lawson had been given a black eye and no mistake. Not that anyone there was shedding any tears on his behalf. We still think he has no right to be calling himself 'Lord Of the Manor' and charging us rents for our grasses up on the fells – not that the Thorneythwaite grasses are worth much, being nowt but rock and bracken, and frozen solid all winter. This wasn't old Sir Wilfrid, mark you, him that was named in the Great Deed. Old Sir Wilfred died childless back in – when was it, Thomas? 1632, that's right, not long before your John was born. With old Sir Wilfrid being barren, for all he married twice, he left Isel Hall to this 'young' Sir Wilfrid's father William, and now the young squire lords it over us, yeomen though we be.

So, as I said, the ale was flowing freely that night, back in '45 as we celebrated Cornet Robert Phillipson who surprised Sir Wilfrid's garrison on St Herbert's Island, in the middle of Derwentwater. Rowed in quiet like, in the middle of the night, and by the time the sleepy-heads had roused themselves they were surrounded and had to surrender to Phillipson's men, good honest King's Men, not like the turncoat who is our Lord. By God, I must have had too much ale, that's dangerous talk – mind you tell no-one. Sir Wilfrid, though, he was leading the Parliamentarians besieging Carlisle. Civil War is a hellish thing, with Cumbrians like him starving fellow Cumbrians to death. Nigh on two years he held them penned in the city – yet his father sent money for the King's cause! Father against son, brother against brother, it's a terrible thing. There are times when living quietly up beyond the jaws of Borradell is the best place you can be.

Now we have what they call a Manorial Court, twice a year down in the Ale-house in Rosthwaite, courtesy of this same Sir Wilfrid Lawson. I don't know why we suddenly need a court to keep us all in line, back in Grand-dad's day everybody just minded their own business and made sure they could eat well and wear enough to keep warm. Myself, I think it's just an excuse for Sir Wilfrid to pass fines and make sure he gets his rents for grasses and tenements. You go in and the room is packed with everybody with any scrappy bit of land, full of baccy smoke which at least takes the edge off the stink of all those unwashed bodies crammed together. You wouldn't dare not go, for fear they'd all start talking about you and bringing all sorts of complaints to the Lord's Steward and his clerk. I'm getting too old for it, to tell the truth, the smoke gets in my wind and I can hardly stagger the couple of miles home in the dark after the court sits. I'll send our John next time, I think.

We're lucky at Thorneythwaite not having any near neighbours. Down in Rosthwaite or Stonethwaite there's always somebody falling out with somebody else, and it doesn't help that everybody is related. As the saying goes, 'kick a Borradell feller's shins and half a dozen start limping.' Our lot, for instance, Birketts, I had a count up in my head and there's at least twenty families of us working in the valley. We must be like a closed flock, with hardly a 'bought-in tup'. It's the same with Braithwaites, Fishers, Jopsons, Harrys, Youdells – there's only half a dozen families spread over virtually all the farms. The Keswick lads have a name for us – 'Gowks' they call us, after the cuckoos that throng the valley every lambing-time. They have a scurrilous tale that once, not so long ago, Borradell fellers built a wall right across the valley to stop the cuckoos leaving, so Spring would stay forever. We might be a bit slow, sometimes, but we've seen plenty of gowks fly over walls.

The first court I remember vividly, because it touched the family, was in the Alehouse in October, 1656, not long after they got going – in the Commonwealth years, of course, when Sir Wilfrid reaped his reward for being on the winning side. It was when our Charles, married then and with a couple of bairns, first took over Gawine Youdell's land in Stonethwaite. Seven shillings a year, Gawine had paid for years, but suddenly in the court Sir Wilfrid upped it to ten shillings, and Charles had to pay. I doubt it's worth that much, but time will tell.

Not long after this Sir Wilfrid decided we needed to have what he called Jurors to keep the peace in the valley. I suppose a lot of parishes have had Jurors for years, but it was new in Borradell and I could see from the start it might be trouble. Sir Wilfrid's steward wanted our John to be one of the first twelve, but he'd have none of it. Find against a neighbour and you've an enemy for life is how he looks at it.

Just as well he didn't take on being a juror, it turns out there are three Birketts out of the twelve anyway. Any more and we really would get a bad name. Old Christopher, one of the main farmers on the Rosthwaite field strip system is one, of course. Charles, who had to jump through the hoops to get married is another, sort of representing Seatoller, and John from Park Yeat in Stonethwaite's the other. I suppose with twelve of them the blame will get spread out, but I still wouldn't want to be getting a neighbour fined.

It's funny how these things snowball. Twenty years ago we didn't have jurors, and as far as I know we didn't have much trouble that couldn't be sorted out over a glass of whisky or two. Then Sir Wilfrid decided we needed jurors, and now, at this latest meeting in 1673 we have to have constables as well, to make sure folk behave themselves. John Jopson and Myles Wilson have taken the job on for this year, to see how it goes. I suppose the trouble is that land is getting tight, and sheep grasses as well. Let's face it, these la'al Herdwicks bring in a tidy income from their wool, even though it's coarse stuff, and they need a lot of ground to thrive. As we say round here, 'A Herdwick's biggest enemy is another Herdwick'. So there's all sorts of roguery out on the high fell these days, with stock being driven onto other folks' grasses, walls deliberately broken down, mebbe even a bit of rustling, though the lug-marks are clear enough.

Mostly the fines at the beginning of a Manor Court are for little things, but little things that can cause a lot of tension if you don't get them sorted. This last meeting was fairly typical. Percival How was fined six shillings and eight pence for calling a juror a liar – didn't say which, but I can guess: him and our Christopher have never got on. The lonning from Longthwaite to Chapel has been getting worse for years, and the court finally found against Lancelot Harry and William Grave who have to make two tracks, one for people, one for horses, both to be kept passable, and to do it before Allhallows Day, on pain of a fine of 20 shillings. That should see it done! It's a good idea to separate horses and those on foot, for the horses make a hell of a mess in Winter.

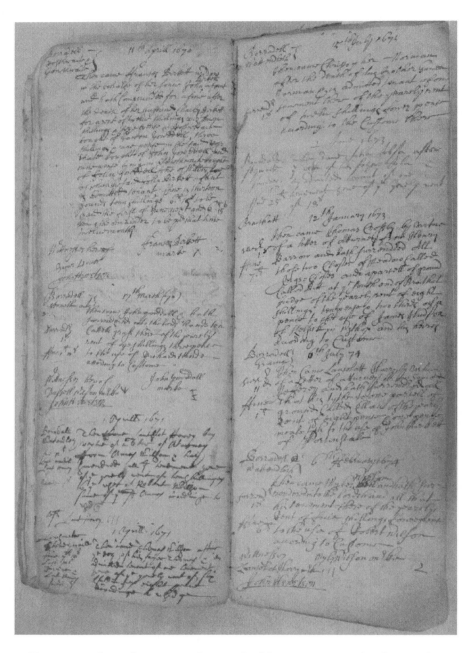

*Two pages from the manorial record of the meetings in Rosthwaite Inn
(now The Royal Oak) from 1670 – 1674. (Carlisle Record Office)*

118

Mainly though, the business is about walls and hedges. Talk about 'Good walls make good neighbours'; if some of these neighbours kept their walls in better order they'd be a lot better neighbours. Even gates come in for the odd fine, though it seems to me that if you don't keep a decent gate on your property it's your own fault if a cow tears up your cabbages. Be that as it may, Widow Agnes Langstrath was fined 6d. for not keeping her gate in good order.

Chapter twenty-three

Daniel and Sarah Jopson; early to mid-1700s

Well, we're in! The first time Thorneythwaite hasn't had a Birkett living in it. Ever, quite possibly. I'm not even married to a Birkett: Sarah's a Youdall frae Stonethwaite. Saying that, no doubt there's plenty of Birkett blood flowing in both of our bodies – and Fisher, Braithwaite, Wren, Grave, Harriman blood to boot. But times are changing, there's a lot more farms changing hands these days. I feel sorry for John and Ann, the last Birketts at Thorneythwaite, to be honest: saddled with three lads who didn't want to farm. Big, strong lads too, John, Jonathon and young Joseph. Funny family, though, if all the truth was known. A bit soft in the head, all three lads –too much in-breeding if you ask me. Anyway, by the time Joseph was nearly grown John and Ann were in their sixties it was clear none of the lads could take over, so they put the farm up for sale – and here we are. Or mebbe it's just that Ann fancied a bit more comfort in her old age, and who could blame her. She had more than her fair share of elderly relatives to look after, and a few sponging younger ones that should have been kicked out on their ear.

It wasn't cheap, but then it's a big fine spot these days. Once old Will Birkett extended the farmhouse back in the Commonwealth days – 1653 according to the carving over the fireplace – it can easily hold two or even three families. The story in the valley is that Lizzie Birkett wouldn't let her father, old John, rest in peace till he provided a halfway decent house for her and Thomas. Fair enough, if you ask me, with her being his eldest lass and expecting to inherit the lot till Will turned out to be John's bastard. Trouble is, if you've a bit of room, some bugger's gonna come and fill it. Better hadn't try it with me, though, I've no time for layabouts. John and Ann were always a soft touch. I would have kicked those three wastrel lads of theirs out a long time before they did. Course old Daniel had a right to pass his last days there, with Ann being his daughter. Another case of a Birkett marrying a Birkett. He died in 1720 if memory serves, same year that Ann's brother, Ben Birkett, had his first lass, Mary. By God but she's grown up a beauty – hope to hell she doesn't marry another of the clan! Ben was living with them too, kind of crept in with old Daniel – just like Ann's three lads when I come to think of it, not able to handle Park Yeat in Stonethwaite without his father there.

You'll maybe be wondering how a feller like me could afford to buy? We were just tenants in Seathwaite, Sarah and me, and it took us till I was forty-six to scrat the brass together – or perhaps I should say the wad.

Part of our holding was a la'al field I'd walled in myself, well up the intake, and folk called it Daniel Jopson's New Close. It was just below the boundary wall, immediately south of Wadhole Gill, opposite the two best seams of wad there was – Low Wadhole and the Grand Pipe, as the miners called it. I was rather proud of it, if you must know. Ya day this feller comes to me and asks if he can dig intill't hillside to open up a copper mine – top corner of my new enclosure. Feller by the name of Hetherington – William Hetherington. Seemingly he'd bought a lease to mine, at £25 each for him and his partner. Seemed a queer place to mine for copper, but he was prepared to pay over the top to put his mine in my field.

Time went on, Hetherington and his partner John Martin built a la'al hut at the entrance to their new mine, to store gear in and make a meal and sec like, and started blasting their way into the fellside. Me, I'd rather be out in the open, even when it's pouring down, but as Hetherington says, there's more money in minerals than sheep. Not that I could see much money in the la'al bits of copper ore they said they were winning from their mine. He was very 'easy come, easy go' was Hetherington, didn't mind folk poking about in his mine – not at all like the heavy guards on the wad mines. Wad had got to be so dear those days that folk were always trying to steal a bit. There were some nights when I looked out from Seathwaite farmyard and could count a dozen la'al lamps on t'hillside – Borrowdale folk mainly, gleaning a couple of pounds of wad from the spoil heaps. Even a pound could bring you more in the George and Dragon in Keswick than a fortnight's proper work on a farm. Seven shillings a pound was the black market price back then. They called it the black market on account of the other name for wad – Black Cawke. Still, Hetherington's mine was for copper, so nobody bothered his spoil heap.

He invited me up to take a look at his mine. Not that I take much pleasure in a hole in the ground, but for neighbourliness sake I went. It was a queer place, beautifully lined with timber for the first ten yards or so – needed to hold the roof up Hetherington said. It went on mebbe another ten yards till it came to a stop. He said they were getting copper ore every yard they went, and it was just a matter of time till they hit a big vein. Course I knew the stories about the German miners nigh on two hundred years ago, and their big copper strikes in Newlands and Borrowdale, but it seemed a shot in the dark to be trying it here. Even with the gunpowder to help blast his way in it was cruel work tunnelling his way in. And something about that tunnel ferreted away in the back of my mind.

It was about three in the morning – pitch black outside anyway, when I woke with a jump and the answer. If the tunnel needed all that timber to start with, why didn't it need it after about ten yards in? And why

121

was there sec a big spoil heap for nobbut twenty yards of mine? The heap was bigger than them outside some of the adits that went in fifty yards and more. Hetherington and Martin often didn't bother coming to their mine, specially on wet, miserable days. A couple of days later seemed perfect – a real Seathwaite downer, with the cloud nearly down to the valley floor, and the rain driving down in bucketfuls. Nobody with any sense was going to be about that day, and there wasn't much I could do on the farm in that weather. I took a couple of lanterns and a flint and climbed up into the cloud for New Close.

T'mine was open as ever, and I checked the shed just to be sure nobody was about. I lit both lanterns in the entrance and bent my way in to the end of the fancy woodwork, ten yards or so. Here the tunnel curved left a bit, so I had a good feel around the timber on the right-hand wall, and brought both lanterns close. Sure enough, there was a door, varra cunningly contrived so there were no straight edges to give it away, but with a bit more prising and breaking my fingernails I found where to get hold of to swing it open. Just as I'd woken up knowing, there lay another tunnel. No timber in here, just a straight drive forward. Superstitiously I didn't shut the door behind me – I hate these tunnels, I always feel sick in them, and the thought of being trapped inside made my guts lurch.

I knew where this would end, long before I got along the twenty-five yards or so that Hetherington and Martin had blasted out, and sure enough it opened out into a ten foot hole at the end. A hole with black cawke all round it. The fly buggers had burrowed their way into part of what the miners called the Gorton Sop, a deep, ten foot wide plug of wad that sank who knows how far down from its top up on Seatoller Common. I got out fast, this was no place to get caught, either by Hetherington or anybody else. This sort of knowledge would need very careful handling, and a good bit of thought. Sarah and I sat up half that night pondering how to make best use of what I'd found.

What we weren't going to do was to let on to James Spedding, Sir James Lowther's steward, that was for sure. Who the hell was Sir James to think he owned the wad in the first place? What with him and the Lawsons lording it over us we were sick of Knights. When we thought about it, that wad was really ours. After all, the mine started off in our field – the field I'd laboured long and hard to create. Then again, if I suddenly started offering wad in the George word would soon get out, and neighbours would get very nosey. Eventually we made a plan we felt should work. The next time Hetherington showed up in the yard I invited him in for a beer, before he went up the hill for more blasting.

"Now then, Willy, good day for hacking out copper is it?" Hetherington looked shifty, he could tell something was afoot.

"Every day's the same twenty yards inside a hill, Daniel," he says, careful like.

"Course you wouldn't need to blast if you were picking out wad, I suppose?"

"You've been in the mine, Daniel, you know there's no wad there. Do you think I'd leave it unguarded if there was wad to be found?"

"Well, however it is, Willy, Sarah and I have been talking about the rent you pay for that corner of our field."

"Oh aye?"

"We think a shilling a year's a bit on the thin side, Willy."

"Well, it's nobbut a few square yards, Dan, they tell me you just pay a penny-halfpenny for a sheep grass that's mebbe ten acres."

"Aye, but there's nae wad under them acres." Show a bit of steel, Sarah tell't me.

"What's aw this talk about wad, Dan, I's mining copper."

"Course you are, Willy, and we wadn't want anyone to hear different, wad we. Course, if you were mining wad, say in Gorton's Pipe, Sir James might have a thing or two to say. Felony, is that. Punishable by a longish spell in Carlisle gaol, so they tell me." Willy sat quiet, like, for a minute or two.

"How much rent were you thinking of, then, Daniel?" he says eventually.

So now you know how come Sarah and I could afford to buy, but nobody else did. Nobody else's business. I wouldn't have told you but that Sir James eventually caught up with Willy Hetherington. It was nigh on 1750 by then, so he'd had a good few years out of the job. Course, he couldn't take too much – selling it on is always the tricky part. But at getting on for ten bob a pound you don't need to sell that much. Sir James sent his steward, James Spedding, to have a good look round, and Spedding spied a few bits of wad on the mine-shaft floor, and worked it out from there. He did eventually stand trial at Carlisle, but kept his neck intact.

Now here's the strange part of Willy's story. After he'd served less than two years for his impudent scheme, Henry Bankes, son of the great Sir John and now a mine owner, took him on as mine superintendent! Case of 'set a thief to catch a thief' I guess, but Willy turned out to be one of the best they ever had. He knew so many of the villains and their ways that they never stood a chance against him. That was in 1754: a few years later Willy drew up a map of the mines, as if you were looking from Jenny Bank, and he brought it round to Thorneythwaite one night for Sarah and me to have a look. Well, I couldn't make head nor tail of it for a bit, till he showed me how to look at it, then he just went on looking at me sort of

123

sideways – expectant like. Suddenly Sarah burst out laughing. "Ha, now I see why thou's brought this, Willie" she says, and bugger me they're both now looking at me expectant. "What?" I says, "What's ga'an on?" Sarah pointed at the bottom right corner, and I finally cottoned on. "Well, bugger me, Willy, whats t'a done that for?" There in the corner he'd drawn our house – the house we'd bought with his wad – and labelled it 'Thorneythwaite where Daniel Jopson resides'. I've copied that la'al detail for you here, so you can see how well we lived in 1759.

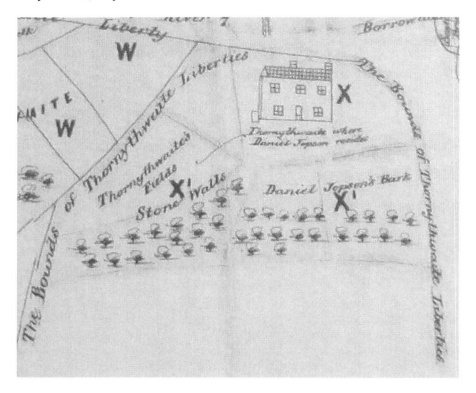

I allus had a sneaking respect for Hetherington and Martin: at least they were clever about their stealing. There were others were a lot less shrewd, and a lot more dangerous. I mind one night, happen about ten years after we came to Thorneythwaite, John White was set on guard in the house the company had built right over the mine entrance, so no-one could get in without breaking into the house first. He'd bolted the door and shuttered the window, but there was sec a load of ugly thugs battering on the door. In fear for his life John was forced to let them in before they burst in anyway, and watch while they took a load of wad that had been left in the mine for safe keeping. It was a different story a few nights later. John had been taken round the back of the Inn in Rosthwaite and told to stop at home that night, if he cared for his life and his home.

Now there's another man I have a respect for. Not only did John take no notice of the warning, but he came round to Thorneythwaite to see would our John and a few others take muskets and help him out that night. There were six of them at the finish, and nine thugs armed with pistols and muskets came battering on the door again. They knew John had reinforcements, of course, and were spoiling for a fight. Yan of them hopped up on t'roof and ripped off a few slates, then blasted off his musket straight into the room below, badly injuring one of the lads John had gathered. Not our John, I'm glad to say. He let off his own musket at the feller on the roof, and killed him stone dead. That was that, the cowardly buggers turned tail and ran, leaving their mate lying on the ground where the shot had thrown him. Daniel Wright, he was, a thief and a murderer.

Still, he was dead, and the law is the law. John and the rest of the guards thought to make themselves scarce for a bit, and travelled off to Coniston while things cooled down. They needn't have worried too much. Henry Bankes now owned a big share of the mine and he made sure the law knew just whose fault the blood-letting had been. Wright had been a thorn in the side a lot of years. There were few to grieve his passing.

We might have owned Thorneythwaite, but Sarah and I soon found out it didn't make a great deal of money, and money was becoming more of a necessity these days. We'd a good bit of land enclosed, and all the sheep rights up on Thorneythwaite Fell and our bit of Glaramara, but it was poverty-stricken land and wadn't keep much stock over winter. We'd not been there long afore our first-born lad, John, married – to a Birkett, of course! Another Sarah – and their first-born was another Sarah. They'd moved back to Seathwaite by then – took on my old tenancy from Sir Gilford Lawson, Lord of the Manor now. A couple of years later our Sarah married out as well... bet you can guess who that was. Johnnie Birkett, from Stonethwaite – yet another of Lawson's tenants. We were left with our Daniel, born in 1728, and a fine strong twenty-year-old when Sarah got married. As long as he stayed we could manage, though we were getting on a bit by now. At fifty-five you can't do what you could at twenty-five.

Chapter twenty-four

Daniel the younger; 1750 onwards.

There's no getting away from it, father was a rogue. Trouble is, a wad mine on your doorstep invites roguery; a wad mine on your land, that no-one else knows about, demands exploitation. It took about five years after father cottoned on to Willy Hetherington's la'al scheme afore Spedding twigged. They say that opportunity makes a thief – well, he wasn't short of opportunity, was he? The main Wadhole was shut up, them years, while the bosses waited for the market to be desperate for wad again – particularly for casting cannon-balls and keeping muskets shiny. There was nobody about for weeks on end in winter – even Hetherington wouldn't turn out to mine his 'copper' when the days were too short to get up and down the valley. All that wad, sitting in a mine no-one knew about – and on his land.

I was just a bairn, though we had to grow up quick at Seathwaite. As soon as I could whistle I had a dog to help gathering the fell. As soon as I could wrap a fleece tightly enough that was my job while father and John clipped the sheep. We were just tenants, of course, in those days. John Braithwaite owned a lot of the houses at Seathwaite then. But our Sarah and I had time to lake about, up on the intakes along what we called Jenny Banks, going along to Thorneythwaite. She was two years older than me, and mebbe getting a bit above exploring with her little brother – till we found our own Wadhole! It was in a cave, well, not so much a cave as a deep hole in a group of gurt big boulders that had fallen from way up on the crags. Course, we knew what wad was; you could hardly live at Seathwaite and not know, and we scurried on home to tell father about it. We thought he'd be pleased, but a gurt thunder-cloud crossed his face and he let out a growl so deep it made our blood curdle.

"If either of you kids ever tell a soul about that wad I'll leather the skin off your arses. Do you understand?" We understood. It wasn't so much what he said – he was allus threatening to leather us – it was the look on his face when he said it. Both frightening and frightened, if you know what I mean. A week or so later I sidled along to our Wadhole. It was empty! As if there had never been anything there. When I told father he just kind of smiled "Never was anything there, was there?" I agreed. It wasn't long after that we moved to Thorneythwaite, and he bought three of the la'al houses at Seathwaite as well, yan for each of us, he said, me, our Sarah, and big John.

John took his up not so long after that, when he'd married another Sarah – Sarah Birkett from Stonethwaite, and they farmed it and had a lot more kids. I wonder if any of them ever found the hole on Jenny Banks? Not that much later our Sarah got married an' all, to Johnnie Birkett from Stonethwaite, t'other Sarah's brother! We don't go far for someone to wed, up t'top end o' Borrowdale. Me, I married my cousin from Rosthwaite, just so she didn't need to change her name, being a Jopson already. First name, well, what do you think? So here we are, farming Thorneythwaite, the second Daniel and Sarah Jopson in a row. We got married in 1759, when I'd just turned thirty. Father and Mother are getting old now, but of course they still own the spot.

Father's been a juror for the Manorial Court more times than I care to think, and knows the customs of the valley as well as any man, being now in his sixties. In 1761 he and the other fifteen jurors had to adjudicate a claim Thomas Willson put to the court. Thorneythwaite nobbut has four stints on Stonethwaite Fell, and they're more trouble than they're worth I sometimes think. They're at the top of Coombe Ghyll, around Coombe Door, and the sheep need to be gone quietly round then driven down into the coombe to come in with those grazing there.

It all started nigh on twenty years ago, when John Jopson the blacksmith sold his little flock of sixty-four ewes to his nephew, Daniel of Chapel's lad, also called John Jopson. Their grasses were at the top of the coombe, on the Langstrath side, and the blacksmith used to drive them up there from the back of Stonethwaite Fell, through Scale Yeat. John carried on the same for a few years, but it was easier from Chapel to go through the coombe and up the route from Dove Nest. Thomas Willson brought a suit against John in the Manor Court, claiming he ought to use the old driving road, to help in its preservation – as indeed the Court had ruled both in 1759 and 1760. In response John attacked on all fronts, presenting a plan which he said showed how Willson's sheep had invaded John's grasses at the top of the coombe, and also showing what he claimed was the ancient road up through Dove Nest, which he had every right to use. Overleaf's the plan he drew, that was put before the jurors.

Father knew perfectly well what was going on, of course. It was true, as Willson alleged, that John's new flock should have been driven to the back of Coombe Head by the old Scale Yeat road, but John was deliberately trying to heaf them on what had been Chapel grasses at the head of the Coombe, so driving back Willson's sheep. And it was true that the road he was driving them up, through Dove's Nest, was the ancient track for the Coombe Head stock. It was a knotty problem for the jurors, and the worse for all being neighbours.

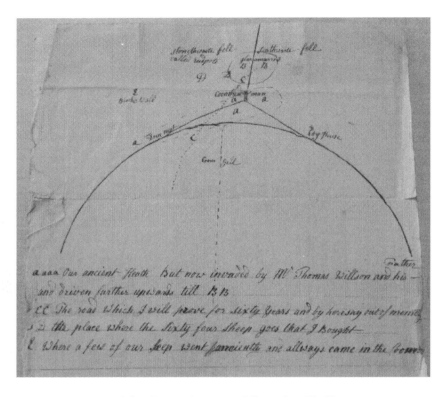

John Jopson's map of Coombe Ghyll

In the end the jurors mebbe exercised the wisdom of Solomon. They directed that John must indeed use the ancient Scale Yeat for this flock of sheep, but that he had a right to take them right over to the top of the Coombe and to drive Willson's sheep back to their rightful grasses. This was a considerable concession, because for a long time there had been a complete ban on anyone hounding any sheep off a grass, ever since the big dispute back in 1703. That year Joseph Wilson and John Birkett had been appointed as Lookers for Stonethwaite Fell to ensure no person put more sheep out than they had stints for, or 'wilfully and maliciously' disturb his neighbour's goods. We'd had lookers ever since, such was the temptation to overstock, and this very year of our Lord, 1761, the court had to settle a dispute between Joseph Wilson of Rosthwaite and Joseph Youdale of Stonethwaite over the hounding and disturbing of each other's sheep. Of course, as soon as someone does overstock, as Willson obviously did, the sheep spill out onto other grasses, as they had on John's.

The court report from 1703

I'd never got on that well with cousin Daniel, of Chapel, forby we shared the same name, but I have to admire the man. He and father were two of a kind, personable rogues, but rogues nonetheless. Chapel was a customary tenancy of the Lord of the Manor – Sir Gilfrid Lawson, it was now. A baronet, as they all had been since the infamous Sir Wilfrid who bought the baronetcy from James II in 1688, using £2,000 of ill-gotten money from the tenants he screwed mercilessly. For all he was landlord, Sir Gilford never spent a penny on his tenements. If a tenant wanted an improvement he had to do it himself; and Daniel desperately needed a barn. All over the valley farmers were pulling down the old shacks that had served as storage for years and putting up new stone-built and slate roofed barns – partly because for once times were better for farmers, and partly because Honister slate mine was up and running properly, so slate was easily come by. Stone had always been easy. Timber wasn't. Timber had to be bought from Sir Gilfrid, and Sir Gilfrid knew how to charge.

Daniel was having none of this, and he and his son John simply went out in the woods behind Chapel and felled a dozen good straight oaks that had been grown for the job, true trunks you could get a roof beam from. Mebbe he thought John Grainger, Lawson's steward, would never get to know. If he did, he was wrong. Thomas Willson was Lawson's bailiff – yes, that Thomas Willson.

129

Grainger was livid, and come storming round to Chapel demanding to know what the hell Daniel thought he was doing, and threatening to throw him off the tenancy unless he paid ten pounds apiece for the oaks. According to the story I heard, Daniel just sat in that old rocker of his, nodding sagely at all Grainger's rants, and when he had finished just says quietly to his missus, "Betty, ga and ratch in t'iron box, and fetch yon Gurt Deed out, will't tha." Daniel could read and write, pretty well as it turned out, and he'd come upon a copy of the old 1614 Great Deed in the iron chest at Chapel. All signatories had had a copy back then, though I don't suppose many were still left uneaten by mice or mildew after a hundred and sixty years. As Daniel read, according to Betty, he got more and more excited.

"Says here, Mr Grainger, in black and white, that we have a right to any of the trees on our land, as tenants."

"Rubbish, Jopson, what are you talking of. Tenants have always paid for their timber."

"Aye, thou's reet theer, and we've allus paid rent for our grasses, and fines whenever a son takes ower."

"So what the hell are you talking about, man?"

"Let me just read you the relevant section, Mr Grainger..." Daniel could talk proper if he thought the occasion demanded it. "Here we are, Sir, let me quote to you...

'*And whereas there are within and parcel of the said manor divers other things which cannot conveniently be apportioned and divided and yet nevertheless are included in the said purchase and are meant intended and agreed on to be bargained, sold and conveyed by the said William Whitmore and Jonas Verdon unto or to the use of the said several persons purchasers before named* – that's us all, Betty! – *for their apportionable benefits* & blah blah blah – here's the rub – *All and every the woods according to the former divisions, which woods are to be enjoyed as formerly they were before the purchase from His Majesty, wastes, commons, stinted pastures, salt springs* – and so on!'

Betty says Grainger blanched before her eyes, seemed almost to shrink, before he pulled himself together and began to bluster.

"Rubbish, man, you've no idea what all that means..."

"Seems plain enough to me, Mr Grainger, but we could test it in court if you like."

"Courts are expensive places to be, Jopson. Do you think you have the funds to match Sir Gilfrid? And mind you understand, lose in court and you lose everything, court case, farm, a chance for your sons. Everything. Shall we see you in court, then?"

"Aye, but if we win, Mr Grainger... do you think your job is safe if you lose Sir Gilfrid his Manor?" Daniel was standing by now, face to face, mebbe just six inches between their noses. Betty felt an unwonted thrill of excitement, quickly submerged in panic.

Grainger flinched first, looking away and coughing. He sat down. Daniel stayed standing. "What's it to be, then, Mister Grainger?"

"Well, I do know Sir Gilfrid is a generous man, keen to help his tenants. I'm pretty sure he would want you to have those trees. Of course, he would need a note of receipt – a note that made it clear this was a one-off gift, and that you recognise you have no rights – absolutely no rights – to any other trees. Better that way than money wasted on lawyers don't you think, Mr Jopson?"

"Shall you write out the note then, and I'll give you my best signature?"

Here's the very note, shown to us all at the next Manorial Court.

Transcript:

May 22nd. 1773

I Daniel Jopson of Borrowdale Chapel in the manor of Borrowdale and county of Cumberland, yeoman, do hereby acknowledge that Sir Gilfrid Lawson of Brayton in the said county, baronet, Lord of the manor aforesaid did of his own free will and out of respect to me make a present to me of eleven or twelve oak trees growing upon part of my customary estate held of the said Sir Gilfrid Lawson Baronet as a parcel or part of the said Manor. And I do hereby further acknowledge that I have not any right claim or pretension whatsoever to any of the oak wood growing on any part of my said customary estate in the said manor, and that I have paid the sum of two shillings to Thomas Wilson bailiff to the said Sir Gilfrid Lawson as an acknowledgement for the tops of the trees which I took away, as witness my hand this day and year above written.

Daniel Jopson. Witness Tho. Wilson.

Like I said, Daniel could write pretty well. I loved the 'out of respect to me' – I could just imagine Daniel dictating that bit, but I wasn't surprised Grainger had then crossed it out. And the two shillings to Willson! Splendid!

That was on May 22nd 1773, as you can see from the letter. On May 25th Father died, just passed away quietly in his sleep. I reckon he was a hell of a man, my father, for all he was a rogue. Born in Stonethwaite, with no chance of inheriting that tenancy, he took on the tenancy of Seathwaite and pulled himself up by the caulkers on his clogs till he owned Thorneythwaite and another three cottages in Seathwaite. He was no farmer, though and by the time he died we were in parlous order at Thorneythwaite. If he would have let me I could have turned it round, but I was forty-five by then. Too late to be learning how to be in charge. Twelve years later I had to sell the spot to John Braithwaite, who'd done so well up at Seathwaite. But at least we stayed on as tenants, so my eldest lad John will have an inheritance.

I treated John a lot better – gave him responsibility early on, like. Well, soon as father died, really. He did well, did John, of course they were good years for farming. We made enough for me to be able to buy the farm back from Braithwaite in 1798. It went into my name. John can wait till I die before he gets that responsibility. I don't suppose it will be long, I was seventy that year.

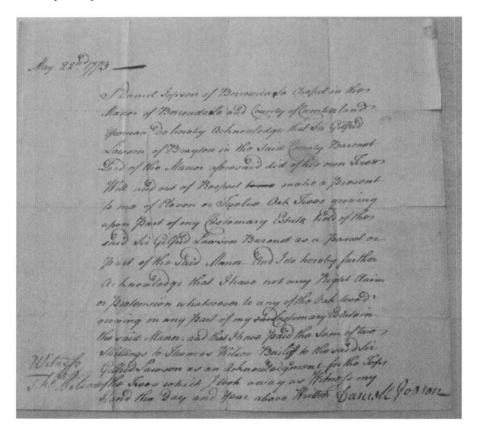

The original letter, transcribed overleaf

Chapter twenty-five

Honister mine and the slaters from Honister living in the cottage at Thorneythwaite, 1781-1833:

Robert & Mary Graves and family;
Joseph & Ann Dawson;
Jonathon & Agnes Thompson;
Daniel and Sarah Jopson still owners.

Daniel's story of those years.

With Thorneythwaite being so big now, and Borrowdale expanding with the workforce for the new quarry up at Honister, Sarah and I thought it wise to make a bit of money from the quarrymen – slaters as we called them. Well, all right, I thought it wise and Sarah had little choice but to gan along with the idea, though she'd have rather had the whole spot to ourselves. We'd kenned Joseph Dawson and his sister Mary since they were bairns, and we were happy enough to take a bit of rent each week from them both. Joseph married Ann Walker frae Stonethwaite, and they never had any bairn when they were with us. Little Lanty wasn't born till they'd gone back to Ann's father's spot. Must have been quite a surprise to them after twelve years wed! Course Mary wouldn't give over teasing her sister-in-law about how long it had taken them to work out how babbies were made... but then, she and her husband, Robert, had had a few by then. Robert Grave, that is, the first of that long line of valley family to work up at Honister. For sure Mary kenned how bairns were made – she was showing clear enough when Robert made an honest woman of her in May, and young Robert was born at the end of September.

Him and Joseph would be up before light, most of the year, for a quick breakfast then over Nichol Dub bridge to join the rest of the slaters in Seatoller for the hour's slog up to the quarry. They could shift, those fellers, for they had to go right up over Fleetwith Pike to Dubs Quarry on the far side. A lot of the slaters lived there all week, in a la'al bothy they'd built for themselves, just going back down to Keswick for Sunday. Some nights Bob and Joe stopped there as well – Bob especially if there was a howling bairn at home. Their first, named Robert after his father, was a terrible tearful babbie, and if I'm completely honest I wasn't that sympathetic when the poor mite died after only a couple of months. Mebbe that's why they moved out over to Seatoller straight after. It was five years till they came back to Thorneythwaite, by which time they had another two toddlers, and Robert the second on the way.

This would be back in, oh, the early 1780s. I know our Jonathon was only about five years old, and he was born in '76. The slate quarry up at Dubs had been going mebbe thirty years by then. Longer, really, but it wasn't till Charlie Norman got hold of it that it started making money. He opened up Ash Gill and Bull Gill as well as Dubs, and they were turning out slate as fast as they could get it away – 400 tons in the year young Robert was born and died, so his father said. Most of it went down Buttermere valley and out to Cockermouth where there was a market locally. Some went by pack horse over the side of Great Gable and so down into Wasdale and on to the port at Ravenglass to be 'ex-ported' as Joseph put it. They called the first part of the way Moses' Trod after Moses Rigg, who led most of the pack trains. Moses made most of the whisky the quarrymen drank, as well, and if you were living all week up on Fleetwith you'd need a bit of whisky each night. There's some lovely peat hags up there, full of perfect water for whisky. Robert and Joseph used to bring a bottle or two down and we had some right merry nights at Thorneythwaite then. Hell of a lot better than paying good money for it down at Rosthwaite.

Robert was built for sledding; strong as an ox and quick on his feet, and sledders could earn more than quarrymen. But it was cruel work, hoss-work as Joseph teased when we sat around the whisky bottle. He ferried a quarter of a ton of dressed slate each load, on a sled weighing about 80 lbs itself, down that long steep incline from Dubs down to Warnscale Bottom, near Gatesgarth Farm. 1200 feet drop in about a couple of miles – then he had to carry the sled on his back right back up to the quarry. I tell tha, I'd rather gather Glaramara twice over than do yan of them runs. I mind well when he landed down one Saturday night, after stopping all week in that la'al bothy they've built themselves – he was that pleased with hissel.

"How many loads does'ta think I've done this week, then, old feller?" They were like that to me, these two striplings, and I suppose I must have been quarter of a century afore them. I'd seen the route and the full sleds ya day when I was fetching a few stray yows frae Willy Richardson's at Gatesgarth, so I'd a fair idea of the load.

"Nay, I diven't know, Bob, what, five loads a day mebbe?" Five loads! Five loads would have killed me, just on one day. He shook out his pipe intil t'fire and spat accurately into the flames.

"Forty-five runs I made this week, Daniel. Forty-five lang hauls up and down that bloody hill. What's t'think about that, then?" Truth was, I thought it both amazing and horrifying, but I was hardly going to let on.

"Nay, Bob, they tell me the record's summat like seventeen loads in a day. That'd make over a hundred in a full week!" Robert spat again, the spittle sizzling on the hot hob.

"Aye, Lanty Wilson did do seventeen loads ya day – but he did nae mair for over a month till he could walk again!"

Joseph joined in at last. He was a quiet one, Joseph, happen brooding on his barren missus. Naebody wants an empty nest. "Thou'll bloody kill thysel, Robert, and leave our Mary widowed with three bairns to feed and nobody to care for her."

"Nay, thou's nae mouths to feed, Joe, you and Ann would see her straight."

Joseph takes a bit more care of himself, working in the quarry itself, but even that's hoss-work in my book. I'll bet it's no safer, either, working with gunpowder and all. They have to prise what they call a clog of slate, mebbe a ton or more, off the quarry wall, belting a gurt lang chisel in up to a yard intil't slate. Then he pours gunpowder into the hole and tamps it down, sticks a plug of dampened slate dust over the top, pricks a hole right down to t'bottom of the hole with a copper pin – wouldn't dare use iron for fear of sparks – sticks a long straw filled with powder down the hole, lights the end – and runs like hell!

No, you wouldn't catch me doing any of the jobs up there. It's all muscle and mind out! Yan of those clogs lands on you and that'll be the end of your working days. And when it's pouring down, and t'winds in t'crack, as they say, blowing fit to bust, you must wonder what the hell you're doing slogging your guts out. I know they get paid mebbe twice as much as a labourer down in the valley, on a farm, but what a life!

It wasn't that long till Joseph saw the light – or mebbe it was Ann not wanting to see her man fading away in front of her. Or mebbe it was just that, without bairns to feed, he could scrat the money together to buy a horse and a cart. Whatever it was, in 1790 Joseph became a carrier, carting the slate from the head of Buttermere along the side of the lake and Crummock Water all the way to Cockermouth, and the market there. Three-quarters of a ton, one trip a day, and Joe was a happy man. It must have made a difference – Lanty was born the year after he changed course.

By then of course both families had quit Thorneythwaite, and in many ways I was glad of that. I wouldn't have wanted to see their decline, not after those evenings we all spent round the fire, when they were in their prime, laughing, bragging, smoking and drinking. They were good years. I mind I saw Robert in1794, mebbe five years after he and Mary and the family left Thorneythwaite. I never saw a man so changed, grown old so quick. His hair was white, his skin grey, his hands gnarled and the veins on his arms stood out in gurt knots. And haggard. All the flesh seemed dropped away.

"How do, Bob. What fettle then?"

"Thou can see for thysen what fettle I's in, old man. Nae mair sledding for me, that's for sure. I still work up at t'quarry, riving slates, but I's hardly fit even for that, if tha wants to know." Riving was old man's work, or so they said. A sitting down job, splitting the slates time and again with a broad cold chisel, till you got to good roofing slate thickness. The only trouble is, sitting down in the cold and rain up at Dubs Quarry isn't that much better than sledding, though not as demanding, and I said so.

"No, it's not so bad" says Robert "we're mining now, more than quarrying, and I can sit in the mine mouth in the dry. Still bloody cold, some days, though."

I wasn't surprised to hear, just the next year, that the poor bugger had died. Only thirty-six. They said it was pneumonia, and I suppose it was, but I would have said he simply wore away.

An old-timer riving slates

I was more surprised to hear Joseph also died, a year after Robert, for he'd always had more sense and looked after himself better. There's not that many make their threescore years and ten in this valley. If the rain and the cold don't get you, the sheer hoss-work will. I give thanks to God that Sarah and I have lived so long and so well. 'Old man' the lads called me, all those years ago. Well, it's over ten years now since I went to both their funerals, and Sarah and I are both in our eighties. Thorneythwaite has been good to us: I'd like to think we've been good to it.

And what an eighty years ours have seen in Borrowdale. My father wouldn't recognise our farming compared to his time. It's mainly in the arable section that things have moved on so fast. I mind well enough the scratty little strips of oats growing down on Rosthwaite town field. It was bloody hard trying to get enough just to feed people through the winter, without trying to feed livestock as well, so most of the cattle were butched and salted. It was often October before the heads were ripe enough to cut and thresh, and by then the ground was sodden and half the crop ruined. Now there's fields ploughed and sown with corn that father would have laughed at, fields with hedges round to protect them from the Herdwicks. At Thorneythwaite we have corn on Nookem and Noon Bank every year, with them being so easy to plough, and John has laid drains across into Black Syke. It's the drains and the lime that's made the difference. I'd like to think I've been part of it, but the truth is it's our John that's the go-ahead farmer here. He's even walled in the intakes along Jenny Bank. Hell of a job and hardly worth the manpower it took to build way up there. It's not as if Jenny Bank is much good for sheep, full of rock and bracken as it is, and the crags at the top are nowt but a death trap, as I tell't him. But John would have none of it – they allus know best, these young 'uns. Myself, I think it was nowt but fashion, everybody was walling round as much land as they could, hiving off the common. But as I said to him 'What's the point? There's only Thorneythwaite sheep out on that fell anyway, so you're not gaining owt.'

Of course the war with Napoleon has helped – it's an ill wind as blows no-one any good, and prices for everything have shot up. There's always losers of course, and a lot of the little holdings have been swallowed up. It's as well Honister and Yew Crag need so many workers, or I don't know what would have happened to the little cottagers with a couple of acres and a cow, a pig and a few hens. There's over a hundred men work up there these days, and they've just built a row of cottages at Seatoller so there's even more families over the beck now.

It's not just the farming that's changed. The whole valley is a different place since I was a lad. It's all opening up, with new folk coming in, and some of the old families leaving. Partly it's the wad mine and the quarries up at Honister, but mainly I think it's that there is a half-decent road down to Keswick now. We get a few folk riding up and standing around gawping, and they tell me there's a pair of poets taken up residence in Keswick – Southey and Coleridge I believe their names. And then of course there's King Pocky. If anyone characterises the changing times it's Joseph Pocklington. His Keswick, his Borrowdale, his Derwentwater are playgrounds, not places to earn a living the hard way. I don't know how he came by his money, but he has a mort of it, and he's not afraid to spend it. Once upon a time Vicar's Island stood for industry, with the German miners building workshops, stores and so on. Now it's a big fancy house, a boathouse looking like a chapel, and regattas on the lake. Him and Peter Crosthwaite – I don't know which is the bigger bairn, or the bigger threat. Both are drawing outsiders in to stand and gawp, folk with more money than sense. It seems all wrong to me, folk with money to burn at one end of Borrowdale, and folk like Robert Grave literally working themselves to death at the other.

Chapter twenty-six

The walls have ears… what if they could talk?

1835 - 1870

I've been here, a building of one sort or another, eight hundred and fifty years: years that have slid past gradually, gracefully. Occasionally one of my guests has thought to modify me a bit – knock a bit down here, build a bit up there, and I've taken it all in my stride. After all, I'm still the same stones I always was. Now, suddenly, the world has gone mad. For centuries I knew the folk I sheltered. They were born within my womb; they died under my protection. I knew their ways, how succeeding generations gradually slid one into the other. The Norsemen, desperate for shelter both from the perpetual rains and their vengeful countrymen, and then their sons and daughters, wives and husbands, and always the babies, the hopeful babies, the tearful babies, the lusty and the doomed babies. They grew up knowing me and my ways, my sagging timbers, the corner where the wind whistled through the small holes that went right through my three-foot walls. And I knew them, I got used to their voices, their loves and hates. The de Borgerdale-Heads, eliding gently through Birkheads to come to rest as Birketts. Mine for the best part of a millennium, till their near relatives the Jopsons took over. I could cope with that, the laughter and the tears were the same, the hopes and fears the same.

Now – all is change. Change upon change upon change. Change in me and change in them, the families I shelter. I am grown fat in my old age, doubled in size. I have spawned my own infant, a three-roomed cottage forever clinging to my skirts. Now there are always two or three families rustling away under my covers. Families forever changing, moving on, before I get the chance to know them. For I give my love but slowly; I need time to grow to know you. Now I feel like a whore, as lovers come and go, scarcely pausing to say either hello, goodbye or thank you. It started with those Jopsons, just when I'd got used to the change from my long-loved Birketts. The times were good to them, with Napoleon's war raising prices so high. They must needs spend the good they'd gained; they it was who doubled my size, in 1822. John and Daniel, brothers-in-arms without a wife between them. What did they want with a home so big? But to bring others in, wild folk, miners, slaters, old women and young.

I could bear it. I could even enjoy the laughter, the constant stream of youngsters, old Mary Birkett, returned and given shelter till she died in my arms. But when they died, John in 1831 and Daniel just two years later, I was left bereft, ownerless, disinherited. It was no surprise to me that Abraham Fisher snapped me up, for Abraham Fisher was greedy for farms, buying here, buying there, increasing his portfolio... It was only the second time in my long life I had been bought, and I felt cheap, diminished, a mere property to be added to a collection. It might have been easier to bear if he'd let someone get to know me, grow to love me, but instead they trooped in at my nice new front door, given by the Jopsons who did love me, and in no time out by the old back door. First it was the Robinsons, William and Hannah, who stayed and farmed just long enough to conceive and bear young George. I felt a brief surge of the old love as I heard his first cry, but no, soon they were off, and in came Joseph and Eleanor Hodgson, who taunted me with their baby, junior Eleanor, before they too took off and left me.

Abraham Fisher, c 1850 (Holt Antique Furniture 2017)

At least I knew the next pair, Henry Dawson and his brand-new wife Mary Dixon.

They could have been good for me, for they were local enough. I knew their parents, aye and their grandparents. I could have grown to love them. Indeed, Henry's grandparents sheltered under my wing a generation ago – Joseph, the slater, and Ann his wife. Henry's wife Mary, now she's the grand-daughter of William Dixon, a man of great distinction in these parts. He and his wife Grace had their first son, Thomas, here in 1826. Old William, even at sixty-six, was still the main agent at the wad mines, with eight of his family working the mines. Among them was Matthew Coates, whose daughter Mary came to me with the Robinsons, a sort of servant. That didn't last long. Soon enough there was the sound of a baby's cry again, her son George, but a son without a father, and that didn't go down well. Another of old William Dixon's grandchildren was Thomas Bennett, a wad miner of course, and Thomas and his wife Mary moved into the cottage – with a quiver full of kids. This was more like it, for me, my rafters ringing with the sound of childish laughter. I snuggled down, a mother hen drawing her chicks under her wing.

So much change! But even change changes, and after Henry and Mary, Thomas and his Mary and all their children I got a proper farming family. Ten years of mayhem I suffered, after Abraham Fisher so cavalierly bought me and foist upon me such a procession of folk I could hardly cope. At last Abraham got a tenant who would stay. Of course, it wasn't just at Thorneythwaite that so much changed so quickly. All over the valley, all over Cumberland – probably all over the country, but I don't get any news from outside – all over farmers were moving on, moving up, trying to better themselves. After centuries of half a dozen families shuffling around the chessboard of the valley head suddenly the new queen muscled in. A pawn sacrificed here, a knight toppled there, a castle demolished; and suddenly, in just a generation it seemed, the old families were checked and new ones took their place. The new churchyard at St Andrews opened in 1775, its registers pristine and ready to record the baptisms and the burials. Check out those names; scarcely a Birkett among them. Rarely a Youdale or a Fisher, a Braithwaite or a Jopson. Now the valley rings to the sound of miners, of quarrymen, of blacksmiths and hoteliers.

And me – who are my new guests? Offcomers! Thomas Walker, from Newlands, and his wife Catherine – not even from Cumberland, but from far off Grasmere, in Westmorland. Ah, but he's a good farmer, is Thomas, and withal he has his father and mother living in my cottage, old Robert and his wife Mary, who farmed long years in St John's in the Vale. Now at last Abraham Fisher may see his land well farmed again: now at last I feel loved once more, secure with three generations settled and happy. Secure for a generation.

Just when I'd got over the upheavals, when I'd got used to my new size, my new families, change hit me once again. I should have seen it coming, Abraham Fisher and his partner John Fisher Crosthwaite never really wanted me for myself. I was only ever a commodity, and it makes me feel so dirty and degraded. I long for the days when my owners loved me enough to live with me, the Birketts and the Jopsons. Those days I fear are long gone. Now I am but a bauble to my owner, a tool to my tenant, and like a bauble I was to be sold again, to the highest bidder, sold with a sitting tenant. So at least I keep my Walkers.

Once again my vital statistics are duly noted, particularised for the sake of an auction. Once again I am paraded like a tart for some rich entrepreneur to feel the frisson of bidding for me. I am a comely farm, though perhaps I says it as shouldn't. 221 acres, 3 roods and 9 perches, more or less – though the reality is that fully 150 of those acres would hardly feed a goat, never mind the 440 Herdwick ewes who adorn my acres. But that's not all, Oh no, I have hidden charms: Grasses and rights on Thorneythwaite Fell (unenclosed, mark you) of fully 104 acres, plus 38 grasses on Coombe Fell for 380 sheep, and a further nine grasses for 90 sheep on Langstrath Fell. These nine come with a history and an element of mystery, for they are Customary Freehold of the Manor of Borrowdale – the only bit of me Sir Wilfrid Lawson ever got his hands on, let me tell you. The rent for these is ninepence a year, so Buyer Beware!

So much for the land, but they have documented my closer secrets too. I comprise a good Dwelling-house containing two sitting rooms and five bedrooms, a large kitchen – and all the usual offices. Plus of course my small three-roomed cottage. I am not without accessories, either.

My buildings consist of a stable with two stalls and two loose boxes, two byres for 24 cattle, four loose boxes and a calf shed and two hay barns, which the auctioneers say are 'of ample size for the holding'. Well! My apportioned Tithe Rent Charge is £2 19s. 9d. Or as you might say, I'm threepence short of a pound, but desirable for all that. H.C. Marshall esquire thought so, and paid well enough. Sitting tenants, my Walker family, didn't put him off, for like all the rest of the newly affluent at the auction, he merely wants a trophy farm, not some land to work himself.

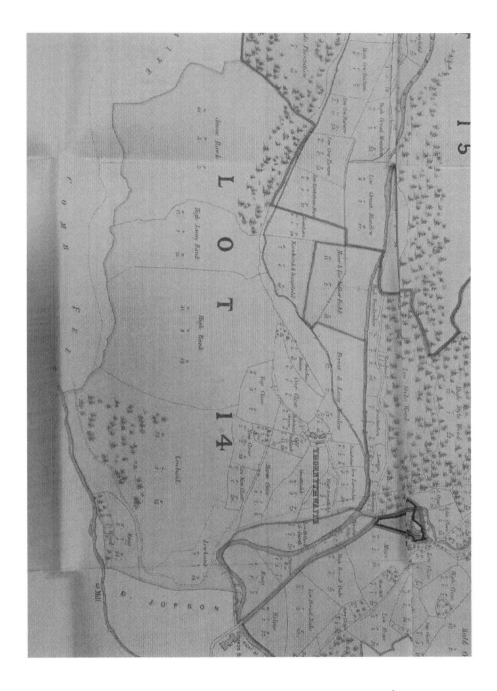

*The plan of Thorneythwaite land for sale on August 27ᵗʰ, 1895
Lot 13 was Seatoller Farm, Lot 15 was all Seathwaite.*

That was in 1868: by then our entire world had changed, and my small heartaches at the cavalier treatment meted out to me was as nothing in the great excitement that gripped the valley and our madam, Keswick. A railway, a mighty steel and steam conveyance to bring the hordes to ogle and to spend their coppers, opened in 1865. They come in their thousands,for the day from Carlisle, Whitehaven, Workington; for the week or even the month from further afield, from the mill towns of Lancashire and the ship-builders of Newcastle. A sturdy new hotel has opened by the station, costing £11,000. My valley was almost as quick off the mark, with the Borrowdale Hotel opening in 1866 and the enlarged Lodore Hotel a couple of years later. Not to mention smaller guest houses built to cope with the summer influx. Thank God I was not required to prostitute myself further – at least not then. For that was how it felt, for the farmers and the miners, the shepherds and the quarrymen, working their health away for a pittance while offcomers milked the mill workers, with their 'picturesque' viewing stations, their boat trips on Derwentwater, their carriage trips over the 'horrors of Honister'. I chuckled to myself as the fine dames and their beaux had to disembark for the long haul up to the top, easily visible from my windows, little knowing they would have to walk down the far side too, as it was too steep to risk a full carriage. Little knowing either, as they set out in sunshine, how likely rain will be at Seatoller.

All things change, then, and an old lady like me finds it hard to handle. But a change was coming that was very welcome. Within the decade following the coming of the rail came back to me my old family. Robert Jopson and his wife Jane, Allison as was, on Lady Day, 25th March 1872, fresh from their wedding at Crosthwaite on 16th March. Robert is Daniel Jopson's son – yes, I know, there's a confusion of Daniel Jopsons! This one was old Daniel Jopson of Chapel Farm's son, the Daniel who was married to Betty and bested Sir Gilfrid Lawson's steward, Mister Grainger. So Robert is family, good and proper, and I feel whole again. He's only thirty: I expect a family of my own again.

Chapter twenty-seven

John Fisher Jopson (1876 – 1969)

My earliest memories of Thorneythwaite are of climbing the great yew tree at the end of the yard, and getting stuck high up and crying like the bairn I was till my father was grumpily extracted from the house to come and rescue me. I have a vivid mental picture of looking down from what seemed a great height to see him emerge sleepy-eyed and tousle-headed from the door into the kitchen, hitching up his braces over his bulky shoulders as he came. I must have been around four or five – lured up there by my big sister Sarah Jane, two years older and several inches taller – so it would be summer, 1882, a decade after Pop and Ma took over the tenancy. It's a well-oiled family story; how they married on 16th March 1872, had a week's honeymoon at Silloth, travelling on the new railway, then moved in here on Lady Day, March 25th, 1872.

Perhaps you should be introduced formerly. Pop is Robert Jopson, proud scion of a Borrowdale family from time immemorial, though he was born in St John's in the Vale, as I remind him sometimes when he gets too nostalgic for the old days. His father, Daniel, was the second son of old Daniel Jopson, the legendary tartar of Chapel Farm. As ever, Chapel was left to the first son, John, so my grandfather had to take a tenancy out of the valley, but it wasn't that long before he wriggled his way back into God's country, taking on the tenancy at Seatoller Farm, just over the beck from us. Pop, Uncle Dover and Aunt Sarah Ann all went to school in Borrowdale… but they're still offcomers, as I tell them occasionally. Ma is truly Borrowdale – an Allison from Stonethwaite. Grandad Thomas and Grandma Sarah still farm there, now in their sixties.

We had farm labourers in those early days, till Frank and I got big enough to help. I go to the new school with Willie Tyson, though he's a couple of years older than me, and taunts me that he was born at Thorneythwaite before I was. Well, maybe so, but his father is nobbut a farm labourer and part-time miner, Wilson Tyson. They live in the cottage across the yard at the end of the la'al barn. There were three of us lads there all of an age, though I was the oldest by two months! Willie's brother, Henry Tyson, and the other labourer's lad, Tommy Scott, whose father I had to call Mr Scott – but I knew he was called Samuel. There were a few years when there was half a dozen of us trooping off down the lane to school at Stonethwaite each day: Willie, Henry, Tommy and our Sarah Jane, me and Frank. I remember one day in February, I suppose it would be 1885 or so. There was a fair covering of snow we had to trudge through on the way to school, and come the break at dinner time we all made a snowman in the yard, and then started on an igloo. Time went on and there was no bell to call us back in, so we just went on till the igloo was complete, with a la'al tunnel to get in by. It was magnificent! It was years later that I realised the teacher must have decided it was better for us to do that than learn our alphabet. It was maybe a mile and a half home, and Frank, who was the youngest of us, went into a drift way over his little boots and cried and snuffled all the way home. Sarah Jane carried him the last half mile up the lane. I pretended I didn't even know him.

I turned fourteen in 1890 and left school properly. I'd been half-left for a couple of years, going only when there were no pressing jobs on the farm. I look back on the next twenty years now with a fondness that belies my contentment with my own wife and family, for those teenage and twenty something years with no responsibilities are unrepeatable. Pop was the boss, and made it very clear he was, and though I often knew better I soon learnt not to say so. I was a big, strong lad, developing muscles I was proud of, happy to work alongside Pop at any job. One of my favourites was walling, putting up the many gaps that Herdwick sheep inflict every year. It's a muscle job all right, but skilled as well, and it took many years before neighbours would concede they didn't know which of us, Pop or me, had mended this or that particular gap.

On the other hand Frank was anything but big and strong. I always felt a bit guilty about that day in the snow, 'cos he was in bed for a week afterwards and somehow never really thrived. We had sheep like him – something seems to eat them from inside and however well you feed them they drag about the fields looking miserable. When he was fifteen Frank developed a terrible cough that went on for months, racking his skinny little body, and he would wake up sweating like a horse at the end of a furrow's ploughing. Pop paid for a doctor, but all he got for his money was a diagnosis – tuberculosis – a disease without a cure. God help me, but by the time Frank died I was heartily sick of it all. Pop and Ma worried themselves half to death, buying this poultice and that. Pop became all lethargic and it was left to me to say what as to be done that day, and then to do it. Ma snapped at everyone, and my four sisters and I learnt to spend most of our time anywhere else but the kitchen, where she worked with a stern set face producing nourishing soups and tasty puddings for a Frank who couldn't face them.

We buried him on Whit Sunday, May 13th, 1894. They tell me it's a corruption of White Sunday because it was the day people got baptised and wore white robes. To me it's white for the opposite reason; it's the day we buried my brother, who was so white by then you'd have said he was translucent. I got up early next day and did what I'd done for the last month, alone. Went round the lambing fields looking for trouble – a yow straining to get a reluctant lamb out, a half-starved lamb bleating for a mother who'd got up and left it. I was halfway round when Pop joined me, for the first time this lambing. He said nowt, just sucked on his empty pipe. Back in the house Ma was up and breakfast was on the table, hot, steamy porage followed by a fry-up. Even the lasses were up, and it not yet half-past six. It would be all right. Maybe not today, but it would be all right.

In another hour she'd be making breakfast for the visitors, booked in long ago and not to be turned away come hell or high water. Both were frequent neighbours at the top end of Borrowdale. Every Whitsuntide we had an influx of climbers, hearty men set on conquering Napes Needle or some crag on Scafell. They'd set out after a monster breakfast, hemp ropes around their shoulders, nailed boots striking sparks on the cobbled yard, and not be back till nearly dark, ravenous for supper forby Ma had put them up sandwiches enough for an army. Darwin Leighton and Braithwaite Andrews are the names I remember, perhaps because they formed the basis of the Fell and Rock Climbing Club that figured so large at Thorneythwaite a decade later. Visitors to the valley came in two types: these hardy pioneers – crag-rats we called them – and the others who hardly walked the fells at all, but took up 'stations' as they called them, where the views were 'picturesque'. They came by train and disgorged on Keswick platform either to walk to a guest house in town or to be transported in trap or carriage to the more select hotels. We didn't get any of these: Thorneythwaite was strictly for fell-walkers and climbers, who didn't mind the dining room in the old outshot that used to be the shed where everything we didn't need was put. Who didn't mind sleeping two or three in a bed, as long as it was cheap – for with seven of us plus Joseph Preston, our labourer, we were already a house full.

Not as full as the la'al cottage across the yard every Saturday and Sunday night though. Mr Marshall let it off to Matthew Pepper and his family, and there you are talking about a full house. Nine Peppers, including Alice's bastard son James, born when she was barely sixteen, plus three quarrymen every weekend who worked all week up at Honister. All the Pepper lads worked at Honister and lived in the bothies all week so the cottage was big enough for old Matthew and Hannah, Alice and James. They had some tales to tell – tales that made me glad to be a farmer, I don't mind telling you. They took to sitting in our kitchen of a Saturday night – after they'd spent most of their wages down at The Royal Oak in Rosthwaite. This was in the '90s, when the Buttermere Green Slate Company was working full stretch on both sides of the pass. Up on Fleetwith Pike they had seven different mines, nearly all connecting to the brand-new Bull Gill incline. John Pepper had been on the team constructing this tramway where the full tubs of dressed slate ran down the slope, pulling the empty tub back up. It was a hellish place to work, cutting into the rock of the crag exposed to all the elements, including that freak wind that sometimes blows at Honister – 'the crack'. John told how old Billy Rigg had been working there with his two lads when a gust had literally blown him off the crag face to his death far below, right in front of his sons, hanging on to the wire rope for dear life.

There were inclines everywhere now, bringing dressed slate down to the Hause, the top of the pass. One from Yew Crag, the fell opposite Fleetwith, one down a new incline from the original quarry and mine at Dubs, on the top of Fleetwith, and now one over Bull Gill. There were over a hundred men and boys working up there, most of them staying five nights a week in the various bothies. The fells both sides of the pass were like rabbit warrens with entrances, exits, connecting shafts and levels all over the place. Made the old wad mines look amateur – or so John said. Of course slate veins are many yards thick, and predictable because of it, so each mine is very big, whereas the wad just comes in quite small cylinders that seem to have been poured into holes way back whenever. One thing John couldn't argue with, though, is that dressed slate only fetches about £5 a ton, against 30 shillings a pound for graphite. Nevertheless, as the Honister mines expanded and invested, the wad mines were coming to the end.

Truth to tell, the wad mine had been in trouble for nigh on twenty years. Even in the legendary Billy Dixon's time – and he was a wad miner and gaffer of huge ability – the wad had been drying up, and he'd ended up being required by the company to sack the eight men still searching for new sops. A new board of directors poured money into the dying company in a desperate attempt to find a big deposit, but it was a waste of time, money and muscle, and on 16th June 1891 the company and the mines were officially wound up. I was fifteen at the time and I can remember a real feeling of mourning in the valley at the news. Not that we're a soft lot – anything but – but wad had somehow got under our skin. There was a pride in being the only place in the world where such quality graphite existed, as if Borrowdale had been marked out by God as a special place. Then there were the stories, the legends; of Moses Rigg and his trod and whisky still; of Black Sal from Rosthwaite who scratted a few bits of wad from the spoil heaps to hide away in the walls of her cottage, only to have it all washed away in a flood. Black Sal was used to scare the kids to sleep, with tales of her end – torn apart by wolf-hounds at the foot of Thorneythwaite Fell. She gave me some bad dreams, I can tell you, living right beside where she died. In a quiet way we loved the notoriety wad brought, the air of mystery, the tourists who came to gape and to gasp at the awesome holes the miners disappeared into each morning. And then of course there were the various pencil factories in Keswick, an ongoing reminder of a once great industry. The tourists still came to visit them and to buy fine cedarwood pencils, but now the lead in them came from Korea, Ceylon and Mexico.

We transferred our pride into our slate. Well, officially it was Buttermere slate, but don't try telling that to a Borrowdale man in the Royal Oak after nine o'clock at night. The road it used to get to the outside world – to the roofs of the Houses of Parliament and half of London Town – came down Borrowdale to the railway at Keswick. Cart after cart for eight long miles, and the first mile so steep you could hardly hold it back, down the side of the beck above Seatoller. It was well into the new century, 1907, before they got their new road built, sweeping down the shoulders of Scawdel before curving back on itself to come into Seatoller through a fine set of high gate posterns, with a stout gate barring entrance to anything but mine traffic, or anyone prepared to pay the hefty toll Mrs Byrd collected. Mainly from the tourist carriages, whose passengers would rather pay a mite more than be obliged to walk up the 1 in 4 mountain-side of the old road. Along with the new road came a monstrous, snorting beast of a machine, a steam traction engine weighing ten tons that could pull two eight ton trailers of slate to Keswick and negotiate this new road. Joe Milbourne was as proud as Mr Punch, sitting up high steering the brute. Carting was a thing of the past.

Not only the road but also most of the miners abode in Borrowdale, and the stock of housing was expanding to meet their needs. At the end of our lane, where it joins the road up to Seatoller, Lord Leconfield granted permission for a terrace of four new houses, to be called Leconfield Terrace, naturally, and held on lease to Leconfield. The good Lord did none of the work at Honister, faced none of the hardships, none of the insecurity, none of the financial traps and snares that bankrupted more than one company at Honister; but made money in good times and in bad, taking his rent, his dividend, his cut – all because he's Lord of the Manor. We've never had much time for Lords of the Manor in this valley, ever since the Lawson days. £700 that first row cost, and as soon as it was built there was need for a neighbouring row, so many were the miners at Honister Hause, miners with families, demanding family homes. We got our own back, in our own little way, on the Lord. It might have been officially Leconfield Terrace, but it was Mountain View to us, right from the start, 1894 to be precise.

In 1910 I was 35, Sarah Jane 37 and Percy (yes, I know it's a silly name for a girl) was 25, Edith 22, and we were still all single. Only

149

Ethel had taken the plunge, and it was looking like I was going to follow old Daniel and John, the last Jopsons at Thorneythwaite, and die with no-one to leave the tenancy to. Partly it was work: I'd always loved the work and only rarely gone out, down to the pub or the whist drives and dances held in the new Village Hall – the Institute – in Rosthwaite. And Pop was 67 now, too old for gathering Glaramara, too old for clipping, but not too old to tell me how things should be done. Nevertheless, it was at just such an event in the Institute, Harvest Supper in October, that I first met Hughina MacLeod. She was a servant at the Vicarage for the Reverend John Ashworth, our new vicar, and obliged to wait on for us farmers. I can't say she was a great beauty, but something about her caught my eye, or perhaps my ear, for she had the most intriguing Scots accent, and it was that which broke the ice.

After the meal the tables were set aside for dancing, something I've never been much good at. I stood by the dado, uncomfortable, itchy in my Herdwick suit, with a pint glass in my hand, largely drained, wondering whether to get another or to call it a day and walk off home. Hughina appeared before me, asking demurely if she should take my glass to the barrel or the sink, and it was something about that intuition of my mood that sparked my interest. Small talk is purgatory for me, but I managed to enquire about her accent, and was rewarded by a lively account of the town of Nairn, on the north coast of Aberdeenshire, and her family of twelve. There's nothing better for a tongue-tied man than a talkative woman, filling in the gaps for him, teasing the yarn from his tangled skein. She learnt about Thorneythwaite, the subject dearest to my heart, and I pointed out my sisters, capering on the floor. By the time the vicar gently asked whether she'd given up work for the evening I felt she knew me better than most of the lasses I'd grown up among.

I'll not bore you with the details of our courtship, which in truth was more her courtship, clod that I am. Suffice it to say that nine months later we were wed at St. Andrews Church, a beautiful day, June 14th, 1911. We held the reception at Thorneythwaite – where else – and Ma put on the best of spreads for the twenty-nine of us present. My only regret was that my sister Ethel, now Mrs. Skedge, living in America, couldn't be with us. Two of Hughina's brothers, Alec and John, and her sister Bella, who was her bridesmaid, made the long trip down from Nairn – twelve hours on trains.

150

*Fisher Jopson & Hughina McLean's wedding day, June 14th 1911.
Reception at Thorneythwaite, (Photo courtesy of their grand-daughters,
Ina Monkhouse, Vera Harris and Ethel Chapman).*

Back row: Bill Nuttall, Jack Cockbain, May Allison, Mr & Mrs Singleton,
Tom Jackson, Tom Allison
Next row:Tom Bird, Ernest Plaskett, Dinah Birkett, Fisher Jopson
(groom), John McLean, Annie Jackson, Daniel Jopson, ?
Next row: Edith Nuttall, Alec McLean, Bella McLean, Hughina Jopson
(bride), Jane Jopson, Robert Jopson, ?.
Front row: Edith Jopson, Alice Bainbridge, Sally Jopson, Percy Jopson,

Chapter twenty-eight

John Fisher Jopson (1876 – 1969): Part two 1911 – 1947

Marrying changed everything at Thorneythwaite. Till that day Pop was the boss and I was the lad. He was 68 and I was 36: suddenly I was a man. A man in a houseful of women, with Hughina added to the 'three sisters' as they were known, and of course Ma. We were outnumbered, Pop and me, and it didn't help that our first born was a girl: Margaret, born in lambing time, late April 1912. I thanked God when the next was a boy, born in 1914, and named him Frank after my ill-fated brother. Maybe I should have known better. The other two girls came regular as clockwork, Vera in 1916 and Ethel in 1918. Three males versus eight females: we didn't stand a chance.

It's a terrible thing to say, but those years of the Great War, when our children were being born, were the best years for farming in a long while. Suddenly the nation needed what we produced, and were prepared to pay for it. News filtered back to Keswick and the valley about the fate of all those 'Keswick Pals' who'd looked so brave and ready for the fight as they caught the train 'en masse' to join up in 1914, and it was news to freeze your blood. Forty men went from the valley to fight, ten were killed and many others wounded. We have more than our fair share of memorials to them, at Stonethwaite, at Grange, atop of Castle Crag, and a plaque on the top of Great Gable to all the members of the Fell and Rock Climbing Club who gave their lives.

Thorneythwaite has a special relationship with this club, for they chose our farm as their Borrowdale headquarters at their inaugural meeting here in 1907. Pop and Ma. made them very welcome, and every Whitsuntide they descended upon us like a secular version of the Keswick Convention. We had climbers and walkers sleeping everywhere. Out in the old cottage, in the barns, in caravans and tents in the garth behind the little barn – they got everywhere, and at five bob a head per night we were glad to have them. Ma and the three sisters produced food and sandwiches with factory precision, and as soon as we were married Hughina joined in doing her share. The rest of the summer was less manic, but we generally had a few Bed and Breakfasters in, though we were short of bedrooms. The farmhouse at that time was a longhouse with an outshot the full length of the back, containing two pantries and the stairwell, and a visitors' downstairs bedroom. Their dining room, I admit, was rather primitive, being the old wash-house outshot to the end wall. Outside was the pump for all our water.

Outside the war years, both before and after, as the Depression of the Twenties bit deep, visitors were a mainstay of Thorneythwaite and most of the other farms in the valley. Some folk came in cars, but most came by train to Keswick then by Willie Agnew's horse coach, and later in Jack Pepper's bus. We certainly had the woman-power to see them well-provided for, and with all those mouths to feed we needed the extra income. Man-power was a bit harder to come by, though the lasses certainly played their part on the farm. For heavier work, now Pop was past it, I had Tom Bird who lived at Mountain View as farm labourer, and things were getting easier and more mechanised. We had two grand horses, Peggy and Jewel, and a load of hay-making gear they could pull – a mowing machine, a tedder and a big old hay rake. These all drove from the wheels turning, so if you went too slowly the mower didn't cut and the tedder didn't ted. It took a while for Tom to get the hang of it. Peggy got her name from her rather withered front inside leg, but it never stopped her working.

Hay time was always a fraught time for me, though everyone else seemed to enjoy it. They got the sunny days, raking, piking, smelling the sweet crop, with a good break for sandwiches and a flask of tea lying in the dry meadow grass, with the bees humming overhead (and the cleggs biting down below). I got the threat of rain, or the reality of it, the crop going mouldy before my eyes and nothing I could do about it. Still, we generally got the barn full of a good enough crop to see us through the winter.

We never fed the sheep in winter. Every farmer knew that if they once got the idea you'd let them in the fell gate and feed them you'd never get them to stay out on the fell again, and they'd just sit around the gate till they starved. How the hell they did survive on that frozen, North-facing fell always amazed me, but we'd never have had enough fodder to feed them. We needed all we could make for the cattle. We milked maybe half a dozen cows just for our own use and to sell to the lodging houses and miners in Seatoller and Mountain View. Milking and selling were Sally's jobs, and she was good at it. The rest, nigh on twenty cows, were sucklers with calves that we took on to about a year before selling them at Cockermouth Mart. The government started a Milk Marketing Board in 1933, but it never seemed worthwhile to gear up to their standards.

And besides, by then it was clear Frank would never be able to take over from me, so why make life difficult? By the time he was in his teens Hughina and I had to admit to ourselves there was something not right about Frank. Even from a baby he was withdrawn, inward-looking as you might say. He was slow to learn to speak, and when he did it was always somehow off-key. He would never look you straight in the eye –

shifty, I called him, God forgive me. He was nineteen when the dam inside his head really burst. We had been gathering the fell that day, a rare hot day, and Frank ran off to take a dip in Nichol Dub, as he often did. He came back shivering, quivering all over, and babbling strange words, some recognisable but unconnected, some just animal sounds. He was … agitated, I suppose you would say, but it was worse than that.

Slowly we understood what he was trying to tell us, though it made no sense even when we did. He was frightened, terrified more, by voices all around him, inside his head, voices telling him he was guilty, guilty, guilty. "Guilty of what, love?" asked Hughina gently. He looked at her: no, he looked right through her. He wasn't seeing his mother, but some devils of his own creation. Frightened, we did look at each other – helplessly. Infinitely gently Hughina persuaded him into the house, and then up to his bedroom and into bed. Next day we sent for the doctor – who had very little more idea of what was wrong then we did.

And so it started, and so it carried on. Doctors, specialists, then psychiatrists, and all costing money. A lot of money when it got to the psychiatrists. And a lot of the time Frank was fine; well, not that fine, but functioning. Then he would have another 'episode'. We were learning the jargon by now. Call it an episode and it doesn't sound as frightening. But you couldn't call it a fit. Fits are what epileptics have, and Frank didn't have epilepsy. Schizophrenia, that's what the experts decided Frank had. Even the word frightened Hughina and me. Schizophrenics murdered people, didn't they?

Only in very rare cases, we were assured, and reassured. And there were treatments, expensive treatments to be sure, but just once with Frank in one of his 'episodes' and you'd pay anything to bring him relief. And us. He had it all, poor son of mine. They pumped him full of insulin till he passed out into a coma I thought he'd never recover from, then pumped him full of sugar till he did. They tried their new-fangled electric shock treatment on him. We weren't allowed to watch, thank God, but inevitably we heard how the shocked body writhes and jerks as the shock hits the brain. All this on my only boy, my heir, my successor who could never be. Frank's schizophrenia slowly sucked the life out of us all, just as the world slid headlong into another war. We drew the line at a lobotomy. They were going to cut into his head and take out a bit of his brain, but Hughina refused point-blank.

I'm sorry, that's a very bleak picture, and of course there were some bleak times. But we had three lovely daughters too, daughters who brought joy as they married, married as Frank never could. Margaret was the first, as was fitting for our eldest. Hughina had been tutting for some time about the state of the house, and how it wasn't really fit for the Bed

154

and Breakfast trade as it was in 1936. "People expect more nowadays, Fisher" she'd say, time and again. "Why, even the Fell and Rock lads and lasses are beginning to turn their noses up at the state of our dining room and the bedrooms. We haven't the space to do the job properly. You must talk to Mr Walker."

Mr Walker was the landlord. Thorneythwaite went through a mort of landlords over the last century. There was Abraham Fisher first off, back in 1833, and when he died his partner Fisher Crosthwaite sold it to Mr Marshall. Then on to Mr Musgrave at the end of the 1800s, and then finally to William Walker, our landlord, who bought it along with High Lodore in 1925. One family living here, seeing off four landlords. William Walker had made his fortune running a tannery in Millom, and Hughina reckoned he was a shrewd enough business-man to recognise the need for investment in his property. No doubt the rent would go up to compensate him, but so would our income, and with Frank to support we needed to make more.

I wasn't confident, as we sat in his estate office at Lowther, uncomfortable in my best suit, with Hughina starchy beside me, waiting to be called in. Hughina did the talking, after all it was a house extension we wanted, her business really. She'd never lost that soft Aberdeen burr on her voice, and she had the figures to hand to back up her case. She wanted to put a complete second storey on top of the outshot that ran the length of the house. "It would give us two more letting bedrooms, Mr Walker, and a bathroom and inside privy. People expect that sort of thing, these days. Without them I really don't think we can go on taking the visitors, and for sure without them we'll never afford the rent."

Of course, at the end it came down to a compromise. Mr Walker would pay three-quarters of the cost of the extension, and we would pay a quarter. And the rent would go up. Significantly. I knew there was no point in arguing, either with Mr Walker or with my wife, so we shook hands on the deal there and then, and left with me wondering where the hell we would find that sort of money on top of what it was costing for Frank.

And that's where our first wedding comes in. Margaret was twenty-four when the builders started on the big extension, ripping off the slates on the outshot, exposing the stairs, the pantries and the downstairs bedroom to the stars and the rain. Among them was Robert Taylor, just turned thirty. Hughina spotted it first, of course, when Margaret kept volunteering to take the builders their tea, and seemed to spend a long time gossiping with them – well, with one in particular. Hughina was right about the extension, it's fairly made the house as a B & B. She was right about Margaret as well. They got the new roof on by the end of August,

1937, and by October Margaret and Robert were wed, and Margaret left us to live in Threlkeld.

You'll have heard enough of my story, I dare say. The war didn't stop the other lasses marrying: Ethel married John Ramsey in 1943, and Vera married George Dixon in 1944. Of course both lads were involved in the war effort, but thankfully as technicians here in England. Hughina and I battled on for a year or two, but with the lasses gone and Frank in Garlands, the mental hospital near Carlisle, the heart had gone out of the place, even if they did bring the grand-children often. By 1946 I was sixty-nine, Hughina sixty, and we knew it was time to go. We had to give a year's notice, which turned out to be a bit of a disaster, as we left on Lady Day 1947 – at the end of the worst winter for snow Borrowdale had known in living memory. I'll not dwell on the state of the sheep, or the money we had to pay for the shortfall in the landlord's stock.

Codicil.

Copy of an Article in Fell & Rock Climbing Club Journal, 1947 by W.G.Pape

When the Jopson family left, and Thorneythwaite ceased to be the Borrowdale Headquarters of the Club, a long and happy association came to an end. It is the passing of the place, as well as the people, from the life of the Club which makes the break more felt. It is difficult to write adequately of the place of Thorneythwaite in Club history, but I must attempt the task.

Thorneythwaite Farm had housed the climber even before the foundation of the F&RCC; Darwin Leighton, Braithwaite Andrews, Thompson and others of the 'ancients' stayed there in pre-Club days.

Old Mr Jopson and his wife entertained the climbers from 1901 to 1923, the Misses Percy and Sally Jopson then took over the hospitality till 1927, and Mrs Fisher Jopson continued in a manner that cannot be equalled up to this year; you have, therefore, an unbroken record of 45 years of unsurpassed hospitality.

Why then should the tradition of Whitsuntide at Thorneythwaite be broken? Our regrets at losing Thorneythwaite must be modified by our sympathy for Mr & Mrs Jopson. The work of running the place fell more heavily upon them when their daughters married, left home, and when in due course, new family members appeared. Finally, ill-health added its troubles, and the burden became too great. Who shall say then, that their retirement had not been earned many times over by a lifetime of kindly hospitality? I understand that they are living in Threlkeld but have learnt with regret that Mrs Jopson has been in Keswick Hospital from shortly after leaving Thorneythwaite up to the present time. May she soon be restored to health, and may she and Mr Jopson enjoy many years at Threlkeld!

Change is so often sad; but memory offers comfort, and there are so many memories tied up with Thorneythwaite – personal memories and Club memories. So let us make memory hold the door for a while.

Thorneythwaite was known as "The F. & R. Club headquarters" in 1908, when the first recorded meet was held there in August, the tariff was five shillings per day.

The accommodation then was about half what it is today. The kitchen was where the dairy is now, some fed in the kitchen, and the conditions were truly rural.

Old Mr Jopson was a strict Sabbatarian and flatly refused to have his photograph taken on a Sunday, and turned his broad and uncompromising back on the camera.

Misses Jopson added a feminine touch by changing round the dining room to the back of the sitting room and reorganising the bedrooms; the present dining room was then a bedroom.

With most commendable enterprise, Mrs Fisher Jopson changed the layout of the farm again, and added all the present amenities, and Thorneythwaite can now justly claim a high standard of accommodation.

The charm of the place has to be seen and experienced to be really understood; in all the moods and conditions of weather, winter and summer alike, it has an atmosphere all its very own.

The old farmhouse and its outbuildings are uniquely situated in such a delightful setting among those giant trees and near the head of the loveliest dale in all Lakeland; the river Derwent winds its way through the meadows close to the farm and the multi-coloured stones (peculiar to Borrowdale) glisten in crystal-clear waters.

And what can one say of that most superb bathing pool just across the field? Can one ever forget those before-breakfast dips, or that exquisite "peace with all the world" feeling after the evening bathe; epilogue to a hot and exhausting day on the crags?

Did I say "Memory hold the door"? Surely it rather throws it wide open when the magic word of Thorneythwaite is mentioned. The campers, the caravanners, the sleepers-out, the members from Seathwaite, Seatoller, Rosthwaite, and of course the inmates of the farm all crowd into the sitting-room or squat on the stones outside, for those never-to-be-forgotten sing-songs; this memory is certainly peculiar to Thorneythwaite and is perhaps the most popular.

And the sitting-room with its 1822 fireplace, its wood fire and low ceiling, its suffocating tobacco smoke and the oil lamp on the table. What memories!

Those three magic words "do you remember" come into their own in any talk of Thorneythwaite and they bring back a thousand happenings, all memorable in their own way, but mostly personal and, therefore, difficult to mention separately.

Yet, do you remember the green covered wagon with the piebald horse which later grew into a palatial motor caravan always in its place by the stream and the caravan which housed the rowdy 'Hullaballoes' from Hull (what a pun)?

Do you remember the campers in the close behind the barn, and in the meadows? Do you remember that night when the rain descended and the floods came and washed the lot completely out to seek refuge in the barns and hayloft? No matter what one's memories are, whether of friends or visitors, of climbs or days on the fells, of the beauty and quiet of the place, (save only the persistent cuckoo) THORNEYTHWAITE, THE JOPSONS, and WHITSUNTIDE are synonymous and have become a tradition of the Club.

Undoubtedly there is sadness in the fact that it is no longer our Whitsun meeting place, and yet:

> "How at their mention memory turns
> her pages old and pleasant"

The Club owes an unpayable debt to Thorneythwaite Farm, and to the Jopsons for that matter, because so many friendships born of the mountains and in the mountains began there; so many members found their love of the hills and the crags there, and so many happy memories on which we continually feast come from there. I cannot do better than quote from Mrs Jopson's letter to me which serves to cement that happy relationship between the Club and Thorneythwaite:

> "I am truly sorry to give the Club up. It was always a great pleasure to see you all at Whitsuntide."

To stand at the gate on the track to Seathwaite and to look up the dale towards Great End is;

> *"To hold converse with Nature's charm,*
> *And view her scrolls unrolled".*

John Fisher Jopson. (Courtesy of his grand-daughters)

Chapter twenty-nine

Betty Hall, 1975.

Betty Hall fired up the little grey Fergie she'd always loved. Fired it up for the last time, to lay out all the implements in long lines in the field behind the sheep sheds they'd built just a dozen years ago. Neat lines of all they owned, ready for the auction sale on Saturday. They were leaving Thorneythwaite, just fifteen years to the day since they'd come, full of hope and promise, full of energy and drive – full of life. They shouldn't be leaving yet; she was just fifty-five, Jim sixty, or at least they would be later that year. And yet they couldn't stay. Without Ian it was just too hard, too pointless, even. It wasn't possible for the two of them to gather the fell properly, especially as she still didn't have a decent dog. They had to go twice or even three times to be sure of getting most of the sheep, and every time Glaramara seemed to have grown another fifty feet higher.

She remembered Ian's excitement when he was offered a place at Oxford, to read Maths, and of course she'd been fiercely proud of him, and glad for the opportunities it would open up for him. But for her and Jim it was almost a prison sentence. Solitary confinement and hard labour till old age caught up with them. She thought back on all the other families she knew of who had, for one reason or another, run out of sons to hand the tenancy on to. Stan Edmondson, next door at Seathwaite, was born and bred there and had satisfied her curiosity about those who'd farmed here before. When she thought of the last two families Ian's reasons for leaving seemed positively benign. Poor Fisher Jopson, with three strapping daughters but an only son disabled by schizophrenia; she shuddered at the thought. Then Billy and Ethel Dixon, who'd come after the Jopsons in 1947 and stayed thirteen years till she and Jim had taken the spot on in 1960. Their only son, Ralph, was simple in the head, poor lad, and quite unable to take over or even to help much, and had ended up in Garlands Mental Hospital outside Carlisle. Why, even Fisher Jopson had lost his only brother to TB, or so she'd been told. Thorneythwaite didn't have a very good track record for sons, when you looked at it. She was grateful Ian had left for the opposite reason.

She and Jim, they really were the first tenants not born to the place, in a sense. Jopsons went back centuries in Borrowdale, and Ethel Dixon was about as local as you could get; one of the Pepper family who had probably come for the mines long ago, and were still working up at Honister. Stan said Ethel's husband Billy was a Braithwaite lad, so again

160

as local as graphite. In their early years Billy, Ethel and Ralph had slept in a wooden hut that still stood in Lamb Close all Summer long, to free up all the farmhouse bedrooms for visitors. Betty had a shrewd suspicion Bed and Breakfast visitors were the only thing that had kept the farm solvent for the Dixons. For sure it wasn't possible to make a decent living just on four hundred odd Herdwick ewes and a small suckler herd, which was all the land could support, even in these days of bagged fertiliser.

Not that they needed a lot of fertilizer: one thing about the battery hen houses was the amount of hen-shit they produced, very strong in nitrogen and ammonia. So strong Jim had to be sparing when he spread it, or a huge crop of chick-weed would grow and be impossible to dry into hay. The hens were their lifeline, because self-catering didn't bring in anything like as much as B & B would, but she was damned if she was going to be a slave to the Aga as Ethel must have been. Coming back to Ethel Dixon in her circular brain, she mused how Ethel had similarly looked after her mother as she grew old – just as Betty had looked after Jim's mother Lizzie. Which brought her full circle back to the sons. Every generation, it seemed, faced the same problems, and never found an answer, but to muddle through. Fisher and Hughina had survived thirty-six years of married life there, Ethel and Billy just thirteen years, she and Jim fifteen. All had left for the same reason: no-one to take it on, no-one to help when the fell got too steep.

"Ach, Betty, snap out of it woman" she muttered savagely to herself. "Your boy has done well, and he's married the girl you wanted for him – and how many do that? And you're a grandmother, twice over very soon. You've done your job, and done it well." Grandmother twice over – oh Gawd, as she always said. Makes you feel so old, and yet not old enough not to work. What would they do, Jim and her? There was one bright spot on the horizon, and that totally unexpected. She had been pretty well estranged from her own father ever since her mother ended her own life – at fifty-five, by malign coincidence. Actually, she'd been estranged from him almost since birth, when her mother had frequently sent her packing to her own grandparents or her aunt to keep her from his influence. So she wasn't expecting an inheritance, and nor did she get one, directly. As soon as her mother had taken her own life, her father Harry had moved in next door with a girl the same age as his daughter, who had been orphaned and inherited her parents' house. Harry's savings from his own house were squirreled away, and when he had died late last year had, quite rightly, been left to Edna – his 'housekeeper'.

That would have been that, had Edna herself not died within the month. At fifty-five. The letter from the Bristol solicitor came…unsolicited, she giggled. And added 'if Edna edn'a died' for good

161

measure. In the law's eyes, so the letter said, if a legatee dies within a month of the legator's death the bequest is null and void, and belongs to the next of kin. Or in plain English, Harry's carefully kept cache was hers. He would have been furious, which made it all the sweeter. It wasn't a fortune, not even a small fortune, but it was just enough to buy a run-down cottage with an acre of land only a mile from Ian and Jen and the grand-children. But they would still need to work, and what sort of work would there be for a sixty-year-old ex-farmer?

Jennifer and her cousin Geoff helping out.

Leaving Thorneythwaite was bitter-sweet, right through to the end: perhaps more bitter than sweet. The looked-for sale day came, and she found she could hardly face it. All day long she skulked in the kitchen, young Jennifer, heavily pregnant, her only company along with her grand-daughter, Catherine, busily licking out the bowls where she had whipped up egg mayonnaise as they turned out plate after plate of sandwiches for the assembled farmers and dealers poring over the tarnished treasures of fifteen years of farming. Muttered phrases filtered through the open window, as a pair of gnarled old men sifted through the boxes of small tools and bric-a-brac. "What a load of old tat!" "Bloody hell, some of this stuff must have come off the ark." Betty bristled, as Jen laid a pacifying hand on her arm. Hopefully the machinery and implements – and the Grey Fergie – would fare better, for there was little else in the bank after buying the cottage.

As it was, most of their most expensive purchases found few bidders. The banks of battery cages for the hens that had been their mainstay were far too specialised for the local farmers. And she and Jim had spent weeks painstakingly dismantling them for ease of sale – to no avail. The usual scrap-metal merchants who haunted farm sales on the lookout for a bargain snapped them all up for coppers. The almost new sheep spraying set-up that they had had to buy once Ian was no longer available for the thrice-yearly dipping only made a tenth of what it had cost them so recently. Even her beloved tractor made far less than it might have in another sale. Normally neighbours can be relied on to run bids on a bit, to give a good send-off. In her bitterness Betty felt let down, by the auctioneer, by the neighbours, by the landlord, and yes, let's face it, by her son.

Why couldn't Ian and Jen have joined them at Thorneythwaite, taken over the traces? He loved farming, she knew that well, and Jen loved animals and would surely have fitted in well. Gawd, they'd known her long enough, she'd been coming up to the farm most of her life. As the day wore on Betty sank deeper and deeper into gloom. She had no idea how Jim was faring, out there alongside the auctioneer, being helpful to the parasites who were picking over their life's work, and scoffing sandwiches as if they hadn't eaten since the last farm sale.

A couple of days later her bitterness found a target, a legitimate target it could fasten on to. A target that could be spoken of. Their relationship with William Walker, the landlord, had never been good since he'd so abruptly stopped their small camping income. When they had put up first the silage clamp then later the large roofed sheep housing, which came to a huge area some twenty yards square, Mr Walker had agreed that if they left they would be recompensed at an independent valuation, since they had borne the whole cost of construction. Now that the moment had come his agent argued that they owed as much in what he called 'dilapidations' as was owed to them for the building. Pressed as to what these dilapidations might be, by a very proud Jim, he pointed to the fell wall above Jenny Banks, a fell wall in a very dilapidated condition. In vain Jim argued that the wall had been in that state when they came, fifteen years ago. He was unable to prove it, and the agent was adamant. No recompense for the building work would be forthcoming.

Perhaps it would have been better to have sought legal advice, but legal advice isn't cheap. And maybe, just maybe, it was actually better to have a legitimate target.

Jim and Betty, 1975

Chapter thirty

The Bland family:

Stuart and Shirley, 1975-2010
Jon and Joanne, 2010-2016

Stuart Bland was a bit surprised to win the tenancy of Thorneythwaite when Jim and Betty gave in their notice. There was some strong competition from other sons of valley farmers, and while Stuart had those credentials he had been a quarryman at Honister for seven of the last fourteen years and working on various construction sites since then. But farming was in his blood. His grandfather Willie Bland came into the valley from Kinniside, over Ennerdale way, taking on Nook Farm in Rosthwaite back in the 1920s. Willie moved about a few times before settling and starting the Borrowdale dynasty. Born in Patterdale in 1883, where his father James and mother Esther had farmed from the mid-1870s, he and the family took on Brotherilkeld Farm, Eskdale, the noted Herdwick valley-head stronghold in 1890. I don't suppose the seven-year-old Willie had much choice in the matter, but what a place to grow up and learn about Herdwick sheep. Brotherilkeld is an ancient Furness Abbey sheepwalk dating back to the 12th Century.

Itchy footed James didn't stay long at Brotherilkeld, moving to Scar Green in Ponsonby parish, Calder Bridge, at the end of the century, taking the teenager Willie and his seven brothers and sisters with him. Ten years later, with a wife of his own, Elizabeth, and three children, Willie was at Kinniside. By the time they were at Nook Farm the family had swelled to seven; the brothers James, John, William, Joe, Nathan and Noble, and Esther their sister. Such flitting was common-place at the end of the 19th and beginning of the 20th centuries. Agriculture was struggling, with many farms empty for years. Indeed, only the Great War years brought any wealth at all for farmers, and when they were over agriculture suffered with the rest of the nation in the Depression of the 20s and 30s. This was a time when the National Trust, spear-headed by the redoubtable Beatrix Potter (now Mrs Heelis), was able to buy up many a valley farm. Nook Farm was one such, and they were glad to take on Willie as tenant.

In the way of these things Willie's children married, and mostly flew the Nook. James to Stonethwaite where he married Mary Birkett Brown, and later to Watendlath. John married Mary Richardson and worked with her father at High Lodore. Joe married Lily Stuart, from neighbouring Cragg Cottage, in 1943 but didn't fly away. Nathan never married, and he and Joe farmed Nook Farm together for the rest of their lives. Their brother Noble married Amy Sawer in 1936 and took the tenancy of Seatoller Farm. By the time young William the other brother, had married his Mary and taken on Croft Farm, in Stonethwaite, the valley was as full of Blands as it had once been of Jopsons. Most of them married to a Mary. If all their children had been the same age they would have filled Borrowdale School unaided.

Stuart was the second of Joe and Lily's four children, two years younger than Kathleen, two years older than Billy, who in his turn was two years older than David. As first-born son he might well have had aspirations of inheritance – but that would be years away. In the meantime Joe and his brother Nathan were well able to run Nook Farm on their own, once Stuart needed paying for his services. Until that time he was, very willingly, at their beck and call. Likewise at his uncle Noble's command. Stuart would be working away on some wall gap – a bit like painting the Forth Bridge – when he'd see Noble in his old mac homing in on him. He knew what was coming. "Is t'a busy?" There was only one acceptable answer, "Nut varra, what's t'a want?" So with a shrug he'd accept the lift up to Seatoller for whatever job Noble needed doing. Later he'd walk back to Rosthwaite.

In September, 1956, the eleven-year-old Stuart boarded Furness's bus for the first of many rides to his new school – the recently opened Lairthwaite Secondary School in Keswick. As the new boys and girls were lined up along the long corridor to be led off to their various classes, he spied Shirley Waters, daughter of the aptly named plumber in Braithwaite, and made himself the promise "I'll marry thee yan day, lass." He did, both aged just twenty-one, and they started married life in a little cottage in Braithwaite. Their daughter Sam was born in 1971, son Jon in 1972. In 1973 they might well have been father-less.

These were the seven years young Stuart worked at Honister mine, quarrying the slate. Dangerous work, with each man looking out for himself and for his workmates. For a time he was a 'rock man', cleaving huge lumps of slate from the overhanging roof. This meant being at the top of maybe a triple-extended ladder, some thirty feet above the floor of the cavern they were hollowing out, working with a compressed air drill to sink a three foot deep hole in the cracked ceiling of raw slate. At any time the huge clog might detach and crash down on man and ladder – certain injury and probable death. To check for any movement the rock man puts a match in the crack and keeps a very wary eye on it while he drills. Any tremor on the match and he's down that ladder like a ferret down a rabbit hole. No tremor, then the next job is to pack the drilled hole with gunpowder, insert a long fuse – long enough to give you time to get down the ladder, move it out of the way, and clear the area. Say five feet.

The bang reverberates around the cavern like a hundred Niagaras, slowly dying away as your hearing returns to normal, mingling with the mighty thump as a clog of slate weighing up to three tons hits the deck. It has to be broken up into manageable pieces, each loaded on a bogie to be railroaded out of the mine and down to Honister Hause for cutting and riving into usable slates. It was this second stage that almost did for Stuart. The incline in the mine is gentle, and the bogie easily slowed by the brakeman walking behind. Stuart, perhaps a bit young and foolish, wrapped the brake chain round his wrist, the better to control the descent. At the mouth of the mine the rail line splits into two directions, controlled by points. Coming down far too fast, as young men will, at the last moment he noticed the points were set wrongly. Feverishly he unwound the chain from his wrist as the bogie careered towards the edge of the waste drop, parting from it as it disappeared into the void. This glimpse into that void stayed with him all his life, reminding him how fragile is our hold, and how inevitable our death.

So this was the excited family that took over Thorneythwaite on Lady Day, 1975. Stuart, Shirley, the three-year-old tomboy Sam, and her two-year-old brother Jon. Kids even younger than Ian had been a generation earlier, but destined to stay a lot longer. That first Summer Shirley thought herself in heaven, as the sun shone, the hay dried visibly, and she and her bairns spent a part of each day down by the little beck below the farm. The next year, the even better Summer of 1976, confirmed her first impressions: this really was heaven. The dependable sun rose as if this were Spain, clipping and hay time were a delight, and the visitors flocked in to her newly refurbished Bed and Breakfast. If she ever forgot to nip down to the end of the lane and clip on the 'No Vacancies' sign she found herself besieged by disappointed potential customers. With four letting bedrooms (and a dedicated visitor bathroom) she was soon making more money than Stuart could generate from the Herdwicks and the small herd of suckler cows he bought in. These were hard days for farming; the early days of the Common Market when French lamb, Danish bacon and the continental milk lake had free access, and national subsidies were verboten. They were very good days for tourism and B&B in particular.

Bed and Breakfast guests made having a house cow a worthwhile project, and how they loved the taste of full fat milk, straight from the cow. Granted, she needed milking but anything to add value to the income generated by the visitors was very welcome. With a slightly wry smile Shirley named the cow Betty, after her predecessor as queen of the kitchen, and unwittingly copied her hand milking each morning, head

167

tucked into Betty's flank, drawing off a few pints for that day's use.Though she was unaware of it, the human Betty had started her farming life in West Cumberland helping Jim milk their herd of Ayrshires, at first by hand.

Stuart found his life seemed to run in seven-year cycles, and those first seven years at Thorneythwaite were poorly recompensed. Seven years he persisted with the suckler herd, till he had to admit that both there was nothing in them financially and that they took far too much of the hard-won winter fodder. The year that they went down the road his fortunes changed, very much for the better. It was a combination of skill, timing and luck that brought the change. His skill was in shepherding, and in his inborn knowledge of how to treat a Herdwick sheep. Where Jim had begrudged the cost of wintering the young females – the gimmer hoggs – away from home and had kept them inside on hay and barley, Stuart had family access to good wintering out near Moresby and knew well the benefits of strong, well-grown hoggs returning ready to face the summer on Glaramara. Seven years of his skilful breeding produced a flock to be proud of, and wethers which fared well in Cockermouth auction mart.

Timing and luck are harder to pin down, but seven years in there came a chance to expand, to buy thirty acres of mixed pasture and woodland just down the road in Rosthwaite. The family Trust that had inherited Hazel Bank when its last owner died offered these acres under the sealed bid system – you decide how much to bid, and all the bids are opened together and the vendor chooses his buyer, usually the highest offer. After many a night's discussion Stuart and Shirley rather forlornly sealed their best offer in an envelope and posted it, well aware it was, necessarily, below the general going rate for land in 1982. What they were unaware of was that the main trustee, John Hayton, was an old-fashioned gentleman with more interest in helping struggling youngsters than in mere money, and he persuaded his fellow trustees to take the lesser offer for the good of the valley and to make a small farm the more viable. (This Hazel Bank is the fine house where Hugh Walpole chose to base his fictional hero Rogue Herries.)

Stuart's second well-timed event, after those first, difficult seven years, was the invention of Big Bale Silage. In the early '80s a strange new sight erupted on the Lake District landscape each July. Every hayfield was cut one day, and instead of the usual four day desperate turning and tedding to get wet grass transformed into dry hay, ready for baling, the very next day the farmer would row it all up neatly and a contractor drive in with a shiny red machine and in an hour or so produce around ten cylinders of wrapped grass per acre, deftly tied up in string. By the end of the day just with the use of a spike on the back of the tractor the farmer had it transported home, each bale protected from the air by a large plastic bag. And there you have it, instant silage in handy half-ton bales, ready for feeding to the sheep all winter.

In perennially rain-drenched Borrowdale, in particular, this invention was heaven-sent, transforming both the misery of hayfields that drag on for weeks on end and the value of the forage collected. Not that Stuart made silage unless he had to: he preferred to mow all the fields at once if the forecast was good, trying to make the hay he reckoned sheep did best on – but with the back-up position that if it did rain he could revert to the big bales of silage. Instead of the age-old adage that Herdwicks should never be allowed off the fell in winter he and his neighbours could now allow them to drift in any time from January onwards, knowing they had enough good-quality fodder to see them through the winter. Preferring muscle to tractor, Stuart liked nothing better than to carry a handy bale of hay up to the intake to feed the grateful fell ewes. At the same time his newly-bought thirty acres allowed him to keep his older ewes which would normally have been sold for a pittance for an extra year, carrying a cross-bred lamb that really would be worth something in the autumn sales. His

169

good husbandry started to bring real returns, vying with the Bed & Breakfast.

The Hazel Bank land brought another opportunity Stuart and Shirley were quick to recognise. Just off the track up to Hazel Bank, as it starts on the old road over to Watendlath, stood an unusual building in these parts, a small barn for general use rejoicing in the name 'Dinah Hoggus'. Hoggus is dialect for Hogg House, a building for sheep to retire from the rain into. Dinah was its occupant nigh on a hundred years earlier: Dinah Youdale, one of the last of that once ubiquitous family. It cost a bit for materials – new doors, a decent ramp, a basic kitchen, some bunk beds, new pointing and a concrete floor – but by the next year Dinah Hoggus was established on the camping barn circuit and soon became well-known as a cheap and cheerful place to stay for a night or two. The Hazel Bank land was paying dividends twice over.

Dinah Hoggus Camping Barn

The Common Agricultural Policy meanwhile was dictating how farmers nation-wide ran their operations, with some bizarre and sometimes contradictory consequences. Farmers in productive parts of the country were paid a lot of money not to farm – to 'set aside' land – while in the valleys sheep farmers were paid 'headage' subsidies, a fixed amount per ewe kept. So the best land went to waste while the poorest land in the country, including Glaramara and Thorneythwaite Fell, was encouraged to carry far too many sheep, each one producing a generous annual subsidy. Big bale silage had arrived not a moment too soon, the guaranteed good

170

winter fodder allowing Stuart to keep more fell ewes than had ever been seen before on the fell, and in the intakes on silage in the winter.

Of course he wasn't alone in this: all over the Lake District the fells in summer were crowded with little Herdwicks nibbling everything in sight, and it wasn't long before various quangos (quasi-autonomous non-governmental organisations to give them their Sunday name) realised a delicate balance had tipped dangerously against the environment. Soon the smart European Union money was used in almost the opposite fashion, paying fell farmers not to over-stock their fells. In 1993 the Ministry of Agriculture, Fisheries and Food set up the 'Environmentally Sensitive Areas' (ESA) scheme with a remit to reverse the devastating effect too many sheep were having on the nation's fells. Borrowdale Commoners Association, the long recumbent successor to Sir Wilfrid Lawson's Manorial Court, suddenly had a purpose – as did all the other valleys' bodies. Farmers everywhere, but fell farmers in particular, will react badly to any big sticks waved in their direction, but dangle a big enough carrot and they will show an unexpected ability to cooperate with each other and with the carrot dangler.

Enough of this intricate detail: suffice it to say that fell farmers throughout the Lakes, including Stuart and Shirley at Thorneythwaite, began to become rich almost for the first time in history. They responded as farmers always have, renting more land and buying bigger and better machines and tractors – ploughing the profits back into the land. In all the valleys there were soon land-rovers with big trailers ferrying sheep; large, fast tractors with even bigger trailers ferrying silage and hay. Suddenly, for the first time ever, fell farmers were richer than their lowland neighbours, as European money skewed agriculture yet again, with myriad unintended consequences.

On 21st February, 2001, nature hit back. Stuart was at Cockermouth Auction Mart selling fat lambs when the news crackled round the ring faster than the fuses he used to set at Honister. Foot and Mouth disease had been discovered in an abattoir in Essex two days earlier, and now the government had banned the export of livestock and meat to the continent. Instantly, the price collapsed, and, along with many others, Stuart was obliged to pass his lambs out and take them home. Two days later even that wouldn't have been an option, as a ban on all movement from affected areas was introduced. A day later the slaughter began. It might be essential; a way of curbing the spread of the disease, but no-one but a farmer can truly understand the full horror of a complete cull of entire stocks. Out on the plains of Cumbria, as indeed all over England, the disease flared with spontaneous combustion, and every outbreak brought an orgy of killing in a three-mile radius, followed all too soon by the fires of hell, where huge bonfires of ex-railway sleepers were fed their fill of carcases, cattle hanging by a leg from the jaws of some insensate brute machine, sheep tipped on in the tractor front loader, and the stench of burning flesh permeating the countryside around.

In no time Stuart's hoggs in Moresby, his shearlings at Mockerkin, two years' worth of breeding sheep, were culled and burnt. Nothing could be brought home to Thorneythwaite, and Borrowdale, along with all the other valleys, held its breath, praying the disease might not spread to the fells, extinguishing the entire world stock of Herdwick sheep. Ministry vets partitioned the valley, and almost every farm was tested for the disease. Somehow, as it had in the days of the plague, the remoteness of the valleys protected the precious ewes on their stints, save for isolated outbreaks in the Duddon Valley, but it was late September before fell farmers felt they could breathe again, though knowing full well that so many of their cousins were broken men and women, trying to raise the energy and will to start again. Many couldn't.

The farmers weren't the only ones to suffer. Tourism in Borrowdale, as in all the valleys, suddenly hit the buffers. No-one came, and an eerie stillness not felt since the early years of the 20th Century paralysed business. No, that's not true – a hundred years before the valley rang to the sounds of enterprise. Honister mine employed over a hundred men and boys. Rigghead quarry, high above Rosthwaite and Quay Foot, beside the Bowder Stone, employed nearly as many again. Every farm had a man or two, for every job needed muscle power: salving sheep to keep the blowflies off, clipping by hand, mowing with a scythe, turning hay by fork and rake, piking, carting by horse – the list is endless. There were blacksmiths, cobblers, carters: a web of industry supporting the community. In 2001, apart from the farms, there was only one industry, tourism; and when its single strand snapped more than one business fell to earth. Across at Seatoller the Yew Tree Restaurant closed for good, and throughout the valley small guest houses and B & B's had to find alternative income for an entire season. Even the mighty YHA countrywide had losses so big they were forced to close down some of their properties.

All things pass, and slowly the valleys and farms resumed business. Many were changed, diversified; the more so out of the valleys where the whole area had lost all its livestock. At Thorneythwaite, as in Borrowdale generally, the first decade of the ESA scheme came to an end, and ushered in its successor. This was more draconian, requiring a much deeper cut in the number of sheep allowed on the fells, with only a token presence there at all in Winter. Grudgingly the valley farmers accepted the prescriptions, and the large cheques that came with it – and had good reason to question the city-based judgements that decreed the next generation of Herdwick lambs hardly got to know their own fell till they were three years old. Fell farming depends on heafing, the instinct in each sheep on the fell to return to where its mother took it as a lamb. Without this instinct flocks could dissipate over tens of thousands of acres in an unmanageable mixture of lug marks and smit. With hoggs, shearlings and many even older ewes taken off the fells and wintered away twin lambs became almost the norm, and twin lambs can't be put back on the fell. The fear, very justified, was that the heafing instinct might well be lost forever.

By the time this decade of ESA had run its course, and Natural England had taken on the mantle of carrot-dangler, their officer Cath Marsh had a new tenant to negotiate with at Thorneythwaite, for in 2010 Stuart and Shirley were both sixty-five and it was time for their son Jonny to take the helm. For the first time in four generations at Thorneythwaite there was a son willing and able to succeed – in every respect. Born and bred to the place, and with a wife and sons of his own, Jonny seemed likely to continue a Bland presence at Thorneythwaite to rival the Jopsons of old, or the Birketts centuries before. Jonny and Joanne and their sons Cameron and Nathan moved in as Shirley and Stuart swapped the ancient walls of Thorneythwaite for the comforts of their modern house in nearby Rosthwaite – just yards from Nook Farm where Stuart was born a retirement-age earlier.

Real life is rarely as neat as fiction, and the reality was that Jonny and Joanne were all too aware of Thorneythwaite's limitations. It could make a very good living on the back of all those subsidies but was severely hampered in any entrepreneurial direction by its very limited tourism potential. Bed and Breakfast was, if not a dying trade, at least an ill one for a farm off the beaten track and not well-marked on the new internet highway. The Vacancies sign at the end of the lane was rarely preceded by the 'No' of Shirley's prime. Camping was still forbidden, and in any case there were four well-established campsites in the valley. Their first temptation was a strong bid for the farm and campsite in Stonethwaite, as Victor Brownlee followed Stuart into retirement, but though they were successful in that bid the ties to Thorneythwaite were just – only just – too strong, and they turned the offer down.

A year or so later came another, even more tempting opportunity, as Joe and Hazel Relph also came to retirement at Yew Tree Farm in Rosthwaite. Here was real potential: a good farm and a well-established secondary business with the appropriately named 'Flock-in' café crying out for just such a couple as Jonny and Joanne. Again they were successful, the National Trust recognising a good team when they saw one.

So Thorneythwaite fell vacant, at a time in history when the price of houses in the Lake District had risen like a hot air balloon propelled by the fires of hell, and when the Thorneythwaite acres were among the very few not yet owned by the National Trust. Myles Walker, son of the landlord William Walker of my father's era, and now himself of retirement age, contacted the local estate agents, Penrith Farmers and Kidd, and the national firm of Savills. And the rest, as indeed all of this, is history.

Stuart Bland 1945-2017

Chapter thirty-one

The National Trust Thorneythwaite Walk: 15th June 2017

Well aware of the strength of feeling still strong in the valley over their pre-emptive bid for the land at Thorneythwaite without the farmhouse and buildings the National Trust arranged a walk for this Thursday evening, open to all residents of the valley. Knowing of my interest the local Countryside Manager, Penny Webb, suggested I come along, promising some eye-opening revelations. Around thirty of us met in the NT car park at Seatoller, and were introduced to the team: Tom Burditt, North Lakes General Manager; Victoria Lancaster, Let Estate Manager, responsible for the eighteen NT farms in the North Lakes; Emma Dewhurst, Communications Manager; and Penny herself. With dark, lowering clouds and spots of rain already in the air the evening promised to be appropriately wet for a Borrowdale walk, and people dressed accordingly.

Over Nichol Dub bridge – its depths not quite so inviting as the rain swept in – and across what we were told is to be the first of four fields to be restored to hay meadows. Restoration is relatively easy – apart from applying lime to reduce the acidity you do nothing, no fertilisers, no weedkillers, and a late mowing for hay. The only drawback is, of course, that it produces far less crop than a rye-grass mix, but we were assured the mix of herbs and flowers make for a better diet. First stop in the corner of this field to admire the very thick double wall, built as a place to throw all the stones picked from the field after ploughing. The leader Tom said such a wall might well go back to the Furness Abbey days of clearance and enclosure. I couldn't help but observe to him that the second such wall, further down the field, isn't shown on the 1840 Tithe Map. A later clearance, then.

With the rain now settling in to monsoon standard we took a welcome break in the smaller barn at the farm, where Emma explained the plans the new steading owners have for it and for their future at Thorneythwaite. Robin Ewart-Biggs and his wife Katherine Bonner were the successful bidders at the auction in August 2016, and intend to move to Thorneythwaite this summer leaving their jobs and London for a venture close to their hearts. Their daughter Flynne died from a brain tumour in February 2016, after two years and more of treatment, and they intend to make Thorneythwaite a centre for teenagers and others suffering from life-changing illnesses to be able to come and mix with fellow travellers down this difficult road. They discovered from Flynne's experience that one of the best therapies she could have was to do adventurous expeditions with others in the same boat. Literally in Flynne's case, for she went sailing twice under the aegis of the Ellen MacArthur Cancer Trust – set up by the yachtswoman who sailed solo round the world. The barn we now sheltered in is in the planning permission stage and will, if approved, form the basis of Robin and Katherine's Centre – Flynne's Barn.

Onward through the farmyard, past the sheep pens, to the high point overlooking the 'field of stones' – huge boulders left by the receding glacier 13,000 years ago, and far too big to be tidied away into stone walls. Here, the bombshell: Penny, the ranger, handed out a laminated sheet; on one side a fascinating map of Low Bank, High Bank and Jenny Banks, the intakes, drawn up for the NT archaeologist, Jamie Lund, showing no fewer than sixty sites; some for charcoal burning, others quarries, possible old shielings, ancient charcoal tracks, water smoots, sheep shelters and so on. Sites I never knew were there in fifteen years of living at Thorneythwaite; sites I'd guess none of the tenants over the last three hundred years knew were there. Sites dating from mediaeval times, from the bloomeries. Sites that I need to put in Chapter Ten!

Turning the sheet over, at Penny's instruction, we tried to make sense of a strange sort of map, described on the bottom of the sheet as a 'Detailed Topographic survey of settlement (Site 15). *(Page 14 of this book)* Settlement? I recognised the superimposition of the cross of walls near the bend in the lane, and had the first intimation of panic, as Penny said what we were looking at was a map showing an Iron Age settlement roughly surrounding the cross of the walls, dating from about 600 BC. My first reaction should surely have been one of elation that Thorneythwaite should prove to be at least a millennium and a half older than everyone has thought till now. Instead, it was 'Oh bugger! I can't bear to start again!' and so I won't. My sub-title is 'The 1,000 year story of a farm and its valley', and so it remains. Tom joined in with Penny's disclosure, pointing out that we have always known Castle Crag was an Iron Age fort, giving the valley its early name of Borgher Dalr, and that of course the people of the fort didn't live there permanently but retired there when under threat. "Here's where they lived!" he proclaimed dramatically. And so, it appears, they did. I guess you'd need an archaeologist's eye and tools to be able to decry the foundations of the bank and settlement huts for yourself, but there they all are on the bombshell map. Nevertheless, I was relieved to hear Tom say the evidence seems to show a long unpopulated period between the Iron Age inhabitants and the first of the Viking/Scandinavians.

Regaining the will to live I hurried on to catch the group up. Surprisingly the rain stopped. I don't remember it stopping once it had got a hold in our days here – I wonder what the climate was in the Iron Age.

Above the ramp where Dad had his near-death experience we stop for the last time for Tom to explain the Trust's intentions for Jenny Banks and the fields Noon Bank and Nookem. Penny hands out more laminates, this time detailing Breeding Birds (a creditable thirty-one species) and others of gruesome-looking insects, some quite rare, which have been found in the fallen and rotting trees that litter the intakes. These, along with the virtually 'rain-forest' lichens growing on the North side of the trees on the intakes are what has so excited the National Trust, making them so keen to own and therefore be able to preserve this rare eco-system.

Penny also handed out another sheet showing the profile of the valley floor from where we had walked to the far side of the valley. It clearly shows that the lower side of the valley is the Jenny Bank side, where we stood, and that the river Derwent must at one time have come down this side of the valley. Again, Tom wondered whether the Furness Abbey monks were the first to canalise the river to the West side of the valley. Again, but this time silently, I very much doubted it was anything like that old, remembering the evidence of the Seathwaite flood in their days which killed many of the brothers and laid waste to the settlement for a generation. The alpha males were at it again.

Penny then introduced Joe Weir, the red-headed great-grandson of the Joe Weir who was at Chapel Farm in our day. Joe has been looking after the Thorneythwaite sheep since the Trust took over, and has just learnt he has the tenancy now of the land – with strings attached. Joe will have to run the livestock, including the 430 landlord's stock of Herdwicks, along very definite lines agreed by the Trust, They will be far more hands-on in this tenancy than most. But on the plus side, who knows with Brexit where fell farming is going? Perhaps being in league with your landlord is a good way forward. In the short term though, there is already a question: Tom and the Trust would like to see a small herd of Galloway cattle grazing Jenny Banks, for the best of ecological reasons. Cattle encourage new tree growth, whereas sheep positively destroy it. Unable to keep silent I have to observe that when my parents did the same fifty years ago, the cattle developed Cancer – bracken being notoriously carcinogenic. Only when the spores are at a particular stage, is the answer, and besides, it's working very well in Ennerdale. Oh, right.

Back at Flynne's Barn it's a still, post-rain evening and the midges are making the most of the conditions and the presence of twenty or so delicate bodies to nibble on. In between swatting the people are nibbling on the delicious carrot cake and cups of coffee the Trust have thoughtfully provided. It's not long before the midges and the hour send most people off to their cars, leaving me alone with the officers. Time for a more searching discussion, since I need to get this last chapter as right as I can. Tom is very ready to put the Trust's case over their purchase of land without farmhouse and buildings – and keen to hear why I feel they have sold their principles short. Trying to rationalise my disquiet I realise that actually it's not rational, but is nonetheless real, if emotional. For me in particular, of course, with so many happy memories of growing up there, of Jen visiting, of working alongside my parents, of reading Hugh Walpole's 'Herries saga', of lying in bed half-dreaming of the wad mines, Black Sal, Moses Rigg and all the other romantic notions in a teenage mind and soul, the place is full of nostalgia.

But it's more than that. This purchase, and the way it was made so deliberately to split land from steading, marks a sea-change in the National Trust's direction. Till now I and most Cumbrians have thought of the Trust as custodians of a way of life – fell farms with Herdwicks, after the Beatrix Potter template. Now it seems the thrust is towards preservation of the flora, fauna, insect life and lichens, even if that is at the expense of a self-sufficient fell farm. The suspicion among farmers is that the fells are to be 're-wilded' as the buzzword goes, and with re-wilding comes a raft of regulations and duties they aren't interested in following. Being kept on as 'custodians of the countryside' – a patronising description – is of no interest to an umpteenth generation fell farmer's son. A bit provocatively I comment that the next logical step for the Trust would be to split up some of their existing fell farms: after all, selling off a farmhouse and buildings could release a million pounds which would go a long way towards re-wilding a valley. Tom answers that all their existing farms are held in perpetuity, and would take an act of parliament to allow such a sale. True, but not quite an answer I feel. He suggests I come and see him for a proper conversation, uninterrupted by midges.

Report of the interview with Tom Burditt: Bowe Barn, Wednesday 28th June 2017.

I came with a few prepared questions and a real wish to hear the National Trust's side of the argument that erupted after they made their exclusive bid for the land at Thorneythwaite, effectively ensuring that it would be split from the farmhouse and buildings. Melvyn, Lord Bragg, was incensed by the auction result and raised the whole question in the House of Lords. He wrote a letter to the Times containing this scathing criticism: "Had a billionaire bullied his way into this disgraceful purchase there would have been a deserved outcry. If the increasingly arrogant National Trust is there to protect anything of our past surely this is a prime example. The National Trust is about to destroy what centuries of working men and women have created. It used a shameful manoeuvre to achieve its aim. Who can check this bullying charity?" Tom Burditt recognised the anger behind Lord Bragg's outburst, and the disquiet I had expressed as a former tenant's son. Here are his considered answers to the questions I put.

IH: The deliberate splitting of land from steading seems to confirm the impression that the NT's mission has changed from the Beatrix Potter template of small working farms producing Herdwick sheep with a separate business, usually tourist related, to a more environmentalist attitude to the land. Is this the case?

TB: To some extent that is the case. Let me show you the pictorial version of our understanding of our role in the outdoors – nationwide. This illustrates the balance the Trust is trying to maintain or achieve both in existing properties and particularly in any new purchases.

This was introduced just before the sale of Thorneythwaite and did inform our discussions on how to proceed in the auction room. You have to realise we could not afford to buy the entire farm. The question we asked ourselves was this: does the purchase of the land without the steading enable us to satisfy the criteria pictured above? If we go round the circle from the top, we felt – and this was at the highest level, including Lady Helen Ghosh, the Trust chair – that we could make improvements in all sectors.

Rich in wildlife: well, it is still, but the trees are all old, with no new growth being allowed by sheep grazing. It needs careful environmentally friendly management to reverse tree loss and to allow the rare insect life and lichen growth we talked about on the walk to prosper.

Beautiful: yes it is, but it would be more so if we could get rid of a lot of bracken and stimulate new tree growth.

Enjoyed: It could be enjoyed by a lot more people with some interpretation of the terrain – especially the Iron-age settlement.

Rich in culture: we accept splitting the land from the steading does diminish the cultural reality of a fell farm, but we feel the experiment of offering work to a local shepherd, who already has a home in the valley, may well open other avenues, new cultures. We also feel that the Trust can enhance the culture to be found here. We now know there is an ancient settlement, numerous charcoal-burning platforms: we know the ecology of the woodland and can seek to preserve and enhance it; we have already restored the fell wall and mended other gaps. The culture of these woodlands is already rich: we feel able to allow it to blossom further, and to interpret it to anyone interested.

Productive: This rocky hillside can never be productive in the sense of producing much food for human consumption; but it can be tremendously productive in environmental terms. This top end of Borrowdale is the only example of a rain forest in Britain – and it truly is, or could be, rain forest, with four metres of rainfall each year. The lichen population bears silent witness to this.

Healthy: currently you would have to say the intakes are not healthy. They have been over-grazed by sheep for over a hundred years, resulting in a very aged tree population. A regime where only cattle forage the intakes will improve the health visibly over a generation. The sheep flock needs to be on the fell or in the inbye land.

IH: You said the Trust could not afford to buy the entire farm. Why was that?

TB: National Trust finances are quite complex, and have changed considerably these last few years. It used to be the case that funds were held centrally and each region had to bid for any capital purchase it wished to make. This meant the central body made decisions on priorities – were the Churchill papers more important nationally than the possible purchase of Croft Farm, for instance. About two years ago the model changed as regional managers now receive grants from the central office and run their own finances much more than before. The downside of this is that there is much less access to central funds – indeed, there are far fewer central funds – if a particular possible purchase comes up. In the case of Thorneythwaite our region, North Lakes, had a long-standing bequest with the specification that it had to be used for a single purchase in the Borrowdale valley. It wasn't enough to buy the whole farm, and we had to use additional capital in hand even to buy the land, and it would have been difficult to access central funds in the timescale available.

We also had to balance the benefits of keeping the entire farm and steading intact with the need, if we bought the house and buildings, to factor in a large endowment for future maintenance. You will know that for many years the National Trust has been unable to accept the gift of any historic property unless it comes with a very substantial endowment to cover future maintenance costs. This is simply good management on the Trust's part. We took the decision – at the highest level – that to purchase the entire farm with such an endowment made the purchase unviable in the larger National Trust portfolio. At the same time, the purchase of the land was affordable, and allows us to invest significant sums in its protection and enhancement. I think you will agree that what you saw on the Thorneythwaite Walk showed a real contribution to everyone's deeper understanding of just what a gem these lands are in cultural terms.

So we took the decision that this once-in-a-lifetime opportunity to obtain at least the land was appropriate. And yes, in order to make as sure as we could that we did obtain the land, we put in the highest bid we could afford and justify.

IH: I understand there was talk of reporting your bid to the Charity Commission on the grounds that it was unjustifiably high and therefore not an acceptable use of charitable money.

TB: There may have been talk, but in fact the whole process was cleared by the Charity Commission after we made the bid. They recognised that the intrinsic value of this parcel of land justified the price tag – a price that was within the professional valuation we had sought before the auction.

IH: I suppose this acquisition does fit the last piece into the jigsaw of your holdings in upper Borrowdale. Is that important to the Trust?

TB: Yes indeed. I don't know whether you know the name John Lawton? He's very influential in National Trust thinking and produced a White Paper for the Coalition Government which in essence made the point that almost all Environmental groups are too focussed on small pockets of land. So we get a wildlife park here, a wetland there, a woodland somewhere else – but they're not joined together. They don't form a corridor, an entire system that nature can run riot in. The reserves are too small to be viable in the long term. With the Thorneythwaite land we now can ensure a complete eco-system enough space to flourish.

IH: I recall James Rebanks came up with a rather snappy phrase to encapsulate the anger people felt about the splitting of land from its steading. He said, more or less, 'Thorneythwaite has sheep, sheep need a shepherd and a shepherd needs a place to live.' It was a good summing up of the mood, I thought.

TB: Yes, that's true, but in Joe Weir, the shepherd we have gone into a partnership with, you could stand that aphorism on its head and say something like 'Here's a shepherd who has a home. All he needs is a flock of sheep.' And I don't think Joe is alone in this: there are lots of farmers' sons unable to follow their father onto the family farm – perhaps they are second or third sons – who can live at home and would love the opportunity to have a flock of sheep to shepherd. I really think this may be the beginning of a new model for the Lake District.

IH: You're not suggesting he can make a full living on the Thorneythwaite flock of 430 ewes, and the few cattle you want him to run on the intakes?

TB: No, it will of course be part-time. But the reality is that almost all our tenants need to supplement their agricultural income – usually with Bed & Breakfast or other tourism projects. And of course there's nothing new in this. Borrowdale farmers have probably always, historically, had other work – as quarrymen, miners, carters and so on. It is true that recently with the extraordinarily generous payments from the Common Agricultural Policy fell farmers have had perhaps their best period ever, but there is no telling what effect Brexit will have on that. I think the future will see more and more National Trust tenant farmers more than happy to enter agreements which guarantee an income in return for more environmentally sensitive practices.

IH: In hindsight do you wish the auction and the aftermath had been handled more sensitively, to use your word?

TB: I won't deny we were set back on our heels by the strength of the reaction, and it has caused serious introspection within the Trust at all levels. Nevertheless, I do believe our motives were positive, and the outcome will be seen to be positive. It could probably have been handled better, but it is still true that buying the land alone was the only realistic option we had and I'm glad we took it. It offers an opportunity for a newer approach in what will be very changing times, and we are seeking creative solutions to cope with those changing times. I know it's sometimes seen as a rather slick strapline, but it is true that the National Trust is here 'For ever, for everyone.' Making that happen does mean changing with those times.

IH: Thank you very much. I feel at least that I understand far better now how that astonishing auction bid came about.

Epilogue

Two important events happened just as I was finishing the first draft of this book: firstly the National Trust published the Historic Landscape Survey Report on their newly acquired land at Thorneythwaite, which gave fresh insights into its history; secondly, UNESCO announced (Sunday, 9th July, 2017) that the Lake District had been inscribed as a site of global significance because it meets the three criteria laid down for inscription under the cultural landscape category. The spectacular landscape of the Lake District has been shaped by farming, industry, picturesque landscape design and the conservation movement. It stimulated poets and artists of the Romantic Movement from the late 18th century and conservationists from the 19th century. The three criteria are:

"Landscapes that exhibit an important interchange of human values, over a span of time or within a cultural area of the world, on developments in architecture or technology, monumental arts, town planning or landscape design".

"Landscapes that bear a unique or at least exceptional testimony to a cultural tradition or to a civilisation which is living or which has disappeared".

"Landscapes that are directly or tangibly associated with events or living traditions, with ideas, or with beliefs, with artistic and literary works of outstanding universal significance".

I find it deeply ironic that eleven months to the day after the break-up of Thorneythwaite such a powerful indication of how Lake District management should henceforth be conducted by public bodies such as the National Trust should eventually emerge. (The Lake District World Heritage Status bid had been pursued for three decades). It is inconceivable following this inscription that the National Trust would ever again feel it appropriate to make such a tactical bid to split a farmstead from its land, since it would be contrary to the criteria above.

The farm of my youth, then, ended its existence as an entity due to a double accident of timing. It came up for sale in two lots at the worst moment in history: a few months earlier the National Trust adopted its new, nationwide policy which in its view justified making that tactical bid for the land alone. A bid that was in a sense a testing of the waters in the re-balancing of its conservation stance versus its cultural heritage stance. A mere eleven months later the World Heritage inscription effectively precludes such a narrowly conservationist view, insisting that in the Lake District the cultural heritage fostered by, among many other factors, the contribution of small family farms is one of the features required for such an inscription.

I can't imagine the National Trust will ever repeat such a gambit. Perhaps that is some small comfort for the sacrifice of a compact farm that had just celebrated a thousand years of continuous existence.

Acknowledgements

Many people have given me information and encouragement in my researches for this book. First and foremost Jennifer, my wife, who shared Thorneythwaite with me from our early teenage years and who has shared also the research and memories involved in bringing this work to fruition. Without her encouragement and belief in the project I doubt I would have persevered.

Helen Cunningham, in the Carlisle Record Office not only provided this history novice with many answers but also told me what were the appropriate questions, and where to begin to look. I owe a great deal to her and to the many other members of the staff there.

The National Trust have been unfailingly helpful to someone who was clearly distressed at their role in the break-up of the farm he grew up in, and afforded me much time and expertise in my researches. In particular Tom Burditt, North Lakes General Manager and Jamie Lund, archaeologist for this area, both allowed me extended interviews which were extremely helpful. Thanks also to Penny Webb, Borrowdale Countryside Manager, and Victoria Lancaster, Let Estate Manager for their help. The two National Trust archaeological reports prepared for them by Oxford Archaeology North – the 2007 Borrowdale survey and the 2017 Thorneythwaite survey – were tremendous sources of information.

The cover photograph is that featured in the Sale brochure, and is used by permission from Penrith Farmers' and Kidd's plc and the photographer, Allen Williams.

I am very grateful to Fisher Jopson's three grand-daughters, Ina Monkhouse, Vera Harris and Ethel Chapman for giving time to talk about Thorneythwaite in their grand-father's time, and for a series of photos which helped enormously in untangling the various strands of the story.

Shirley Bland, Stuart's widow, took the time to read through and suggest improvements to the chapter on her and Stuart's forty year's connection to Thorneythwaite, as did Jane Sutton (née Edmondson) on chapter nine.

The new owners of the farmstead and thirteen acres, Katherine Bonner and Robin Ewart-Biggs, also gave me time for an interview and talked of their aspirations to make the place a suitable centre for children and others with life-changing illnesses to come together for mutual support. I wish them well in their enterprise – a fitting purpose for a farm that has meant so much to me.

Any errors (and I am sure there are many) are of course mine.

Historical Notes

Prologue

The pre-emptive strike by the National Trust in effectively ensuring by their large opening bid for the land at Thorneythwaite that it would not remain as a small farm was extensively criticised in the press by such luminaries as Melvyn Lord Bragg and James Rebanks, amongst many others. The Trust defended its decision robustly, saying it saw its main duty in this particular instance being to secure and therefore protect the rare and valuable eco-system on the Thorneythwaite intakes 'for everyone, for ever'. It didn't feel able to buy the whole farm, taking on the liability for upkeep of an ancient farmhouse and buildings.

Chapter one

Jim and Betty Hall, and their eleven-year-old son Ian, took on the tenancy of Thorneythwaite on Lady Day 1960 (25th March) and farmed it for a fifteen year period. I am that Ian, and my memories of Thorneythwaite over those years are my chief reason for writing this book.

Chapter two

It is a matter of conjecture whether any descendants of the Iron Age people who built Castle Crag hillfort around 500 BC remained in the valley even by Roman times, let alone till the 10th Century. The highly informative *Historic Landscape Survey* commissioned by the National Trust in partnership with the Oxford Archaeological Unit, published in 2007 collects and collates most of the archaeological evidence on what were then the Trust's holdings, and notes the two stone-axe workings high on Glaramara, exploiting natural outcrops of the volcanic 'tuff' which Neolithic man found easy to chip into sharp-edged axes. However, it found very little evidence of Iron Age populations, beyond the existence of the hillfort on Castle Crag and another in the Watendlath valley on Reecastle Hill. It did note that widespread clearance of the forest by felling and, principally, by burning, seemed not to have taken place before the Norse clearances of the late 10th Century.

However, after their purchase of Thorneythwaite land in 2016 the National Trust commissioned a further survey by the Oxford Archaeological Unit, appropriately entitled *Land at Thorneythwaite Farm,*

Borrowdale. It documents the find of what is presumed to be an early Iron Age settlement though the report does admit it may prove to be of Viking origin. It is centred about 100 metres East of the present farmhouse, on the same terminal moraine, and its boundary is D-shaped in plan, measuring around 85 x 80 metres. For my story I have assumed the older origin, but excavation may refute this.

Chapter three

I first discovered the field names used at Thorneythwaite many years ago. In my late teens I spent an afternoon in the Carlisle Record Office, then based in Carlisle Castle, tracing their map of the farm and the field names, I think from the 1840 Tithe Map, though I am not sure. Black Syke is well-named, syke coming from the Old Norse meaning a small sluggish drainage channel through a marsh. Only in hindsight have I realised how innovative and full of energy my parents were, though in truth many of their 'book-learnt' ideas and intentions fitted only moderately into the harsh conditions of Borrowdale. They persisted with their experiments and collaboration with the Ministry of Agriculture throughout their time at Thorneythwaite.

Interestingly, Jim was unwittingly following in historical footsteps in cutting down holly and ash branches for winter fodder for the sheep. It was common practice in mediaeval times – with elm being even more sought after. Pollen analysis points up the periods in pre-history when elm was so used, for the farmers of the day virtually stripped their woodland of elm, as shown by the lack of pollen at certain periods of history. (*The Lake District: Pearson and Pennington, chapter 13)*

Chapter four

Professor John Birks conducted pollen core research in Johnny's Wood, a few hundred yards to the North of Thorneythwaite, and concluded it was part-felled, not burned, in the earliest days of the Norse settlement of the valley, in the 10th Century. The post-glacial woodland was dominated by oak and elm, with much alder in the wetter areas. After the clearances birch and silver birch sprang up amongst the oak, along with some mountain ash and holly. More recently sycamore and larch have been introduced.

Almost without exception the ancient place-names in the valley are of Scandinavian origin, suggesting that the Norse settlers took over virtually virgin land. All the ancient farms and hamlets have Norse names:

Seathwaite (The clearance in the sieves and sedges); Seatoller (The summer farm by the alder tree); Thorneythwaite, Stonethwaite, Longthwaite – all obvious. Rosthwaite apparently means 'the clearing with the heap of stones'. Langstrath is a tricky one: etymologists don't recognise any usage of the 'strath' part until 16th Century Scotland, where it does mean a broad river valley, as indeed is the case for Langstrath. And yet it was inhabited at least by shepherds' shielings in Norse days, so may be derived from the Old English 'strod', meaning a marsh. Certainly it would have been a long marsh – indeed still is to some extent.

I have suggested the early settlers built stone houses, in defiance of the accepted view that they used wooden walls, covered with sods. I have lived in Borrowdale, and consider the climate sufficiently wet and cold to require better than wooden walls. It is true that Viking houses in Greenland at that time were stone-built, and I see no reason why they wouldn't apply the same skills in Borrowdale. There is, after all, no shortage of suitable stone!

Chapter five

The more I remember of our early days at Thorneythwaite the more impressed I am by my parents' vision, tenacity and ability to produce great things on a shoestring. They were certainly very strapped for cash throughout their tenancy at Thorneythwaite, but nevertheless brought in many innovations, such as the silage clamp and the battery hen houses (there were two prefabs eventually.) The connection to Mary and Harold Wilson is astonishing, but true. The more so in that Gladys Mary Wilson (née Baldwin) was a Southerner who only came to Carlisle specifically for the secretarial courses being held at the Gregg School. She and my father corresponded fitfully all his life, and on the Wilson's visit to Penrith, when they invited Jim and Betty to dinner, she presented them with a lovely porcelain figure of a shepherd and his dog which Jen and I still have. Later she send a slim volume of her poetry, published in 1970, which sadly has been misplaced, but which I have now replaced. I can't read those early poems – The Virgin's Song; Winter Parting; and The Train – without a whimsical wonder as to how deeply they were involved with each other.

Chapter six

The two Alice de Rumillys are a fascinating study in their own right. I am indebted to volume 7 of the *Early Yorkshire Charters*, edited by William Farrer and Charles Travis Clay, and '*Skipton Castle and its builders'* by Richard T. Spence, for the details of their lives included in this chapter. We are now in recorded history, and the records show Alice the elder was a woman of great power and prestige. She kept her mother Cecily's maiden name presumably because it was through her mother's line that she inherited the 'Honour of Skipton', and also the Barony of Copeland. Alice's father, William le Meschin was granted the Barony in 1120 by King Henry I, and it was he who first built a Motte and Bailey Castle at Egremont

She was obliged to marry one of the sons of King Duncan II of Scotland, one William Fitz Duncan, notorious for his cruelty in warfare. King David I of Scotland, William's uncle, was sweeping through Northern England, subduing it to Scotland. He sent part of his army under William's control to invade Lancashire, Lonsdale and the Skipton district of Yorkshire. Under William the army ravaged and plundered the North West, destroying the fledgling Furness Abbey and putting whole villages to the sword. It is even possible he took Alice the elder and her mother Cecily prisoner. Certainly he demanded of King David to marry Alice, coveting her Copeland barony and the Honour of Skipton which she was to inherit on Cecily's death. He was then able to influence Cecily, and there are several charters in Skipton granted under their joint names.

They had one son, Ranulph, who died young and without issue, and was posthumously known as the Boy of Egremont. He it was who died trying to cross 'The Strid', a narrow chasm on the River Wharfe, near Fountains Abbey. They also had three daughters, Annabel, Cecily and Alice the younger. The continued Lordship of the Manor of Egremont should interest us, as it still exists today, and mineral rights still attain.

The falconer's strange question "What is good for a bootless bene?" comes from Wordsworth's poem *'The boy of Egremont'* – it is the first line. In the poem Wordsworth has the distraught Alice giving Bolton Abbey to the monks of Embsay in memory of Ranulph, a nice poetic touch, but unjustified as the charter giving the land to the monastery is signed by both Alice and her son. This does not preclude her seeing the new Abbey's realisation as a fitting tribute to the boy taken by the river which runs beside it.

It is Alice the younger, however, who moves Thorneythwaite's story forward. Indeed, she is fundamental to the ensuing story of the whole area of Borrowdale and Keswick and the Derwent Valley. Her gifts or sales (it is not entirely clear which) of the entire valley well down to Bassenthwaite to the two Cistercian Abbeys of Fountains and Furness ushered in the centuries of monastic control which prevailed till Henry VIII's dissolution in the sixteenth century.

189

Chapter seven

Not much to add, here. I do remember various disastrous hay times, and the self-inflicted difficulties caused by my parents' unwillingness to cut more than one field at a time, which meant the season dragged on through late July, all of August and often into September. They were unlucky that Big Bale Silage wasn't invented till nearly a decade after their retirement. It has been the salvation of the fell farmer, enabling a field to be cut one day, and turned over then baled as silage the next, producing nourishing fodder for the Winter full of the nutrients which were so frequently leached out at Thorneythwaite.

Chapter eight

We are now well into the realm of recorded history, for the abbeys of Furness and Fountains kept accurate records of their dealings, in what are known as their Cartularies. The main through routes in the valley reflected the influence of the abbeys, with Furness favouring the Sty Head Pass and Grains Gill routes through Seathwaite, while Fountains went over Watendlath, then either over Walla Crag to Castlerigg or steeply out of Watendlath and over to Thirlmere via Harrop Tarn. Both abbeys sent wool by pack horse up Langstrath and over Stake Pass into Langdale, bound for Kendal. Surprisingly, it seems there was no major route into Keswick: perhaps the monks were forbidden the delights of the town?

Chapter nine

My chief source for this chapter was Jane Sutton, (née Edmondson) who was a nine-year-old at the time, and has vivid memories of what must have been a harrowing time for the adult population of Seathwaite. Thorneythwaite, as always in flood events, was virtually unscathed; a tribute to the foresight of its original founders. Part of the National Trust's declared aim in buying the Thorneythwaite land is to allow the River Derwent in this upper reach to meander over the erstwhile flood plain between Thorneythwaite and Seathwaite to mitigate flooding further down the valley. The river there currently is constrained by walled banks to pass through this plain as quickly as possible, though of course when it does overflow it does so into these fields.

Chapter ten

The historical dispute between the two abbeys – Fountains and Furness – over the land at Stonethwaite is well documented (if you can read Latin!) in both *The Chartularies of Fountains Abbey* and the *Coucher Book of Furness Abbey*. Carlisle Record Office holds a transcript in English of the Grant which Alice de Rumilly (called therein Alize Rumley) 'gave unto the Abbey of Furnass touching the Liberties and Bounds of Borrowdale' in 1211. It seems very precise as to the area under Furness control, but you need a detailed knowledge of the valley's landmarks and their ancient names to be sure of what is and is not within the purlieu of Furness. The relevant section covering Stonethwaite reads: 'From Ashness Beck where it descendeth into Derwentwater and so ascending up to the top of a mountain which is between Watendlath and Borrowdale by the height of that mountain until Lowdoor, and so ascending up to Highdoor and from there up to Marthbuth and from there ascending unto Dock Tarn and so by the top of the mountain ascending unto Greenup Edge and from there along the top of the Raise called the Huttrell and so over along unto Bredmegillhead, and so it descendeth into Langstrath Beck and thence to a lake called Angle Tarn....' Drawing this on a map appears to make it clear all Stonethwaite is within Furness Abbey control. However, it clearly was not the case, for Fountains Abbey certainly had a vaccary (dairy herd) at Stonethwaite from the earliest times. It must, presumably, be the case that Alice, or her cartographers, unwittingly gave or sold the Stonethwaite area twice over. The subsequent battle for control of the area was inevitable.

Chapter eleven

I'm ashamed to say every word of this chapter is true.

Chapter twelve

I am indebted once more to the Oxford Archaeology survey for the National Trust for the bones of this chapter. An archaeological survey at Seathwaite revealed the colluvial fan that had covered a large area. Under it were traces of a mediaeval wall and fences, carbon dated to the early 14th century, and also evidence of coppicing of hazel and ash. The Black Death visited the region in 1348, 1361 and 1362, but it is likely not to have penetrated the remote valleys. Murrain was a generic term for a variety of sheep and cattle epidemics, literally simply meaning 'death'. Borrowdale is notorious in sheep circles for liver fluke, which prosper in wet conditions and might well have become widespread after the appalling weather apparently suffered in the period immediately before. It may well have been the main cause of that particular 'murrain'. The first recorded use of slate as a roofing material is in 1287, in North Wales, another famous slate area. It seems likely to me that in an area where it occurred naturally and was visible as outcrops – an area moreover where the rainfall is legendary – that enterprising locals may well have realised its potential as a better roofing material.

The oldest part of the present house at Thorneythwaite is the kitchen, which is square with walls of three feet thickness. I have no way of knowing how old that part is, but I could well believe it may be 14th century.

The years 1315 – 1317 were years of great famine throughout Northern Europe. Abnormally severely cold Winters were followed for at least three Summers by torrential rainfall, blighting any attempts to grow crops. One can only imagine the rainfall in already over-burdened Borrowdale, and the effect on a population living a hand to mouth existence and housed in hovels. On the other hand they may have had enough stock able to survive the elements and keep themselves alive on grass for the population to weather the storms by judicious slaughtering over the famine period. Whatever the reality, it must have been a horrendous three-years, and any aged, weak or infirm must have perished from the cold and wet, even if enough food could be found.

The almost complete failure of three harvests meant there was virtually no bread to be found in Britain and its European neighbours, and it is documented that even King Edward II's servants, when he passed through St Albans on 10th August 1315, were unable to find bread for the king's table. (*The St Albans Chronicle: Chronica Maiora Volume II 1394 - 1422;* Thomas Walsingham).

Probably exacerbated by the famine the Border Reivers were much in action in this fourteenth century, although Borrowdale itself seems not to have been a target – the open and fertile Eden Valley and the coastal strip offering richer pickings. Nevertheless, the monasteries could, and did, require able-bodied men from their holdings in Borrowdale and elsewhere to serve some time under the Warden of the Marches in the policing of the (non-existent) border between England and Scotland.

Chapter thirteen

Astonishing as my father's escape from death seems, it is an unembroidered fact. As a footnote, I left them to the last of the hay-making the following year, too, once again touring Europe this time with two new-found University friends. This time Dad managed somehow to be behind the buck rake with its malevolent sharp prongs, meant to slide under hay or grass before lifting the load. This time as Ma reversed she skewered his foot with one of the tines, and again he spent a couple of nights in Carlisle hospital, and a couple of weeks on crutches. I didn't take any more Summer holidays abroad.

Chapter fourteen

Once again I am indebted to the National Trust survey of 2007 for the background information surrounding Agatha's story. They point to the British Museum *Add MSS 24764 f 6*, in Elliot 1961 for the primary source of the Fountains Abbey survey which counted 41 farms in their part of the valley, and suggest this was roughly half the valley. This is, to my mind, refuted by Alice de Rumilly's description of the land sold/given to Furness Abbey, which includes all the hamlets save Watendlath and, possibly, Stonethwaite. The state of the woodland at that time is documented in Pearsall & Pennington *'The Lake District'*.

Chapter fifteen

What can I say? It's only when you're a grandparent yourself, with your own children grown away, that you realise how much heartache your parents must have suffered on your account. Perhaps it's even worse with an only child.

Chapter sixteen

The account of the Dissolution of Furness Abbey, and others referred to in this chapter, comes from 'Houses of Cistercian monks: The abbey of Furness', in *A History of the County of Lancaster: Volume 2*, ed. William Farrer and J Brownbill (London, 1908), pp. 114-131. There is of course no way of knowing how strictly the Duchy of Lancaster ran its new-found properties in Borrowdale and elsewhere.

Ralf's account of the works he had undertaken, rebuilding the house and barns, fetching slate from Honister, building walls etc. is in line with the structures to be found at Thorneythwaite.

Chapter seventeen

My mother died, aged eighty-five, of a brain tumour. We discovered that, somewhat surprisingly to laymen, such tumours bring no pain, the brain having no nerve ends, which at least makes the end a little easier to bear. We also discovered that brain tumours progressively disinhibit the sufferer. The downside of this was that my mother acted impulsively, kicking out at carers, throwing plantpots out of her (upstairs) window and so on. The interesting side was that she became more than willing to share family secrets she never would have before her illness. This is how I know of my father's indiscretions, assuming, that is, that brain tumours do not also cause a tendency to lie and deceive.

Chapter eighteen

After centuries of extremely scant documentary evidence of life in Borrowdale, we now hit an embarrassment of material. The Augsberg parent company of the Company of Mines Royal required meticulous accounts of expenditure and living conditions in the Keswick Company. W G Collingwood's scholarly *'Elizabethan Keswick'* goes back to these primary sources, translating and selecting for the modern reader's benefit. These accounts cover the foundation period 1564 – 1577.

M B Donald's equally well-researched *'Elizabethan Copper'* goes deeper into the characters and make-up of the original company and its shareholders, making documented judgements on the main players: Daniel Hechstetter; Thomas Thurman; Hans Loner; William Cecil and many, many others.

At roughly the same time (1562) St Kentigern's Church, Crosthwaite, began keeping records which are still extant on Baptisms, Marriages and Burials for all the surrounding area, including Borrowdale. The earlier ones contain scant detail, but quite soon they list places of residence. Thorneythwaite itself isn't mentioned until 1589 when the record of the baptism of 'John, son of Christopher Birkhead of Thonythwaite (sic) and Alice' is recorded. This may in fact be a misprint for Thornethwaite, a village three miles North-West of Keswick, which is mentioned many times in connection with the Birkhead clan. Sufficient to say Thorneythwaite is not mentioned again for many years, and there is no further record of Christopher, Alice or John.

Instead, the records speak of Seatoller as the place of residence for many Fishers and Birkheads (among others). It is not till the Great Deed of Borrowdale (1614) that we get a definite reference to John Birkhead, yeoman, of Thorneythwaite. This one is incontrovertible, and informs my choice of Birkheads as the family at Thorneythwaite over many years, since Richard and Elizabeth did bear a first son John, born in 1566, who would be an appropriate age by 1614 to be the John named in the Great Deed. There is no reason to believe that other families said to be 'of Seatoller' were the inhabitants of Thorneythwaite, though of course it is possible.

The Great Deed makes it clear just how numerous was the Birkhead clan. Birkheads mentioned as landowners in the deed are:

Thomas, of Seathwaite
John, of Seatoller
Robert, of Seatoller
John, of Thorneythwaite
Nicholas, of The Chapel
Edward, John, Christopher and Thomas, of Rosthwaite

A total of nine different holdings, or parts of holdings, in Birkhead hands.

For comparison, there are six Fishers; six Braithwaites; only one Jopson – a family that became very numerous in later centuries. The other names – Dickson, Hudson, Vickars, Richardson, Youdell, Harris (Harry), Wood, Banks, Lambert and Hyne (Hind) are the solitary standard-bearers of families which continued, generally, for many centuries in the valley. Birkhead has of course long elided to Birkett or Birkitt, still common Lake District names.

George Bott's *'Keswick: the story of a Lake District Town'* concisely brings together many of the strands in the previously mentioned sources.

The murdered German miner was called Leonard Stoultz, and in a letter to Hans Loner Hechstetter affirms the ringleader of the assault was 'one Fisher'. *(Collingwood, P 17)*. Collingwood deduces from the Crosthwaite registers that in fact Leonard Stultz was a baby, probably killed accidentally, but I find his evidence unconvincing and insufficient to justify Daniel Hechstetter's angry tirade against the lax English authorities who failed to bring Fisher to justice. I have no justification beyond a novelist's imagination for deciding it was a John Fisher of Seatoller.

As a rider to Queen Elizabeth's insistence that any mine producing any amount of silver or gold, however small, was a Royal Mine, with the entire output of all minerals belonging to the crown, the judgement governed mining till 1688 when, under William and Mary, a statute declared 'no mine of copper, tin, iron or lead shall hereafter be adjudged a royal mine although gold or silver may be extracted out of the same'.

Chapter nineteen

The first mention we get of Frances Hudson is in the Crosthwaite Registers, where the birth of her son William is recorded thus:

March 23rd, 1588. William, son of John Birkhead of Borradell and Frances Hudson. Base Gotten.

There are a few things to note here: firstly we are still on the old pre-Gregorian calendar, where new year's day is Lady Day, 25th March. William therefore is baptised on almost the last day of 1588. Secondly, base gotten is the phrase then in use for illegitimate. Thirdly, you may wonder why I should decide this John Birkhead in fact lives at Thorneythwaite, since only 'Borradell' is mentioned. The trail in fact resembles a detective story, and is never completely water-tight. All the later children born to John and Frances are always said to be 'son/daughter of John Birkhead of Seatoller, and Frances'. He seems the only candidate to be the John Birkhead named as yeoman of Thorneythwaite in the Great Deed (1614), so I have to assume he is indeed of Thorneythwaite in these earlier references.

Frances appears to be married to him for these later births – none is referred to as 'base gotten' – but there is no record in the Crosthwaite registers of any such marriage ever taking place. As to Frances' somewhat elevated birth, I have no justification whatsoever, beyond a need for a Thorneythwaite connection to the Hechstetter family who are so important in the area at this time, but this tale is 'one eye open, one eye closed' and as long as I don't commit demonstrable error I am content to stretch the truth somewhat.

The Crosthwaite registers note the death of Frances Birkhead of Seatoller in 1625. The only likely death of John is John Birkhead of Rosthwaite, in 1645. He would have been 79.

I am indebted to Ian and Jean Tyler's *'Seathwaite Wad and the mines of the Borrowdale Valley'* for most of the information on the Wad Mine at this time. John Hudson may or may not have been a brother to Frances, and may or may not have resided at Thorneythwaite, though it is clear some wad miners did.

Going through the Crosthwaite registers one cannot but be struck by the number of infant deaths, and the dates given for Frances' sons deaths – and Henry's baptism – are to be found therein. For the sake of completeness, here are the baptisms and funerals of John and Frances Birkhead's children from those registers.

Baptisms:

Mar. 23rd 1588: William s. of John Birkhead of Borradell and Francis Hutton, base gotten.

Dec. 12th 1591: John Birkhead s. of John of Seatoller and Francis.

Nov 1st 1593: Henry s. of John Birkhead of Seatoller and Frances.

Mar 2nd 1594: Elizabeth d. of John Birkhead of Setaller and Frances.

Jun 12th 1600: Jennet d. of Johne Birkhead of Seataller and Francis.

Nov 7th 1602: Anne d. of Johne Birkhead of Seataller and Francis.

Funerals:

July 23rd. 1589: William Birkhead of Seateller, infant.

Oct 4th 1593: John Birkhead of Stonethwaite, infant.

Mar 1st 1593: Henry Birkhead of Seataller, infant. (Note pre-Gregorian calendar.)

Chapter twenty

The Sir Wilfrid Lawson of the turn of the century and advent of King James I is a prominent man in the history of the Borders at that time. This is the last throes of the Border Reivers, with the Graham family the chief thorn in the side of King James. On his way South to his coronation in London to unite England and Scotland, while James was at Berwick on the East coast border the Grahams led a destructive foray deep into Cumberland, penetrating as far as Penrith. King James instituted a regime to control the Borders as a Crown colony – under the jurisdiction of a royal commission led by Sir Wilfrid Lawson. This was in 1603. The commission, and Sir Wilfrid, were determined to be rid of the Graham family. A hundred and fifty Graham men were forcibly enlisted in the army, and when that failed to work they were exiled to Ireland, with some of the most extreme being hanged. This was in 1606 – the very year when Sir Wilfrid was able to buy all of Walter Graham's Borrowdale holdings. Walter's grandfather, Richard Graemes (Graham) of Eske in Netherby bought the forfeited Fountains Abbey holdings in Borrowdale for £134 14s 2d in 1546. One might wonder why Henry VIII would sell to such a lawless Reiver , but he did. (Bouch & Jones: *A short economic and social history of the Lake Counties 1500 – 1830,* Manchester). The deeds of conveyance make it clear Sir Wilfrid paid properly for his acquisitions, but one cannot help but wonder whether Walter Graham had a choice as to selling. (See Molly Lefebure's *'Cumberland Heritage' pp.49,50.*)

Moving on to the Great Deed of Borrowdale, 28th November 1614; there is a copy of the deed in English at Carlisle Record Office, and a trenchant criticism of much of the later rather flowery conjecture as to the nature of Borrowdale Yeomen at the time in Susan Johnson's article in the Cumberland & Westmorland Archaeological Society's Transactions. *(Volume TCWAAS(2nd series), vol 81 (1981) pp.63 - 72)* In it she makes clear that Sir Wilfred Lawson appears to have no legal backing from the Deed itself for proclaiming himself Lord of the Manor and setting 'fines' (rents) for commons grasses. She strongly queries the later view by such as J. Fisher Crosthwaite in the 19th Century that the Borrowdale farmers after the Deed were freemen. I quote:

'Anyone supposing, like J. Fisher Crosthwaite in 1876, that once the Great Deed was signed each freeholder would share in the ownership of the manor, no longer paying suit to a Lord, must be surprised by the 17th Century manorial documents now at the Record Office, Carlisle. To the Lawsons the tenantry of Borrowdale already in October 1632 had "fynes to be payd tow medlen day next 20d.," and rents such as Edward Birkett's of 10d. Those who had fines "to be payd" include John Longthwaite, Myles Birkett, Gawyen Norman and John Youdall Jr. Of these the Great Deed 18 years earlier had listed Edward Birkett of Rosthwaite and John Youdall of Chapel – in the old manor of the Furness monks. It is, therefore, plain that already the Lawsons had arrogated to themselves the manor, claiming both rents and fines'.

We will have opportunity to return to this article regarding later acquisitions of Thorneythwaite in the 19th Century. The farm gets many a mention in her disposition.

In fact, it becomes perfectly obvious from the Lawson papers held in the Carlisle Records Office that Sir Wilfrid Lawson had every right to claim at least many tenant rents, though not necessarily that he was of right 'Lord of the Manor'. In 1606 he is very busily buying many 'tenements and messuages' in Watendlath, Stonethwaite, Seathwaite and Grange. *References: D/Law/1/155 – 157* A quick count in these documents shows he owned at least twenty-seven properties in Stonethwaite and Rosthwaite alone, plus several more in Watendlath, and one at least in Seathwaite.

There is, however, no indication that he ever bought Thorneythwaite, which adds to my assertion that John Birkett bought it as a sitting tenant somewhere along the line.

D/Law/1/160 is a particularly important document, being a separate agreement between Sir Wilfrid Lawson and William Whitmore and Jonas Verdon, made just days before the 'Great Deed'. For the sake of completeness, I here quote it in paraphrase.

Bargain and sale for "a certain competent sum" (not further specified) *by William Whitmore of London, Esq., and Jonas Verdon of London, gent, to Sir Wilfrid – freehold tenement at Seathwaite, rent 18s 0d, tenant William Braithwaite, and freehold tenement in Rosthwaite, rent 15s 0d, tenant Hugh Yowdale, both being "parcel, or reputed parcel of the Manor of Borrowdale. Together with all "buildings, barns, stables, dovehouses, orchards, gardens... Woods... underwoods... fishings, mines, quarries winterx" as granted them by letters patent, "under the great seal of England the Duchy Seal of Lancaster and the County Palentyne seal of Lancaster dated the twelveth day of March 1612/13" excepting to the crown "all grate trees being Tymber; and such further timber for building repairs that the crown should decide to sell in the next three years, after the date of the said letters patent, with right to fell and carry it away; excepting to Whitmore and Verdon "All that salt well and salt water within the manor of Borrowdale, all those wadholes and Wad commonly called Black cawk within the common of Seatoller or else within the commons and wastes of the manor of Borrowdale aforesaid with liberty to dig, work and carry the same." 23rd November 1614 (*five days before the great Deed).

In the light of this document the 'Great Deed' seems significantly diminished. Borrowdale farmers were still, in the main, customary tenants of Sir Wilfrid Lawson, who also somehow arrogated to himself the Lordship of the Manor to boot. Their precise standing is attested in the Duchy of Lancaster Surveys, 25 year of Queen Elizabeth's reign, as printed in H Hall, *Society in the Elizabethan Age* (London 1886) pp 154-5. In 1583, then this was the description of Borrowdale tenants 'customary tenancy'.

1. The customary tenants enjoy the ancient custom called tenant-right, namely 'To have their messuages and tenements to them during their lives, and after their deceases, to the eldest issue of their bodies lawfully begotten. And for lack of such issue, the remainder hereof to the next persons of the same blood, paying yearly for the same the rents accustomed to the lord or lords of the said manor, at the feast days of St. James the Apostle and St. Wilfred, by even portions'.

199

2.   The tenants shall be ready at the bidding of the Lord Warden of the West Marches, to serve at their own cost, namely as horsemen in summer and footmen in winter.

3.   The tenants shall pay on change of the lord one gods penny, and at their death or on change of their holdings one year's rent.

4.   The tenants shall pay a fixed tithe-commutation.

5.   They shall have all their fishings at the usual rents.

6.   They shall have all underwood and tops (not being timber).

7.   They shall have sufficient timber for the repair of their houses, hedges, and implements by view of the bailiff.

There are other references to Thorneythwaite Births, Marriages and Deaths in the registers of the early 17th Century which seem peripheral to the main story, but for the sake of completeness, here they are.

Marriages:

Christopher Nichollson of Seatoller to Grace Richardson of Thornethwaite (sic) in Borradell. Feb 27th 1602

Thomas Birkhead of Resthwaite to Elizabeth Birkhead of Thornnethwaite (sic), July 19th, 1628. It seems reasonable to place this Elizabeth as the daughter of John and Frances, born in 1594. They go on to have many children, the last born in 1645, when Elizabeth would be 50, which may be why she died in 1646. In truth, this Elizabeth (Thomas's wife) may not be John and Frances daughter, especially as her death is recorded as:

Nov 14th 1646: Elizabeth Birkhead, daughter of John of Seataller.

Baptisms:

Thomas, son of Christopher Birkhead and Eleanor of Seatoller. 1601. I have assumed that Christopher was living at Thorneythwaite at the time, and that he is John's brother, though there is no record of his birth. His death is recorded.

William, son of Christopher Birkhead and Eleanor, of Rosthwaite. 1606.

I have assumed he too is John's nephew, and it is certainly true that Thomas and William take on Thorneythwaite sometime before 1636. See chapter 22.

Chapter twenty-two

A chief source now, as they will so frequently be in later chapters, are the records of the manorial court held in 'the Inn at Rosthwaite' as it is later described. (These earlier meetings are simply said to be in Rosthwaite.) They are held in the Carlisle Record Office as D/Law/2/5 and D/Law/2/32., which simply stands for Documents/Lawson! The earliest, referred to in Susan Johnson's essay (chapter 19) is in 1632, but mainly they run continuously from 1652, which is the first I quote from.

The 1660 Court record documents twenty separate requirements on individuals and occasionally groups to effect various repairs: to hedges (walls are rarely mentioned, but are probably what are meant by 'hedges'); to 'water edges' (four different people are named, all in the same field, where presumably a flood has damaged the banks); and to repair their houses. This last seems strange to me, unless it is a landlord's requirement of his tenant – strengthening the thesis that Sir Wilfrid Lawson in fact bought many of the farms and tenements from William Whitmore and Jonas Verdon in 1614. At each meeting of the court all the tenants are listed, but unfortunately not which property they hold. Occasionally the appellation 'of Rosthwaite', 'of Stonethwaite' etc. is added, but only to distinguish between tenants of the same name. (There are, for instance, several John Birketts.)

Not all tenants are men, though generally women mentioned are widows. In this 1660 document, Ann Wilson is named four times: to repair a hedge on pain of a fine of 6/8; to repair a water bank on pain of the same; along with others to repair a boundary wall (same fine); and to repair her house.

These early court records are characterised by Sir Wilfrid Lawson repeatedly seeking to strengthen his claim to be Lord of the Manor. For instance, each list of tenants begins with the phrase 'Tenentes ad voluntate domini secundit consueludine Manuorii,' which is poor Latin but roughly is rubbing in the fact twice over that the farmers hold their tenancies at the Lord of the Manor's pleasure. A tentative translation runs: 'Tenants at the will of the Lord after the customs of the manor.' After he has bought the Baronetcy, making him First Baronet of Isel, the heading becomes 'Curia Baronis Wilfrid Lawson mil dom Manuorii' – roughly, The court of Baron Wilfrid Lawson, soldier and Lord of the Manor'. I get the feeling he is constantly reinforcing his slightly tenuous claim to the Lordship of the Manor, and the sense that ' the Lord doth protest too much'. A feeling very much backed up by Susan Johnson's article, above.

The justification for placing both Thomas and William at Thorneythwaite comes from the quite unusual entries in Crosthwaite Registers, both on marriage and baptisms, which name the farm. Much more usually people are simply said to be 'of Seatoller' even when we know from other sources they are in fact from Thorneythwaite. This is not particularly surprising: Thorneythwaite is seen as being part of the hamlet of Seatoller for all it is across the river and really quite separate. The other usual Borrowdale appellations are 'of Rosthwaite'. 'of Seathwaite' etc. However, when Thomas married Elizabeth the record shows:

Thomas Birkett of Rosthwaite and Elizabeth Birkett of Thornnethwaite (sic), July 19th 1628.

This might be confused with Thornthwaite, a village near Keswick, except that there are several mentions of that village on the same page, all spelt Thornthwaite. Then again, a little earlier (September 2nd, 1621) we have:

Robert Jopson of Seathwaite in Borrowd. and Alice Willson of Thornythwaite.

It's all very tricky, and apart from anything else reminds us that rarely did one family alone occupy Thorneythwaite – here for instance there is Alice Wilson. Is she a servant, or the daughter of another family living there and perhaps working in the wad mine? The same dilemma arises in 1602, where on February 27th Christopher Nichollson of Seatoller married Grace Richardson of 'Thornethwaite in Borradaile'. This is clearly Thorneythwaite, but is spelt as the village of Thornthwaite is frequently spelt in the registers. Therefore, some of the 'Thornethwaite' abodes which I have eschewed as being probably the village could be the farm.

To return to Thomas and Elizabeth and their children, as recorded being baptised at Crosthwaite, we have:

Oct 1st 1636: Thomas Birkett son of Thomas and Elizabeth of Thorniethwaite (sic).

Sept 11th 1641: Christopher Birkett son of Thomas and Elizabeth of Thornethwaite.

Jan 24th 1645: Elizabeth Birkett of Thornnethwaite daughter of Thomas and Elizabeth.

Note: by now Thornthwaite has become standard for the village near Braithwaite.

In the burials section of Crosthwaite records we find:
Thomas Birkett of Thorniethwaite (sic) August 9th 1670

And for William and his wife Elizabeth, their marriage may be that recorded as:

202

July 22nd 1634: William Birkett of Chapel in Borradell and Elizabeth Birkett of Seathwaite. I can find no other William and Elizabeth marriage or baptisms.

Their children's baptisms are recorded as:

April 14th 1638: Jayne daughter of William Birkett of Thornythwaite and Elizabeth.

May 9th 1640: John son of William Birkett of Thornythwaite and Elizabeth.

Nov 1st 1641: Isabel daughter of William Birkett of Thornythwaite and Elizabeth.

Feb 2nd 1643: Elizabeth daughter of William Birkett of Thornythwaite and Elizabeth.

March 25th 1647: Thomas Birkett son of William Birkett of Thornythwaite and Elizabeth.

Note: we are still on the old calendar, when March 25th was New Year's Day.

Since these records are concurrent, however, we might well wonder why Thorneythwaite might be spelt consistently as Thornythwaite in the case of William's family, but in varied ways in the case of Thomas's. Clearly, we can be much more confident that William was at Thorneythwaite than that Thomas was.

There is an interesting note following the entry of Nov 26th 1653 in the Crosthwaite registers that:

Here beginneth the registering of the births of infants according to an Act of Parliament dated 24th August 1653. Another, after the entry of October 23rd 1654 notes that : *Mr Ratcliff enters vicar.* I don't know whether the Rev'd Ratcliff objected or became ill or lazy, but ironically the entries from 1658 – 1668 are sparse to the point of extinction, taking only two pages. The same is true of the marriage register and of the burial register. Who knows what information on Thorneythwaite and of course everywhere else is lost. I have to assume at least that William's death was in that period, as he is at no time mentioned in the Manorial Court records. But then, if I am right in assuming Thorneythwaite is held freehold, its owner would not be named in general in the Court records, as those named are specified as 'Tenants at the will of the Lord after the customs of the manor.' I assume, however, a Thorneythwaite representative would attend the Court, and might very well be a juror.

John's death may well be that described in the burials register as: John Birkat of Thornethwaite in Borradale, Dec 12th 1708.

Again we have the spelling problem, only solved in this case by the added 'in Borradale'.

In the end I have decided to have William and Elizabeth, followed by John, as main owners, with Thomas and his Elizabeth living in a separate dwelling at Thorneythwaite. On balance, this seems justified, and I need a Thorneythwaite resident to be part of the Wad Mine story, as the early to mid-1600s were an important time in its history. Thomas is then to be that man.

Sir John Bankes was a noted philanthropist for Keswick, and his bust still stands in Fitz park as a memorial. His ownership and dealings with the wad mines are catalogued in Ian Tyler's *'Seathwaite Wad'*, pp 82-87.

Chapter twenty-three

The brief outline in the story of Daniel Jopson, the first non-Birkett owner-occupier of Thorneythwaite, is very much the tip of the iceberg of the huge amount of source material. Sometimes the very weight of material becomes confusing, as does the repetitive use of the same Christian names in families. There are at least five Daniel Jopsons in the valley in the mid-18th Century, and many more Sarah Jopsons and John Birketts. It wouldn't do to overwhelm the story with the intricate detail, but here in the notes I would like to give a flavour of the overlapping webs.

From the Land Tax returns deposited in the Carlisle Record Office we can trace ownership changes that century. The earliest is 1767, and shows a Daniel Jopson as both owner and occupier of Thorneythwaite. A Daniel Jopson continues to be the occupier right up to 1807, when John Jopson takes over. However, ownership fluctuates. A Daniel owns the farm up to 1785, but by 1788 a John Braithwaite is the owner, and continues so till 1807, when a Daniel again is owner and occupier. By 1820, the owner occupier has become John Jopson. (There are no records between 1807 and 1820).

Crosthwaite registers give up their information in a complex fashion. It is necessary to study Baptisms, Marriages and Burials to build up the picture of who's who: a picture complicated by the presence or absence of place names. Fortunately the soubriquet 'of Thorneythwaite' or 'of Seathwaite, Stonethwaite, Rosthwaite' occurs enough to tease out the details. I note the highlights – highlights that took me a long time to disentangle. I have designated the five Daniels as (a) (b) (c) (d) and (e).

204

We have, to go on, five Thorneythwaite deaths recorded in Crosthwaite registers for the period 1670 onwards:

August 9th 1670 – Thomas Birkett of Thornietwhaite (sic).

Dec 12th 1708 – John Birkat of Thornethwaite in Borradale

Dec 3rd 1720 – Daniel Birkett of Thornywhate (sic)

March 3rd 1723 – William Birkett's childe of Thornywhate.

March 20th 1727 – John Wilson's daughter of Thornythwaite.

Notes: 1)The spelling 'Thornywhate' is interesting in that currently the local way of saying any 'thwaite' is to miss the 'th' entirely and say 'waite'. So Thorneythwaite is indeed Thornywhate.

2) There is clearly a Wilson there in 1727, as there was in 1621 when Alice Willson got married from Thorneythwaite.

In terms of baptisms, we have the following probably attributable to Thorneythwaite, in the Crosthwaite records 1670 onwards.

1695:William, son of John Birkett of Seataleor and Isebell.

1709: John, son of John Birkett of Thornethwaite in
    Borradell and Ann.

1719: Jonathon, son of John Birkett of Thornythwaite and Ann

1720: Mary, daughter of Benjamin Birkett of Thornythwaite and
    Mary his wife.

1723: Joseph, son of John Birkett of Thornythwaite and Ann

1744: Sarah, daughter of John Jopson of Thornythwaite and Sarah.
    But note..

1748: Elizabeth, daughter of John Jopson of <u>Seathwaite</u> and Sarah!

And in marriages we find:

1676:Edward Birkett and Elizabeth Hine. No place names.

1681:John Birkett and Ann Bowe. No place names.

1707:Robert Grave and Elizabeth Birkett. No place names.

1707:Hugh Birkett of Borradell and Dorothy Harrison of Patterdale.

1708:Daniel Jopson of Borradell Chapel and Elizabeth Birkett.

1714:Thomas Birkett of Seatoller in Borradell and Judith Wren of
    Longthwaite.

1717:Benjamin Birkett and Margaret Braithwaite of Hawkshead.

1743/4:John Jopson of Thornythwaite and Sarah Birkett of
    Stonethwaite.

1747:John Birkett of Stonethwaite and Sarah Jopson of
    Thornythwaite.

Any, or indeed all, of these could be based at Thorneythwaite. It is tempting to go for John and Ann Birkett 'of Thornythwaite' as main owners/tenants, with children Jonathon and Joseph as above, but if married in 1681 it is impossible they would be having children in the 1720s. It is quite possible that the Benjamin and Margaret, married in 1717, are Benjamin and Mary, parents of Mary in 1720, with a mis-spelt or transcribed Mary/Margaret. The only Benjamin Birkett baptised is in 1678, son of John and Mary Birkett, of Portinscale. In the Manorial Court records for 1705 there is a name crossed out – Gawine Wrenn– and Dan Birkett is written in. This is his first time in these records, and he comes between William Hinde and John Youdale sen., who have both entered at the same time, as previously Gawine Wrenn was between John Youdale jun. and John Birkett de Chappell. We must surely be able to say he has something to do with Thorneythwaite dying there in 1720 and being one of the Borrowdale tenants from 1705. Where was his tenancy? Presumably, from his position in the list, the last Stonethwaite tenement before Chapel.

The only 17th Century Daniel Birkett baptism I have found is that of:

Daniel, son of Thomas Birkett of Wythburn and Margaret. November 30th 1650.

However, as previously noted, there is a ten-year gap in the Crosthwaite records, from 1660 – 1670, so it is much more probable that Daniel was born in this period, to one of the Stonethwaite Birketts.

The fact that he died 'of Thorneythwaite' might signify only that he retired to relations living there; presumably John and Ann, above. His position in the manorial record strongly suggests he is a tenant in Stonethwaite, the last holding before Chapel. It certainly doesn't indicate a Thorneythwaite holding. He is still there in the 1711 record, which is the last in that set. I don't think the records from 1711 to1730 exist.

On Feb 10th 1776 one of the first baptisms in St Andrews, Borrowdale, is that of

Jonathon, son of Daniel and Sarah Jopson, of Thorneythwaite.

So, all we're missing is the period 1723 – 1743, where the change from Birketts to Jopsons takes place. There is an array of family baptisms from Thorneythwaite from then on.

Grace, d of Joseph Dawson and his wife Ann, of Thorneythwaite 18/02/1781

Robert, s of Robert Grave and Mary his wife. Thorneythwaite. 1/10/1782

206

Dinah, d of Robert Grave and Mary his wife. Thorneythwaite. 9/8/1784

Robert, s of Robert Grave, slater, and Mary (late Dawson) his wife, Thorneythwaite 5/12/1788

John, s of Robert Grave, slater, and Mary (late Dawson) of Seathwaite. 6/10/1792

Elizabeth, d of Jonathon Thompson of Thorneythwaite, slater, and Agnes his wife (late Coward). 30/11/1806

George, s of Jonathon Thompson of Thorneythwaite, slater, and Agnes his wife (late Coward).5/6/1809

Edward, s of Jonathon Thompson of Thorneythwaite, slater, and Agnes his wife (late Coward).28/07/1811

It is sad to note some of the above children died very young, and are noted in the St Andrews registers, viz.:

Robert, s of Robert Grave and Mary his wife, of Seatoller. 22/12/1782

Robert Grave (himself), slater, Seathwaite. 13/08/1795

Hannah, d of Jonathon Thompson of Thorneythwaite, slater, and Agnes his wife (late Coward). Aged 9 years. 18/06/1807

George, s of Jonathon Thompson of Thorneythwaite, slater, and Agnes his wife (late Coward). Aged 14 years. 04/09/1808

George, s of Jonathon Thompson of Thorneythwaite, slater, and Agnes his wife (late Coward). 30/07/1810

Clearly, Jonathon and his wife had a second George who also died in infancy, and Robert and his wife a second Robert.

Since both Graves and Thompson are slaters we must presume they were renting accommodation there. Here's a possible timeline for these passing tenants and the resident owner-occupier farmers. Note there are five different Daniels, denoted (a) to (e) and likewise many Sarahs.

Another source of documentation are the Land Tax returns, 1767 to 1829, which are excellent for establishing all owners and occupiers in the valley, and the amount of annual land tax they had to pay. Given this too we can make a pretty watertight assessment of who was at, and owned, Thorneythwaite from 1670 onwards.

1694: Daniel Jopson(a) born to Edward and Dorothy Jopson, of Stonethwaite. He will later (about 1740) own Thorneythwaite, after moving to Seathwaite.

1707: A John Birkett of Portinscale married Ann Woodall of

the same. They are the only John and Ann I can find marrying about the right time. But there are gaps in the records in the late 1690s.

1709: Owned by John and Ann Birkett, who have John, their first-born.

1715: Daniel(a) Jopson of Seathwaite marries Mary (Sarah)(a)Youdall of Stonethwaite. They will later take over Thorneythwaite, in about 1740.

1720: Still owned by John and Ann Birkett. Also living there is Benjamin Birkett and his wife Mary (or Margaret), who have a child, Mary. Also living (and dying) there this year is Daniel Birkett, who had farmed in Stonethwaite since 1705.

1720: John Jopson, who will marry Sarah(b) Birkett of Stonethwaite in 1743, is born to Daniel(a) and Mary Sarah(a) Jopson, of Seathwaite.

1723: Still owned by John and Ann Birkett, who have a second son, Joseph, this year.

1726: Sarah(c) Jopson, who will marry John Birkett of Stonethwaite, is born to Daniel(a) and Mary(Sarah)(a) Jopson, of Seathwaite.

1728: Daniel(b), son of Daniel(a) and Mary(Sarah)(a) Jopson of Seathwaite, is born there.

1740 (circa): Thorneythwaite taken over by Daniel(a) and Mary(Sarah)(a) Jopson, who have at least two more children; John and Sarah(c) (above). They were previously at Seathwaite.

1743: John Jopson, son of the family above, marries Sarah(b) Birkett, one of the Stonethwaite Birketts – possibly Daniel's daughter?

1744: John and Sarah Jopson have their first child, Sarah(c). (And lack imagination!)

1747: Another Sarah(d) Jopson, John's sister, living at Thorneythwaite, marries John Birkett of Stonethwaite – quite possibly Sarah(b) Birkett's (above) brother!

1746: Daniel(c) Jopson is born to John and Mary Jopson, Chapel House.

1748: John Jopson and Sarah(b) (née Birkett) have moved to Seathwaite, and have a second child, Elizabeth.

1761: Daniel(d) Jopson is born to John and Sarah(b) Jopson at Chapel House. (Feb 17th)

1767: The land tax return says Daniel Jopson owned and occupied Thorneythwaite and paid 10s 6d tax per year. Which one? Probably (b) as (a) would be 73 by now. (b) will be 39. (c) seems to stay at Chapel, according to Land tax. There are two Daniels in Land tax from 1769 – 1788, presumably (b) at Thorneythwaite, (c) at Chapel. Definitely (b), as he dies there in 1813.

1773: Daniel(a) and his wife Sarah(a) both die.

1776: Daniel(b) and Sarah Jopson, of Thorneythwaite, baptise their son Jonathon at St. Andrews, Borrowdale, newly able to perform baptisms and funerals, but not weddings. (Feb 14th). I found no record of their marriage. Is this Daniel(b) or (c)?: (b) would be 48, (c) would be 30, but was born at Chapel. The land tax documents show a Daniel Jopson at Chapel throughout these years. Presumably (c), so let's assume (b) is father to Jonathon, even though old. Seems right, there is a John inherits. I don't know who Sarah is, and can find no marriage in Crosthwaite registers.

1778: Daniel(b) and Sarah have Daniel(e).

1781: According to the land tax, Daniel(b) and Sarah Jopson are still owners, but also living there are two slaters and their families: Robert and Mary (née Dawson) Grave and Joseph Dawson and his wife Ann.

1788: John Braithwaite buys Thorneythwaite, but a Daniel Jopson is still the occupier. (Land tax returns: tax has been still 10s 6d, but goes up for the 11- 20 years Braithwaite owns it to 12s 3d.) I think this is (c) because the Jopson at Chapel has changed to John, Daniel(c)'s son. Looks as if he has taken on Chapel while his father has taken the tenancy of Thorneythwaite, after Braithwaite has bought it. Daniel (c) is 42, a good age to take it on. However, Daniel (b) and Sarah are still there, aged 60.

1792: Robert and Mary have moved to Seathwaite, where John is born. Perhaps then Jonathon Thompson, another slater, moves in to their place.

1793: Daniel, husbandman, of Chapel dies.

1795: Robert Grave dies.

1796 – 1803: Somewhere in this period Braithwaite sells to a Daniel Jopson again. Is it the same Daniel? Probably (c). Tax returns to 10s 2d.

1800: John, husbandman of Chapel dies.

1803: Daniel, husbandman of Chapel dies.

1805: Betty (nee Wilson), widow of Daniel of Chapel dies.

1806: Jonathon Thompson has married Agnes (née Coward) and they have a daughter, Elizabeth, followed by George in 1809 and Edward in 1811, all at Thorneythwaite. NOTE: This Thompson is said to have found wad in a slate he split on Castle Crag. *Tyler p.129*

1807: Daniel (c) still owner and occupier, tax 10s 2d.

1808 – 1820: In this period John Jopson takes over as owner and occupier. Tax continues at 10s 2d. John is presumably (c)'s son: need to find his birth. No, don't think (c) is involved.

1813: Daniel(b), of Thorneythwaite, dies aged 85

1829: John Jopson still owner/occupier, at 10s 2d.

1831: John Jopson, of Thorneythwaite dies aged 67. The John, son of Daniel and Sarah, should just be 55 this year. Is this a mistake? If not, who was this John Jopson? If he was born in 1764, as implied by his stated age at death, the only recorded candidate is John, son of John and Agnes Jopson of Chapel House, baptised 1762.

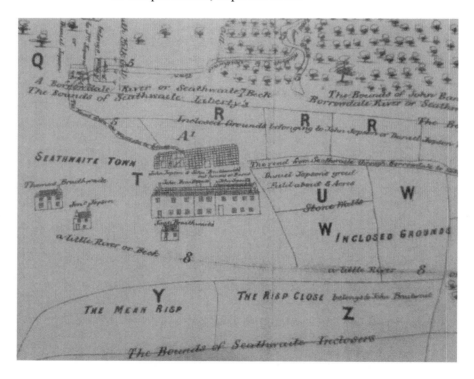

Detail from Hetherington's map of 1759

For the story of William Hetherington's audacious scheme and later elevation to mine superintendent I am indebted to Ian and Jean Tyler's *'Seathwaite wad and the mines of the Borrowdale Valley'*. William Hetherington's map of 1759 is in the Carlisle Record Office, CRO (C) DX/294/9. Here's a detail from it showing 'Seathwaite Town' in 1759. The row of cottages is substantially as it is today.

210

Chapter twenty-four

The Lawson papers, D/Law/1/168 held at Carlisle Record Office are the chief source for this chapter. I was so excited to find the actual plan of Coombe Ghyll, and the Jopson letters, that I couldn't resist putting them in the main story. Ian Tyler is the source of my story that Daniel Jopson was less than totally honest. I quote from Seathwaite Wad page 108:

'John Bankes, in 1765, purchased one of the few houses in Seathwaite from John Braithwaite who at this time owned most of the property. The rest was owned by Daniel Jopson of Thorneythwaite, his eldest son John of Seathwaite and Jonathon Jopson, also of Seathwaite. Between them they owned at least three of the other houses, all having been recently purchased from John Braithwaite. Daniel had lived in the valley for many years, and he and his family had been involved in land ownership and the mine and also, regrettably, some clandestine operations.'.

Interesting, then, that Daniel, his son, should have needed to sell Thorneythwaite back to Braithwaite in 1786, only to buy it back again in 1796, as recorded in the Land Tax returns held at the CRO.

Other than that, we are still working with the Crosthwaite parish registers as noted in the previous chapter's notes, and, from 1775 the St Andrews, Borrowdale, parish records. From that year the chapel was allowed to perform and register baptisms and funerals, but for some reason not weddings. The first wedding there was in 1866, some 90 years later.

The period covered is Daniel (b) Jopson's time, say 1773 – 1813, ie from when his father Daniel (a) dies till when he dies himself. The Land Tax returns for Borrowdale cover the period 1769 to 1829. They are best approached in reverse order, starting at 1829, because then the various holdings are named along with owners and occupiers. Earlier years become increasingly sketchy, but fortunately the same order prevails throughout, so it is possible to work out which owner and which occupier are in which holding. Not all years' returns exist, but it is easy to see the overall pattern of ownership.

Also in Carlisle Record Office is a complete book of the Borrowdale Manorial Court records from 1765 to 1782, plus many loose records of the Court sittings from as early as 1632 to as late as 1856, all held under the umbrella of D/Law/1 with various subheadings. It would be a fascinating study in itself to sift through the entire library of such papers which would tell, in minutiae, the dealings of the valley's farmers over more than two centuries. I have simply picked one or two with some relevance to Thorneythwaite.

There seem to be a variable number of jurors, from twelve to at least eighteen, and from the early 1700s a pair of 'constables' or 'fell lookers' appointed at the court on an annual basis to regulate sheep and cattle numbers and adjudicate differences, notify changes of tenancy, and so on.

Major events in the records in this period:

The dispute over John Jopson's sheep, of Chapel, being driven up Coombe Head thereby displacing sheep belonging to Thomas Wilson and his father.

The list of sheep grasses in 1761

Jurors: In 1761 Daniel Jopson is one such. Might be Daniel (a) or a Daniel from Chapel?

The 11th June 1761 court papers are interesting as well in that they detail a dispute between Joseph Wilson of Rosthwaite and Joseph Youdale of Stonethwaite over the hounding and disturbing of each other's sheep.

Sheep lookers, in 1793 court record.

The 1761 papers also include a list of all the tenants and four columns, headed 1765, 1763,1762,1761 with ticks, presumably signifying rents paid. It is useful for tabulating who was where, then.

Chapter twenty-five

There are a lot of dates and people involved in this chapter – indicative of the changing times and growing farmhouses. Here's a timeline of the principal dates, abstracted from Crosthwaite Parish registers, the Land Tax registers, and Borrowdale St Andrew's registers, where baptisms and burials take place from 1775. The vicar from 1751 to 1804 was the Reverend John Harrison, and I have included some of the register references to him and his family.

1781: According to the land tax, Daniel(b) and Sarah Jopson are still owners, but also living there are two slaters and their families: Robert and Mary (née Dawson) Grave and Joseph Dawson and his wife Ann.

1779: Joseph Dawson married Ann Walker. Nov. 4th 1779

1782: Robert Grave married Mary Dawson, 18th May

1782: Robert, son of Robert and Mary Grave, born at Thorneythwaite. baptised October 1st.

1782: Robert, s of Robert and Mary Grave dies, at Seatoller. November 22nd.

1784: Dinah, d of Robert and Mary Grave born, Seatoller

1786: David, s of Robert and Mary Grave born, Seatoller

1788: Robert, s of Robert and Mary Grave born, Thorneythwaite.

1791: Lanty, s of Joseph Dawson (carrier) and Ann (Walker) baptised

1792:The Rev'd John Harrison's son John, or as he commonly subscribed his name John Wilson, surveyor of the port of Workington died. His mother was Mary née Wilson. They lived at Rosthwaite.

1795: Robert Grave the elder dies.

1795: Joseph Dawson, the slater turned carrier, dies at Rosthwaite.

1801: Mary (Wilson) wife of Rev'd John Harrison, dies

1806: Jonathon Thompson has married Agnes (née Coward) and they have a daughter, Elizabeth, followed by George in 1809 and Edward in 1811, all at Thorneythwaite.

1809: Their daughter, Hannah, dies at Thorneythwaite, aged 9 years.

1814: Ann, d of Jonathon Thompson and Agnes born at Thorneythwaite.

1813: Daniel (b) Jopson dies, aged 85

1815: Sarah, his wife dies, aged 76

1823: Mary Birkett dies at Thorneythwaite, aged 86. 1826: Thomas Dixon, son of William, a miner, and Grace born at Thorneythwaite.

1831: John Jopson dies at Thorneythwaite, aged 67.

1833: Daniel Jopson dies at Thorneythwaite, aged 55.

1837: George Robinson, son of William and Hannah, farmer at Thorneythwaite is born.

1837: Robert Coates, son of Mary, a spinster, born at Thorneythwaite.

1839: Eleanor Hodgson, d. of Jos and Eleanor, a yeoman of Thorneythwaite is born.

1840: Margaret Bennett, d of Thomas and Mary, a miner, of Thorneythwaite is born.

There were a number of books and guides published around the turn of the nineteenth century, notably Hutchinson's *'Cumberland, vols 1 & 2'* in 1795 and Lyson's *'Magna Britannia'* in 1816. I have made use of one or two comments from each in this chapter. From these we learn:

Borrowdale 'lately enfranchised' by Sir Gilfrid Lawson, so about 1800

Sheep fair held in Borrowdale 1st Wednesday of September; in Newlands 1st Friday.

Sir Francis Radcliffe was created Earl of Derwent water by James II, but the second earl, James, was engaged in the rebellion of 1715 and had his head cut off. The lands were forfeited to the crown, and settled upon Greenwich Hospital by act of parliament. The Radcliffes built a fine house on Lord's Island, still extant in 1815. St Herbert's cell was still visible on the island in 1539 (Leland). Peter Crosthwaite established his museum in 1780, continued by his daughter.

Keswick School was well-established by 1815, and indeed Lyson says the company of mines royal gave £20 to it way back in the 16th C.

Chapter twenty-six

Again, a timeline of significant events may help.

1823: Mary Birkett dies at Thorneythwaite, aged 86.

1826: Thomas Dixon, son of William, a miner, and Grace born at Thorneythwaite.

1831: John Jopson dies at Thorneythwaite, aged 67

1833: Daniel(e) Jopson dies at Thorneythwaite, aged 55. He was a son of Daniel (b) and Sarah, born in 1778 at Thorneythwaite.

1833: Abraham Fisher buys Thorneythwaite from the Jopson estate.

1837: George Robinson, son of William and Hannah, farmer at Thorneythwaite was born.

1837: Robert Coates, son of Mary, a spinster, born at Thorneythwaite.

1839: Eleanor Hodgson, d. of Jos and Eleanor, a yeoman of Thorneythwaite was born.

1840: Margaret Bennett, d of Thomas and Mary, a miner, of Thorneythwaite was born.

1840: Tithe map states Abraham Fisher is both Owner and occupier of Thorneythwaite. It also shows him as owner of many other properties in the valley.

1841: Census gives two families at Thorneythwaite. Henry (agricultural labourer) and Mary Dawson, both 25, born in 1816: and Thomas (30) and Mary (30) Bennett and family. He's a black lead miner. Their children are James (12), Joseph (10), William (7), Dinah (4) and Margaret (1). As so often, dates in the census are unreliable: Henry was actually born in 1814, son of William (husbandman) and Mary Dawson, of Seatoller.

1851:Census notes the following at Thorneythwaite. Thomas Walker (34), farmer of 250 acres; Catherine (33) his wife; Robert (7), Edward (4) and Hannah (1) their children; Margaret Hinde (17) house servant and Thomas Edmondson (25) farm labourer. Also there, in the cottage, are Robert Walker (66), retired farmer; his wife (58) and daughter (19). These last two are not named, but in the 1861 census we discover his wife is Mary.

1868:Abraham Fisher and his partner J. Fisher Crosthwaite, sell Thorneythwaite to H.C. Marshall.

1872: Robert Jopson (30) marries Jane Allison (25) at Crosthwaite Church. His father is Daniel Jopson, a farmer of Seatoller. The witnesses are Dover Jopson, Robert's brother, and his sister Sarah Ann Jopson. Neither Robert, Dover nor Sarah Jane were baptised at St Andrew's, Borrowdale, so I assume their father Daniel, the second son of Daniel and Betty at Chapel Farm, moved away to make his fortune before returning to Seatoller sometime between their births and Robert's marriage. In fact, in the 1841 census he is registered at Keswick Mill, High Crosthwaite, Keswick. Daniel is registered as just born. Also living with them is one John Dover, clearly Ann's father: hence the second son being christened 'Dover Jopson'. Jane's birth is recorded at St Andrew's as:

1847: Jane, daughter of Thomas and Sarah Allison, of Rosthwaite, a husbandman.

The road is still poor, but Jack Cawx managed to enter Borrowdale in a chaise, though he nearly overturned at Grange. Farming has moved on apace, with a lot of arable on drier and meadowland on the wetter places – often surrounded by hedges, not walls. Artists, poets and writers abound, and the tourist industry gets under way.

It is clear from the timeline that John and Daniel Jopson are the last of the line there for the time being, with William and Hannah Robinson taking over, probably around 1833. It looks as though Abraham Fisher bought it in 1833 – he is the owner (and 'occupier') in the 1840 tithe map and schedule, though clearly he has farm labourers doing the work (The Robinsons). Thorneythwaite was sold again in 1868 to H.C. Marshall. The Marshalls sold to John Musgrave, a solicitor from Wasdale Hall and Whitehaven, in 1896. (together with Seathwaite Farm, for a total £8,000 according to pencilled notes on the catalogue at Carlisle Record Office). Musgrave sold to William Walker in 1925. Jopsons then were just tenants when they returned in 1872. In the 1800's the dwelling was a farmhouse and there was a three-roomed cottage at the West end of the current smaller barn, hence all the dual occupation. The farmhouse was just one long building (Tithe map, 1840) probably with an outshut roof at the back containing the stairs and various pantries, as described of Skellgill, Newlands, by Molly Lefebure in *'Cumberland Heritage'*. The fireplace in the big sitting room is dated 1822, which is the likely date of extension and addition of the cottage. Why are there wooden partitions for the two sitting rooms? If we can trust the tithe map to be accurate, the house was one long house without the back bits in 1840, but by 1864 on the OS 1:2,500 map it has at least a single storey back element. Likewise the big barn has grown from a long narrow building to its present shape.

In 1801 the following were able to vote:
John Jopson, Chapel, gent.
John Fisher, Seatoller, gent.
John Atkinson, Rosthwaite, gent.
John Wilson, ditto
John Harris, Watendlath, gent.
Daniel ffisher, ditto
Caleb Fisher, Grange, gent.
John Threlkeld, ditto
William Jopson, Stonethwaite, gent.

By 1820 the list was:
Joseph Birkett
John Jopson
John Fisher
John Allison
William Birkett
John Wilson
Thomas Wilson
John Threlkeld
John Weightman
Miles Wilson

There is an important connection to the wad mines again for this chapter. In the 1841 census, the 'Head' is given as Henry Dawson (25) husbandman, married to Mary (also said to be 25, but in fact just 20). Also

216

living in the cottage are the Bennett family, comprising Thomas (30) a black lead miner, Mary, his wife (30), James (12), Joseph (10), William (7), Dinah (4) and Margaret (1). We know Abraham Fisher owns, and is said to occupy, Thorneythwaite, so Henry is farming it for him. Abraham Fisher was single, 30 years old, living in Seatoller (census 1841) with his mother, Agnes, and three servants. By the 1851 census his mother is dead, and Abraham is described as 'County Magistrate & Landowner'. He lives next door to the young Daniel Jopson (aged 10) and his family: Daniel the elder is described as 'Farmer of 70 acres'.

Henry is the son of William and Mary Dawson, husbandman, of Seatoller, so has done well to get the farm at his age. (Born 1814). It would be worth investigating if he is descended from the Dawsons who lived at Thorneythwaite in 1781 – 60 years earlier. His wife Mary is Mary Dixon, daughter of Daniel and Mary Dixon, of Seathwaite. Daniel is part of the wad mine Dixons, who are fascinating in their own right. Tyler tells us (*'Seathwaite Wad', page 140*) that old William Dixon had built quite a dynasty there. In 1818 he was 66, the main agent for many years, under investigation by John Farey. Daniel is one of his sons, then aged 20, married and living at Seathwaite. His elder brother, William (junior) is 28, married, and living at Thorneythwaite. His eldest brother, John, (31) is married and living at Seathwaite. He is assistant agent. These all earn 3/6 for an 8 hour day.

Also related by marriage is James Bennett (41), who is a blind miner, married and living at Seathwaite, also on 3/6 a day; his son Thomas Bennett (13) a labourer on 1/6 a day; Matthew Coates (24), a brother-in-law, a miner living in Rosthwaite: Benjamin Dixon (32) another son-in-law living at Grange. All on 3/6 per day.

Presumably, then, the Thomas Bennett at Thorneythwaite in 1841 is this one above, born around 1805. He would actually then be nearer 36 in 1841, but we know the census ages are pretty random at that time. If it is he, then he and Mary Dawson (nee Dixon) were both brought up at Seathwaite.

It seems clear, then, that Thorneythwaite was sold in 1833 when the last Jopson brother Daniel died, aged 55, and was bought then by Abraham Fisher. The first tenants seem to have been William and Hannah Robinson, whose son George was born there in 1837. Henry and Mary Dawson presumably took over at Lady Day 1839, having married four months previously. They had no children while in the valley, and seem to have moved on and out some time in the next ten years. Also living there in 1837 is Mary Coates, daughter of Matthew Coates, a son-in-law of William Dixon, the mine agent. She has an illegitimate son Robert, father unknown.

By 1839 there are more tenants, Joseph and Eleanor Hodgson, described as a yeoman, who have a daughter, also called Eleanor, while there. It seems then that Abraham Fisher went through tenants/labourers at a rate of knots, there being at least three sets in eight years: Robinson, Hodgson then Dawson, to be followed sometime soon by Thomas and Catherine Walker, who were there in 1851 census, and described as 'Farmer of 230 acres'. The Walkers are much more persistent, still being there in the 1871 census; but by 1881 Robert Jopson has taken possession.

Chapters twenty-seven & twenty-eight

I am very grateful to Fisher Jopson's three grand-daughters, Ina Monkhouse, Vera Harris and Ethel Chapman for giving time to talk about Thorneythwaite in their grand-father's time, and for a series of photos which helped enormously in untangling the various strands of the story. They it was who spoke of young Frank's schizophrenia and also produced the fulsome article in the Fell and Rock Climbing Club magazine which provides such an insight into the farm at the beginning of the 20th Century. They also provided the date of the large extension of the farmhouse, connecting it with the courtship of Margaret Isabella Jopson and Robert George Taylor in 1937.

Timeline dates are:

1874: William, son of Wilson (farm labourer) and Violet Tyson, born at Thorneythwaite.

1874: Sarah Jane, daughter of Robert (farmer) and Jane Jopson, born at Thorneythwaite.

1876: John Fisher, son of Robert (farmer) and Jane Jopson, born at Thorneythwaite.

1876: Thomas, son of Samuel and Elizabeth Scott, born at Thorneythwaite. (Farm servant)

1876: Henry, son of Wilson and Violet Tyson, miner, born at Thorneythwaite.

1878: Frank, son of Robert and Jane Jopson, born at Thorneythwaite.

1880: Ethel, daughter of Robert and Jane Jopson, born at Thorneythwaite.

1881: Elias, son of Edward (quarryman) and Mary Thomas, born at Thorneythwaite.

1882: Percy Ann, daughter of Robert and Jane Jopson, born at Thorneythwaite.

1885:Edith, daughter of Robert and Jane Jopson, born at Thorneythwaite.

1891:Census shows two big families living at Thorneythwaite.

Jopson: Robert (45), Jane (44), Sarah Jane (17), John Fisher (15), Frank (13), Ethel (11), Percie (8), Edith (6) and a farm servant Joseph Preston (35).

Pepper: Matthew (72), Hannah (62), Edward (34, slate quarryman), Alice (22), John (20, slate river), Addison (16, slate river), George (14, quarryman), James (6, grandson), and three lodgers in Pepper quarters: John Shaw (57, slate dresser), Michael Coupland (41, slate quarryman) and William Hartley (29, slate quarryman). A total of 20 people.

1892:Matthew Pepper died at Thorneythwaite, aged 73.

1894:Frank Jopson died, aged 16. Buried Whitsunday, May 13th.

1898:Mountain View becomes the new name in the registers of what was Leconfield Terrace.

1911:Census (Sunday April 2nd) records Robert Jopson (68), farmer: Jane (63); Sarah Jane (38) single daughter, dairy; Fisher Jopson (35), single son, working on farm; Percy Jopson(28), single daughter; and William Greenhow (16), single farm servant.

1911:June 14th, John Fisher Jopson marries Hughina McLean. Reception at Thorneythwaite.

1912:Margaret Isabel, daughter of Fisher and Hughina Jopson, born at Thorneythwaite.

1914:Frank, son of Fisher and Hughina Jopson, born at Thorneythwaite.

1916:Vera McLean, daughter of Fisher and Hughina Jopson, born at Thorneythwaite.

1918:Ethel Caroline, daughter of Fisher and Hughina Jopson, born at Thorneythwaite.

1922:Robert Jopson died, buried at St Andrews, Dec 22nd. Aged 79

1923: Jane Jopson died, buried at St Andrews, Nov 11th. Aged 73

1957: Jessie Pepper died at Thorneythwaite, aged 77. Almost certainly Ethel Dixon's mother.

The H.C. Marshall who bought Thorneythwaite in1868 lived on Derwent Island, and was a keen environmentalist and protector of the area. He thwarted the efforts of the Buttermere Slate Company to drive a railway down Buttermere to Cockermouth station. He also opposed the creation of a tarmacked road over Sty Head. In 1879 he contributed £20 to the Borrowdale Church Augmentation fund *(noted in St Andrew's Church*

Records). Why did he sell to Musgrave who was keen to see a road over Sty Head, and bought Thorneythwaite and Seathwaite as an investment for when the road might exist?

The only one of Fisher Jopson's sisters to marry was Ethel, who became Ethel Skedge. She died in 1972, aged 92. She and her sister Edith emigrated to Detroit in the USA in the early 1930s. Ethel married an American, Ernest Skedge, and stayed till he died in 1957, when she returned and lived with her sisters Edith and Percy in Beech Croft, Threlkeld. Fisher's daughter Margaret lived next door in West Dene with her husband Rob. Fisher and Hughina moved in with them in 1947, but Hughina was so ill she spent most of the next two years in Keswick Hospital, till her early death at 63. Fisher's other sister, Sally (Sarah Jane), ran a boarding house in Southey Street, Keswick, with her sister Percy till her death in 1940. She was 66. I am indebted to Fisher and Hughina's granddaughters, Ina Monkhouse, Vera Harris and Ethel Chapman for all these details.

Fisher's daughter Ethel (24) married John Ramsey (32) in 1943
Margaret Isabella Jopson(25) married Robert George Taylor (31) in 1937, a mason who lived in Threlkeld (Brookside). These are Ethel junior's parents.
Vera MacLean Jopson(27) married George Dixon (34) in 1944. These are Ina and Vera's parents. Ina was born 4th quarter of 1947, birth registered in Penrith. Vera was born first quarter of 1946, Baptised at St Andrews 3rd February 1946, registered in Cockermouth. Robert George Taylor (Ethel's father) was a godfather, along with Eleanor Porter and Dorothy Pettigrew.

Chapter thirty

For the first time in this book I was able to interview the players themselves, though under difficult circumstances. I knew Stuart and Shirley quite well, and they had always been very welcoming. My first visit was ill-timed as I discovered on my way from my car to their door that Stuart had suffered a recurrence of the cancer he had a couple of years ago. He had been warned he only had a few months to live. I debated abandoning the visit, but his sister-in-law, Elizabeth insisted he and Shirley would be glad to talk about their time at Thorneythwaite. Stuart was on good form and happy to talk about his large extended family, and of the many purchases and rentals of land he and Shirley made in their time there.

They talked a little too of Jonny and Joanne's wish for a more rounded enterprise.

I was able, via census records and church registers, to fill in the details of his father and grandfather's generations at home, and looked forward to another visit to check what I had written, only to be phoned by Shirley just a few days later with the news that Stuart had died. His funeral was a fitting tribute to a man who had lived life to the full, fell-running, working and holidaying in wholesome balance. In my second visit to Shirley alone I learnt of their gruesome experiences in the Foot and Mouth epidemic of 2001 and more of the history of the Dinah Hoggus – including who Dinah had been.

They, followed briefly by Jonny and Joanne, were destined to be the last true tenants of Thorneythwaite. I'm glad they made such a success of it.

Cath Marsh, the Natural England officer responsible for Borrowdale and many other valleys, generously allowed me an interview to explain the various agreements Thorneythwaite and the other Borrowdale farms sharing Langstrath Common entered into since the establishment of the Environmentally Sensitive Areas scheme in 1993.

Chapter thirty-one

I am deeply indebted to the National Trust officers in the Borrowdale/North Lakes area for the amount of time they have offered me, and for the interest they have shown in my enterprise. The Oxford Archaeology North survey of Thorneythwaite came out late in my work on this book, and necessitated quite a lot of correction and revision in several chapters! In particular I am grateful to Tom Burditt, head of operations in the North Lakes, and to Jamie Lund, their archaeologist, for the interviews they granted me.

Bibliography and references

Adams, John: Mines of the Lake District Fells
Atkinson, J. C. & Brownbill, J.: The Coucher Book of Furness Abbey
Bott, George: Keswick – the story of a Lake District town
Bouch, C. M. L. & Jones, G. P.: The Lake Counties, 1500 – 1830
Cambridge Library Collection: Early Yorkshire Charters, Vol 7
Collingwood, W. G.: Elizabethan Keswick
Donald, M. B.: Elizabethan Copper
Hutchinson: Cumberland (1794)
Lefebure, Molly: Cumberland Heritage
Lysons, Daniel & Samuel: Magna Britannia, Vol 4, containing Cumberland (1816)
Marshall, J. D.: Old Lakeland
Oxford Archaeology North: Borrowdale, Cumbria; historic survey for the National Trust
Oxford Archaeology North: Land at Thorneythwaite Farm, Borrowdale
Pearsall, W. H. & Pennington, W.: The Lake District
Spence, Richard T: Skipton Castle and its builders
Tyler, Ian: Honister Slate, The history of a Lakeland Slate Mine
Tyler, Ian: Seathwaite Wad & the mines of the Borrowdale valley
Wilson, Mary: Selected poems

Articles and Records in Carlisle Record Office
D/Law/1/155-177 Lawson Deeds and manorial records relating to Borrowdale.
Susan Johnson: Borrowdale, its land tenure and the records of the Lawson Manor. *Transactions of the Cumberland & Westmorland Archaeological Society. (2nd series), vol. 81 (1981). pp. 63 – 72*
Crosthwaite Church Records
Borrowdale Church Records
Great Deed of Borrowdale 1614
Alice de Rumilly's sale of West Borrowdale to Furness Abbey
Tithe Map of Borrowdale, 1840

Printed in Poland
by Amazon Fulfillment
Poland Sp. z o.o., Wrocław

51978709R00130